The Googlization of Everything

The publisher gratefully acknowledges the generous support of the General Endowment Fund of the University of California Press Foundation.

The Googlization of Everything

(AND WHY WE SHOULD WORRY)

Updated Edition

Siva Vaidhyanathan

UNIVERSITY OF CALIFORNIA PRESS

Berkeley   Los Angeles

University of California Press, one of the most distinguished university presses in the United States, enriches lives around the world by
advancing scholarship in the humanities, social sciences, and natural
sciences. Its activities are supported by the UC Press Foundation and
by philanthropic contributions from individuals and institutions. For
more information, visit www.ucpress.edu.

University of California Press
Berkeley and Los Angeles, California

© 2011 by Siva Vaidhyanathan

First paperback printing 2012

Library of Congress Cataloging-in-Publication Data

Vaidhyanathan, Siva.
The Googlization of everything : (and why we should worry) /
Siva Vaidhyanathan.
    p. cm.
Includes bibliographical references and index.
  ISBN 978-0-520-27289-7 (pbk : alk. paper)
  1. Google (Firm).   2. Internet industry—Social aspects.
3. Internet—Social aspects.   I. Title.
  HD9696.8.U64G669 2010
  338.7′6102504—dc22   2010027772

Manufactured in the United States of America
20   19   18   17   16   15   14
10   9   8   7   6   5   4   3

This book is printed on Cascades Enviro 100, a 100% post consumer
waste, recycled, de-inked fiber. FSC recycled certified and processed
chlorine free. It is acid free, Ecologo certified, and manufactured by
BioGas energy.

For Jaya,
who is learning to be patient in a very fast world

It does not break wills, but it softens them, bends them, and directs them; it rarely forces one to act, but it constantly opposes itself to one's acting; it does not destroy, it prevents things from coming into being; it does not tyrannize, it hinders.

Alexis de Tocqueville

CONTENTS

Preface   xi

Introduction: The Gospel of Google   1

1. Render unto Caesar: How Google Came to
    Rule the Web   13

2. Google's Ways and Means: Faith in Aptitude
    and Technology   51

3. The Googlization of Us: Universal Surveillance
    and Infrastructural Imperialism   82

4. The Googlization of the World: Prospects for a
    Global Public Sphere   115

5. The Googlization of Knowledge: The Future
    of Books   149

6. The Googlization of Memory: Information
    Overload, Filters, and the Fracturing of
    Knowledge   174

    Conclusion: The Human Knowledge Project   199

Acknowledgments   211
Notes   219
Index   257

PREFACE

Google seems omniscient, omnipotent, and omnipresent. It also claims to be benevolent. It's no surprise that we hold the company in almost deific awe and respect. But what do we gain and what do we lose by inviting Google to be the lens through which we view the world? This book describes the nature of that devotion as well as a growing apostasy, and it suggests ways we might live better with Google once we see it as a mere company rather than as a force for good and enlightenment in the world.

We may see Google as a savior, but it rules like Caesar. The mythology of the Web leads us to assume that it is a wild, ungovernable, and thus ungoverned realm. This could not be further from the truth. There was a power vacuum in the Web not so long ago, but we have invited Google to fill it. Overwhelmingly, we now allow Google to determine what is important, relevant, and true on the Web and in the world. We trust and believe that Google acts in our best interest. But we have surrendered control over the values, methods, and processes that make sense of our information ecosystem.

This book argues that we should influence—even regulate—search systems actively and intentionally, and thus take responsibility for how the Web delivers knowledge. We must build the sort of online ecosystem that can benefit the whole world over the long term, not one that serves the short-term interests of one powerful company, no matter how brilliant.

Still, questioning the role of Google in our lives and the faith we have in it is not easy. Google does much good and little direct harm to most people. And I did not expect to be the person to do this job. From the early days of personal computers, I counted myself among the champions of all things digital and networked. I saw great transformative, democratizing potential in the technological changes of the past three decades. In the 1990s—heady days of global prosperity, burgeoning freedom, and relative peace—I saw in digital networks the means to solve some of the problems we faced as a species. Back then I took seriously the notion that the world had stepped beyond the stalemate of the Cold War and had settled on a rough consensus on competitive open markets, basic human rights, and liberal democracy—even if the road to those goals was still long and rocky in much of the world.[1] I assumed digitization would level the commercial playing field in wealthy economies and invite new competition into markets that had always had high barriers to entry. I imagined a rapid spread of education and critical thinking once we surmounted the millennium-old problems of information scarcity and maldistribution.

But in the early part of this century, my mood soured and my enthusiasm waned. I saw my great hopes for an open and free Internet corrupted by the simultaneous pressures of inadequate security (in the form of fraud, spam, viruses, and malware) and the attempts at a corporate lockdown of culture and technology.[2] I saw that the resistance to openness, transparency, accountability, and democracy was stronger than I had imagined and present in parts of the world—including my own—where I thought the forces of light had triumphed long ago.[3] I worried that the environment generated by the global reach of the Internet was pulling us in opposite directions—toward both anarchy and oligarchy—and draining the institutions and environments that would foster more reasonable, republican virtues, such as measured deliberation, critical thought, and mutual respect.[4] I noted the ways in which those who promoted the digitization and networking of all things reverted to simplistic and wrongheaded views of how technology works in society.[5] I grew weary of others' attempts to describe technology as an irresistible force that young people have mastered and old people must conform to or wither away trying to resist.[6] And I had an intellectual allergic reaction to the growing notion that one company—Google—could or would solve some of the greatest and most complex human problems simply by applying the principles of engineering.[7]

So I sought a way to explore both my disenchantment with and my approval of changes in our global information ecosystem. I wanted to embrace and champion values and goals such as liberty, creativity, and democracy while offering criticisms of trends and trajectories that I consider harmful or dangerous, such as blind faith in technology and market fundamentalism. And Google exemplifies all these trends.

Because books move more slowly than large, rich Internet companies, I have not attempted to catalog or analyze the company's recent initiatives. Instead, I have tried to discern broad and significant themes and patterns that should hold constant for some years. If Google has dramatically changed course between the date that I finished this text and the date you begin reading it, I apologize in advance. Tracking Google was never my goal; instead, I seek to explain why and how Google tracks us.

Previous books about Google have focused, understandably, on the company's rise and triumph. They have revealed the unique story, culture, and principles that have made Google one of the most pervasive and important institutions in the world. These books have exposed the inner workings of the company, its bold technologies, its brilliant methods of generating revenue, the peculiar vision of its founders, the talents of its chief operating officer, and the revolutionary nature of its approach to making sense of the Internet. I could not write a biography of the company or an exploration of the science of Web search; there are already many excellent examples of such projects. Nor could I write a primer on how one might replicate or learn from Google's success; another recent book fulfills that function. Nor does this book purport to "get inside" the minds of the visionaries who run the company, as other, more connected writers have.[8]

This book is not about Google; instead, it is about how we use Google. It explains the ways we have embraced Google and invited it into a wide variety of human activities. It also examines the resistance to and concern about Google, which is growing as its reach spreads across the globe. It explores the terms of the relationships between Google and its billions of users, and it considers the moral consequences of Google's actions and policies.

This book is much more about us—how we use Google, what we expect of it, and what we give to it—than about Google. My modest hope is that you will approach that screen with the friendly search box and clever logo with a keener sense of what happens when you type the name of the thing you're looking for. To search for something on the Web using Google is not unlike confessing your desires to a mysterious power. If nothing else, I hope to deflate hyperbole about the company, its services, and the Web in general, and to shift the tone of public conversation from one of blind faith and worship of the new to one of sober concern about the wrenching changes we have invited and unleashed. Most of all, I hope we will all approach the future of human knowledge with wisdom and trepidation rather than naive, dazzled awe.

INTRODUCTION

THE GOSPEL OF GOOGLE

In the beginning, the World Wide Web was an intimidating collection, interlinked yet unindexed. Clutter and confusion reigned. It was impossible to sift the valuable from the trashy, the reliable from the exploitative, and the true from the false. The Web was exciting and democratic—to the point of anarchy. As it expanded and became unimaginably vast, its darker corners grew more remote and more obscure. Some had tried to map its most useful features to guide searchers through the maelstrom. But their services were unwieldy and incomplete, and some early guides even accepted bribes for favoring one source over another. It all seemed so hopeless and seedy. Too much that was precious but subtle and fresh was getting lost.

Then came Google. Google was clean. It was pure. It was simple. It accepted no money for ranking one page higher in a search than another.

And it offered what seemed to be neutral, democratic rankings: if one site was referred to more than another, it was deemed more relevant to users and would be listed above the rest. And so the biggest, if not the best, search engine was created.

This, in brief, was the genesis of the enterprise known as Google Inc. Like all theological texts, the Book of Google contains contradictions that leave us baffled, pondering whether we mere mortals are capable of understanding the nature of the system itself. Perhaps our role is not to doubt, but to believe. Perhaps we should just surf along in awe of the system that gives us such beautiful sunrises—or at least easily finds us digital images of sunrises with just a few keystrokes. Like all such narratives, it underwrites a kind of faith—faith in the goodwill of an enterprise whose motto is "Don't be evil," whose mission is "to organize the world's information and make it universally accessible and useful," and whose ambition is to create the perfect search engine.

On the basis of that faith—born of users' experiences with the services that Google provides—since the search engine first appeared and spread through word of mouth for a dozen years, Google has permeated our culture. That's what I mean by *Googlization*. It is a ubiquitous brand: *Google* is used as a noun and a verb everywhere from adolescent conversations to scripts for *Sex and the City*. It seems that even governments are being Googlized, or rendered part of the vast data storm that Google has taken as its challenge to organize and make available.[1]

Google puts previously unimaginable resources at our fingertips— huge libraries, archives, warehouses of government records, troves of goods, the comings and goings of whole swaths of humanity. That is what I mean by the Googlization of "everything." Googlization affects three large areas of human concern and conduct: "us" (through Google's effects on our personal information, habits, opinions, and judgments); "the world" (through the globalization of a strange kind of surveillance and what I'll call *infrastructural imperialism*); and "knowledge" (through its effects on the use of the great bodies of knowledge accumulated in books, online databases, and the Web).

Google consequently is far more than just the most interesting and successful Internet company of all time. As it catalogs our individual and collective judgments, opinions, and (most important) desires, it has grown to be one of the most important global institutions as well. As we shift more of our Internet use to Google-branded services such as Gmail and YouTube, Google is on the verge of becoming indistinguishable from the Web itself. The Googlization of everything will likely have significant transformative effects in coming years, both good and bad. Google will affect the ways that organizations, firms, and governments act, both for and at times against their "users."

To understand this phenomenon, we need to temper our uncritical faith in Google and its corporate benevolence and adopt an agnostic stance. That is, we need to examine what Google has told us about itself, its means, and its motives as it makes the world anew in these ways, and to interrogate and evaluate both the consequences of Googlization and the ways we respond to it.

One way to begin is by realizing that we are not Google's customers: we are its product. We—our fancies, fetishes, predilections, and preferences—are what Google sells to advertisers. When we use Google to find out things on the Web, Google uses our Web searches to find out things about us. Therefore, we need to understand Google and how it influences what we know and believe.

Because of our faith in Google and its claims of omniscience, omnipotence, and benevolence, we tend to grant Google's search results inordinate and undeserved power.[2] These results offer the illusion of precision, accuracy, and relevance. Psychologists at the University of California at Berkeley have even published a study claiming that Google's Web-search technique mimics the way human brains recall information.[3] So it is understandable that we have come to believe that Google's search rankings are a proxy for quality of information, simply an extension of our collective judgment. But this belief is unhealthy and wrong. The rules of the game are rigged in certain ways, and we need a much clearer idea of how this is done.

If I can convince you that we should be concerned about the ease with which we have allowed everything to be Googlized, I hope I can lead you to consider some remedies as well. I am confident we can find ways to live more wisely with Google. My argument comes from a perspective that is too often lost in accounts of the details of technological innovations and their effects on our daily lives: the pursuit of global civic responsibility and the public good. Hopes for a more enlightened future rest in our ability both to recognize the assumptions embedded in our faith in Google and to harness public resources to correct for them. So this book is also overtly political. It calls for a reimagination of what we might build to preserve quality information and deliver it to everyone. It examines the prospects for the creation of a global public sphere, a space between the particular domestic spheres where we live most of our lives and the massive state institutions that loom over us—a space where we can meet, deliberate, and transform both the domestic and the political. We can't depend on one or even a dozen companies to do that equitably and justly. Google seems to offer us everything so cheaply, easily, and quickly. But nothing truly meaningful is cheap, easy, or quick.

After years of immersion in details of Google's growth, I can come to only one clear judgment about the company and our relationship with it: Google is not evil, but neither is it morally good. Nor is it simply neutral—far from it. Google does not make us smarter. Nor does it make us dumber, as at least one writer has claimed.[4] It's a publicly traded, revenue-driven firm that offers us set of tools we can use intelligently or dumbly. But Google is not uniformly and unequivocally good for us. In fact, it's dangerous in many subtle ways. It's dangerous because of our increasing, uncritical faith in and dependence on it, and because of the way it fractures and disrupts almost every market or activity it enters—usually for the better, but sometimes for the worse. Google is simultaneously new, wealthy, and powerful. This rare combination means that we have not yet assessed or come to terms with the changes it brings to our habits, perspectives, judgments, transactions, and imaginations.[5]

Faith in Google is thus dangerous as the airplane and the automobile have proved dangerous in ways their pioneers did not anticipate in the 1920s. These technologies of mobility and discovery are dangerous not just because they physically endanger their users but because we use them recklessly, use them too much, and design daily life around them. Thus we have done tremendous harm to ourselves and our world. As early as 1910, the technologies of motorized transportation were impressive and clearly revolutionary. It was not hard to see that human life would soon be radically transformed by the ability to move people and goods across continents and oceans in a matter of hours. Only a few years later, life on earth was unimaginable without these systems, and by the close of the twentieth century, the entire world was reorganized around them.

The dangers arose because we let the automobile companies and airlines dictate both public discourse and policy. The rules of the road were worked out rather quickly and almost entirely in favor of the automobile: more people became motorists, and fewer were pedestrians. Soon after World War II, flying and driving became elements of daily life for most of the developed world. Yet the externalities of both these transport systems—from global climate change to global terrorism to global pandemics—have left us wondering how we made so many bad decisions about both of them. We did not acknowledge all the hazards created by our rush to move and connect goods and people, and so we did not plan. We did not limit. We did not deliberate. We did not deploy wisdom and caution in the face of the new and powerful. We did not come to terms with how dangerous planes and cars really are. Even had we acknowledged the range of threats that they generate, we would not have wished for a world without them. But we might well have demanded better training, safeguards, rules, and systems early on and thus curbed the pernicious results while embracing the positive, liberating effects they have on our lives.

We have designed our environments to serve cars and planes instead of people. Our political systems have been used to favor and subsidize these industries, even as they have been held up as models of free enterprise. And thus we have become dangerously dependent on them. We began to recognize the problems that they posed only in the 1960s and now are all too aware of them. But it's far too late. As Elvis warned us, "Fools rush in."[6]

Google and the Web it governs are nowhere near as dangerous as our automobile system. People aren't made ill or run over by Web pages. Nonetheless, blind faith in Google is dangerous because Google is so good at what it does and because it sets its own rules. Unlike the automobile, which regularly kills people, Google causes damage mostly by crowding out other alternatives. Because of its ease and power, because it does things so cheaply and conveniently, it may cause us to miss opportunities to do things better. Google's presence in certain markets, such as advertising or book search, retards innovation and investment by potential competitors, because no one can realistically wrest attention or investment from Google. And when Google does something adequately and relatively cheaply in the service of the public, public institutions are relieved of pressure to perform their tasks well. This is an important and troubling phenomenon I call *public failure.*

The power of this young company is so impressive, and its apparent cost to its users so low (close to free), that the strongest negative emotion it generates in the United States is unease; anger at Google (as well as use of and dependence on Google) is much stronger in Europe. We see so clearly how it makes our lives better, our projects easier, and our world smaller that we fail to consider the costs, risks, options, and long-term consequences of our optimistic embrace. That is what the following chapters set out to do.

LIVING AND THINKING WITH GOOGLE

As with any system of belief, ideologies underlying the rise of Google have helped shape the worldview of those who created it as well as those who use and believe in it. For some, seeking wisdom and guidance in navigating the world in the early years of the twenty-first century, Google looks like the model for everything and the solution to every problem.[7] To most people, Google seems helpful and benevolent. For some would-be reformers, particular practices of the company demand scrutiny within the faith. For apostates, Google has fallen from its heights of moral authority.[8]

Google's ideological roots are well documented.[9] Google's founders and early employees believe deeply in the power of information technology to transform human consciousness, collective and individual. Less well understood are the theories that inform how Google interacts with us and how we interact with Google. Increasingly, Google is the lens through which we view the world. Google refracts, more than reflects, what we think is true and important. It filters and focuses our queries and explorations through the world of digitized information. It ranks and links so quickly and succinctly, reducing the boiling tempest of human expression into such a clean and navigable list, that it generates the comforting and perhaps necessary illusion of both comprehensiveness and precision. Its process of collecting, ranking, linking, and displaying knowledge determines what we consider to be good, true, valuable, and relevant. The stakes could not be higher.

For those of us who trudge through torrents of data, words, sounds, and images, Google has become a blessing.[10] More than guiding us to answers and opportunities, it filters out noise: it prevents us from being distracted by the millions of documents that *might* serve our needs by guessing fairly accurately what we *do* need. So it's almost impossible to imagine living a privileged, connected, relevant life in the early twenty-first century without Google. It has become a necessary—seemingly natural—part of our daily lives. How and why did this happen? What are the ramifications of such widespread dependence?

To answer those questions, we must ask some other hard questions about how Google is not only "creatively destroying" established players in various markets but also altering the very ways we see our world and ourselves.[11] If Google is the dominant way we navigate the Internet, and thus the primary lens through which we experience both the local and the global, then it has remarkable power to set agendas and alter perceptions. Its biases (valuing popularity over accuracy, established sites over new, and rough rankings over more fluid or multidimensional models of presentation) are built into its algorithms.[12] And those biases affect how we value things, perceive things, and navigate the worlds of culture and ideas. In other words, we are folding the interface and structures of Google into our very perceptions. Does anything (or anyone) matter if it (or she) does not show up on the first page of a Google search?

Here are some of the big questions facing us in the coming years: Who—if not Google—will control, judge, rank, filter, and deliver to us essential information? What is the nature of the transaction between

Google's computer algorithms and its millions of human users? How have people been using Google to enhance their lives? Is it the best possible starting point (or end point) for information seeking? What is the future of expertise in an age dominated by Google, bloggers, and Wikipedia? Are we headed down the path toward a more enlightened age and enriching global economy, or are we approaching a dystopia of social control and surveillance?

IMAGINEERING GOOGLIZATION

This book employs what I call a "technocultural imagination."[13] A person who relies on a technocultural imagination asks these sorts of questions: Which members of a society get to decide which technologies are developed, bought, sold, and used? What sorts of historical factors influence why one technology "succeeds" and another fails? What are the cultural and economic assumptions that influence the ways a technology works in the world, and what unintended consequences can arise from such assumptions? Technology studies in general tend to address several core questions about technology and its effects on society (and vice versa): To what extent do technologies guide, influence, or determine history? To what extent do social conditions and phenomena mold technologies? Do technologies spark revolutions, or do concepts like *revolution* raise expectations and levels of effects of technologies?

The chapters that follow attempt to answer such questions. The first two chapters explore the moral universe of Google and its users. I don't really care if Google commits good or evil. In fact, as I explain below, the slogan "Don't be evil" distracts us from carefully examining the effects of Google's presence and activity in our lives. The first chapter argues that we must consider the extent to which Google regulates the Web, and thus the extent to which we have relinquished that duty to one company. The company itself takes a technocratic approach to any larger ethical and social questions in its way. It is run by and for engineers, after all. Every potential problem is either a bug in the system, yet to be fixed, or a feature in its efforts to provide better service. This attitude masks the fact that Google is not a neutral tool or a nondistorting lens: it is an actor and a stakeholder in itself. And, more important, as a publicly traded company, it must act in its shareholders' short-term interests, despite its altruistic proclamations. More important yet, Google is changing. Each week brings a new initiative, a new focus (or a new distraction) for the company, and a new enemy or challenge. Such rapid changes, and the imperatives of corporate existence, are the subjects of chapter 2.

One of the great attractions of Google is that it appears to offer so many powerful services for free—that is, for no remuneration.[14] But there is an implicit nonmonetary transaction between Google and its users. Google gives us Web search, e-mail, Blogger platforms, and YouTube videos. In return, Google gets information about our habits and predilections so that it can more efficiently target advertisements at us. Google's core business is consumer profiling. It generates dossiers on many of us. It stores "cookies" in our Web browsers to track our clicks and curiosities. Yet we have no idea how substantial or accurate these digital portraits are. This book generates a fuller picture of what is at stake in this apparently costless transaction and a new account of surveillance that goes beyond the now-trite Panopticon model. Google is a black box. It knows a tremendous about us, and we know far too little about it. The third chapter explains how we fail to manage the flows of our personal information and how Google fails to make the nature of the transaction clear and explicit.

Google is simultaneously very American in its ideologies and explicitly global in its vision and orientation. That's not unusual for successful multinational corporations. Microsoft is just as important a cultural and economic force in India as it is in the United States. Google, however, explicitly structures and ranks knowledge with a universal vision for itself and its activities. This comprehensiveness generates a tremendous amount of friction around the world—not least in the People's Republic of China. Between 2005 and 2010 the Chinese government regularly shut down portions of Google's services because the company just barely managed to remain in the good graces of the Communist Party. Yet for all its deftness in dealing with China, Google for years drew criticism from global human rights groups for being part of the problem, rather than part of the solution, in China. Then, in early 2010, the company surprised the world by giving the Chinese government exactly what it wanted: Google shut down its Chinese-based search engine while leaving intact those portions of its business that supply jobs and revenue to Chinese nationals. This move left Chinese Internet users with fewer sources of information, did nothing to reduce the stifling level of censorship, and put government-backed search engines in firm control of the Web in China. This was an empty and counterproductive gesture. By choosing to be a passive, rather than active, partner in Chinese censorship, somehow the company drew applause from human rights organizations. The fourth chapter covers the trials of Google as it has tried to apply a single vision of information commerce to a wide array of cultural and political contexts across the globe.

In chapters 5 and 6 the book considers the consequences of Google's official mission statement: "To organize the world's information and make it universally accessible." In chapter 5 I assess the controversial Google Books program. This program, launched in 2004, was meant to help fulfill the mission of organizing the world's information, but it served several engineering and commercial goals as well. The audacity of the program, which aimed to copy millions of copyrighted books from university libraries and offer them in low-quality formats to a broad market of readers, was the first case in which Google clearly moved beyond its previously venerated status. Because of the mistakes Google made in the Books program, federal regulators and many important segments of the reading public grew concerned with the scope of Google's ambitions.[15]

In the public mind, Google's informal motto, "Don't be evil," resonates more than its formal mission statement. But the mission statement is far more interesting. It is a stunning statement. What other institution would define changing the world as its unifying task? The Web-using public has adopted Google services at an astounding rate, and Google has expanded to master widely used Internet functions such as Web search, e-mail, personal "cloud computing," and online advertising. Chapter 6 and the conclusion consider how Google is changing and challenging both the technologies and the companies that govern human communication. The book concludes with a call for more explicitly public governance of the Internet. Such governance might take the form of greater privacy guarantees for Web users or strong antitrust scrutiny of companies like Google. The particular forms and instruments of governance are not as important as the general idea that what Google does is too important to be left to one company. But any criticisms and calls for regulation should be tempered with an honest and full account of Google's remarkable and largely beneficial contributions to our lives. Google figured out how to manage abundance while every other media company in the world was trying to manufacture scarcity, and for that we should be grateful.

As I finished this book, it seemed that the instruments that traditionally supply knowledge for public deliberation were collapsing all around us. Newspapers in the United States and Europe were closing at a startling rate. Many newspaper leaders blamed Google because it alone seemed to be making money. Book publishers were also panicking, as readers suffering from a recession steadily held back their disposable cash, and moves by Amazon, Apple, and Google to serve as cheap-book vendors generated as much anxiety as opportunity. After weighing the various claims and arguments about the fate of journalism and publishing during a crippling global recession, I conclude that we should invest heavily in a global library of digital knowledge, with universal access and maximum freedoms of use. This proposal does not entail a simple bailout or subsidy to any industry or institution. It means that we should embark on a global, long-term plan to enhance and extend the functions of libraries in our lives. So the concluding chapter of this book proposes what I call a Human Knowledge Project. It takes a broad, ecological approach to the idea that we need to infuse the public sphere with resources, energy, and incentives. It is based on the premise that we can do better than hand over so many essential aspects of human endeavor to one American company that has yet to reach even its adolescence.

The youth and inexperience of Google lie at the root of my concerns. Among our major institutions, global information-technology corporations change and adapt faster than any others. This is generally good for them and good for us. But when we grant one—or even two or three—firms inordinate influence over essential aspects of our lives, we risk being jolted by sudden changes of direction, burned by the heat, and blinded by the light. The one thing we can't assume about such companies is that they will remain the same. The Google of 2021 will not resemble the Google of 2001—or even of 2011. Much of what we find comforting about Google may be gone very soon. The imperatives of a company that relies on fostering Web use and encouraging Web commerce for its revenue may understandably morph into a system that privileges consumption over exploration, shopping over learning, and distracting over disturbing. That, if nothing else, is a reason to worry.

ONE

RENDER UNTO CAESAR

HOW GOOGLE CAME TO RULE THE WEB

Google dominates the World Wide Web. There was never an election to determine the Web's rulers. No state appointed Google its proxy, its proconsul, or its viceroy. Google just stepped into the void when no other authority was willing or able to make the Web stable, usable, and trustworthy. This was a quite necessary step at the time. The question is whether Google's dominance is the best situation for the future of our information ecosystem.

In the early days it was easy to assume that the Web, and the Internet of which the Web is a part, was ungoverned and ungovernable. It was supposed to be a perfect libertarian space, free and open to all voices, unconstrained by the conventions and norms of the real world, and certainly beyond the scope of traditional powers of the state.[1] But we now know that the Internet is not as wild and ungoverned as we might have naively assumed back at its conception. Not only does law matter online, but the specifics of the Internet's design, or "architecture," influence how the Web works and how people behave with it.[2] Like Jessica Rabbit in the film *Who Framed Roger Rabbit*, the Internet is not bad—it's just drawn that way. Still, architecture and state-generated law govern imperfectly. In the People's Republic of China, the state clearly runs the Web. In Russia, no one does. States such as Germany, France, Italy, and Brazil have found some ways to govern over and above Google's influence. But overall, no single state, firm, or institution in the world has as much power over Web-based activity as Google does.

So Google, which rules by the power of convenience, comfort, and trust, has assumed control, much as Julius Caesar did in Rome in 48 B.C. Before Caesar, there was a state of chaos and civil war. Rome was presided over by weak, ineffective leaders who failed to capture the support of the people or to make the city livable. Like Caesar, Google has found its mandate to rule through vast popular support, even in the absence of a referendum. And like Caesar's, Google's appeal is almost divine. Because we focus so much on the miracles of Google, we are too often blind to the ways in which Google exerts control over its domain.[3]

So how, exactly, does Google rule the Web? Through its power to determine which sites get noticed, and thus trafficked, Google has molded certain standards into the Web. Google has always tended to degrade the status of pornography sites in response to generic or confusing search terms, thus making it less likely that one will stumble on explicit images while rarely blocking access to such sites entirely.[4] Google has ensured that the Web is a calmer, friendlier, less controversial and frightening medium—as long as one uses Google to navigate it.

Through its advertising auction program, Google favors and rewards firms that create sites that meet explicit quality standards set by Google, such as simple pages that load quickly, lack of flashy animation, and coherence in search terms that helps ensure users are not tricked into clicking on a pornography site when seeking travel advice.[5] Google has limited access to sites that place malicious programs on users' computers. This fight against "malware" is one of the keys to keeping the Web worthy of users' trust and time. If too many sites infected users' computers with harmful software, people would gravitate away from the relatively free and open Web into restricted and protected domains, known as "walled gardens" or "gated communities," that seem less vulnerable to electronic pandemics.[6] Google also, extremely rarely, directly censors search results when they are troublesome or politically controversial, or when the company determines that a firm or group is trying to rig the system to favor its site. When that happens, Google usually places some sort of explanation in the search results to explain and justify the policy.[7]

Overall, these policies have the effect of cleaning up the Web, ensuring that most users have a comfortable experience most of the time. Google can usually achieve this goal without stooping to raw censorship. The net effect is the same, however, because the protections that we rely on, including "safe search," are turned on by default when we first access Google, and our habits (trust, inertia, impatience) keep us from clicking past the first page of search results. Google understands the fact that default settings can work just as well as coercive technologies.[8] Overall, Google orders our behavior and orders the Web without raising concerns that it is overbearing. It's a brilliant trick.

Nothing about this means that Google's rule is as brutal and dictatorial as Caesar's. Nor does it mean that we should plot an assassination, as killing off Google might have the same effect on the state of the Web as Julius Caesar's death had on Rome: a return to unbearable chaos and fractured alliances. In fact, the institutions waiting in the wings to assume governance of the Web, such as commercial telecommunication companies and media conglomerates, are definitely less trustworthy than Google is today. In many ways, we should be grateful that Google governs so well. Google has made Web commerce and communication stable, dependable, and comfortable. By hiding how it does all this behind its simple and clear interface, Google convinces us that it just knows how to make our lives better. We need not worry about the messy details.

But how did we get to this state of affairs? How was Google able to assume this role so quietly and profit so handsomely from it? What sorts of trouble is Google causing for states and firms? And how—if at all—should we consider regulating the regulator?

THE SCOPE OF GOOGLE

Google is sui generis. At its core, it's a Web search-engine service. The primary reason anyone uses Google is to manage the torrent of information available on the World Wide Web. But as the most successful supplier of Web-based advertising, Google is now an advertising company first and foremost.[9] Its search function is why we visit Google. Advertising is what keeps it going. However, there were search-engine companies before Google, and several competitors still do just as good a job linking people to information as Google does. And there were Web advertising companies before Google, just as there are now other firms, such as Facebook, that try to link a user's expressed interest in subjects to potential vendors of goods and services that reflect those tastes. But there has never been a company with explicit ambitions to connect individual minds with information on a global—in fact universal—scale. The scope of Google's mission sets it apart from any company that has ever existed in any medium. This fact alone means we must take it seriously.

Google has expanded in recent years into a general media company because it delivers video and text to users, even if much of that content is hosted on other institutions' sites. Its 2006 acquisition of YouTube, the clear leader in hosting short videos contributed by users, made Google a powerful disseminator of video content.[10] This role has put Google and YouTube at the center of major world events, such as the antigovernment protests in Iran in the summer of 2009 and the election of Barack Obama as president of the United States in 2008.

Since about 2002 Google has steadily added to the roles it plays in people's lives, thus complicating the Web's taxonomy. It now hosts e-mail for millions of users. Google purchased the innovative and free blog-hosting service Blogger in 2003. It runs a social networking site called Orkut that is popular in Brazil and India, but nowhere else. Google Voice offers a voice-over-Internet-provider (VoIP) that competes with Skype's long-distance Internet phone service. It facilitates payment for Web-based commerce through Google Checkout.

Google is also a software company. It now offers online software such as a word processor, spreadsheets, presentation software, and a calendar service—all operating "in the cloud" and thus freeing users from managing multiple versions of their files and applications on different computers, and easing collaboration with others. In 2008 Google released its own Web browser called Chrome, despite many years of collaborating with the Mozilla foundation in supporting the open-source Firefox browser. And in 2009 it previewed its Chrome operating system for cloud computing, a direct assault on Microsoft's core product, Windows. It hosts health records online. On top of all that, since its beginning in 2004, its Google Books project has scanned millions and millions of volumes and has made many of them available online at no cost, simultaneously appropriating the functions of libraries on the one hand and the rights of publishers on the other. In 2007 Google announced plans for a mobile-phone operating system and attempted, but failed, to change the ways that the United States government allocates radio bandwidth to mobile companies in an attempt to open up competition and improve service.[11] And since 2005 the company has been Googlizing the real world through Google Maps, Street View, and Google Earth, a service that allows users to manipulate satellite images to explore the Earth from above. Only one company does all that, so it does not even need a label beyond its increasingly pervasive brand name.

This diversity of enterprises has confused and confounded other firms that compete with Google. Because no other company, not even Microsoft, competes in more than a handful of these areas, it's also hard for regulators to get a sense of Google's market power. In most of these arenas, such as e-mail, applications, blogging, photo-image hosting, health records, and mobile-phone platforms, Google is far from the dominant player. But in online video, out-of-print book searches, online advertising, and of course Web search, Google has such an overwhelming lead that other competitors can't hope to develop the infrastructure needed to compete with Google in the long run.

Google thus has been the victor in the winner-take-all race to serve as the chief utility for the World Wide Web. In 2010, in the midst of a massive two-year economic downturn that hampered every sector of the global economy and devastated some, Google was worth more than

US$120 billion and made more than US$4 billion in total net income. More than twenty thousand people worked for Google in 2010, although the company shed a few thousand through layoffs in 2008.[12]

FRICTION

Because of its presence in a broad array of markets and its brazen unpredictability, many established industry players have taken aim at Google and have demanded either regulatory intervention to pressure Google or regulatory relief for themselves. When Google in 2007 made a strong case to the U.S. Federal Communications Commission that newly released radio spectra should be licensed only to firms that promised openness in mobile-phone design and business practice, the major American telecommunication companies banded together to stifle and limit the proposal. When Google proposed collaborating with Yahoo in online advertising placement, U.S. regulators quickly squelched the plan because advertisers feared total market domination by the two companies, which would hold 90 percent of the search market in the United States. When Google moved to purchase the leading placement service for website banner advertisements, DoubleClick, national advertising companies demanded intervention—unsuccessfully. When Google refused to prevent YouTube users from potentially infringing copyrights and instead relied on the provisions of copyright law that protect service providers such as Google from liability, Viacom sued in a naked attempt to change the law. And when telecommunication companies that act as Internet service providers tried to alter how the Internet works by charging fees to services that might wish to have their content delivered faster—and thus downgrade service for those that didn't pay—Google lobbied to preserve "network neutrality." Google thus has made many powerful enemies in a very short period. Many of Google's positions correspond roughly with the public interest (such as giving empty support to a network neutrality policy and "safe-harbor" exemptions from copyright liability). Others, such as fighting against stronger privacy laws in the United States, do not.[13]

When confronted with questions about its dominance in certain markets, Google officials always protest that, on the Internet, barriers to entry are low, and thus any young firm with innovative services could displace Google the way Google displaced Yahoo and AltaVista in the early days of the twenty-first century. With Google unable or unwilling to leverage its advantages though some sort of lockdown, such as holding users' content and data hostage with technology or exclusive contracts so that they must continue to use Google services, they point out that users could easily migrate to the next Google-like company. As Google's lawyer Dana Wagner says, "Competition is a click away."[14]

Of course, that argument relies on the myth that Internet companies are weightless and virtual. It might be valid if Google were merely a collection of smart people and elegant computer code. Instead, Google is also a monumental collection of physical sites such as research labs, server farms, data networks, and sales offices. Replicating the vastness of Google's processing power and server space is unimaginable for any technology company except Microsoft. Wagner's argument about user behavior could be valid if boycotting or migrating from Google did not incur significant downgrades in service by losing the advantages of integration with other Google services.

Google's argument also ignores the "network effect" in communication markets: a service increases in value as more people use it.[15] A telephone that is connected to only one other person has very limited value compared with one connected to 250 million people. YouTube is more valuable as a video platform because it attracts more contributors and viewers than any other comparable service. The more users it attracts, the more value each user derives from using it, and thus the more users it continues to attract. Network effects tend toward standardization and thus potential monopoly.

The network effect for most of Google's services is not the same exponential effect we saw with the proliferation of the telephone or fax machine. If only one person in the world used Gmail, it would still be valuable to her, because it can work well with every other standard e-mail interface. But if only a few people used Google for Web searching,

Google would not have the data it needs to improve the search experi- ence. Google is better because it's bigger, and it's bigger because it's better. This is an arithmetic, rather than geometric, network effect, but it matters nonetheless. Opting out or switching away from Google services degrades one's ability to use the Web.

It may seem as if I'm arguing that Google is a monopoly and needs to be treated as such, broken up using the antimonopoly legislation and regulations developed over the late nineteenth and early twentieth centuries. But because Google is sui generis, business competition and regulation demand fresh thinking. It's such a new phenomenon that old metaphors and precedents don't fit the challenges the company pre- sents to competitors and users. So far, Google manages us much better than we manage Google. Just because Wagner's defense of Google is shallow does not necessarily mean that we would be better off sever- ing the company into various parts or restricting its ambitions in some markets. But the very fact that Google is nothing like anything we have seen before both demands vigilance and warrants concern. That fact also means that there is no general answer to how competing firms or regula- tors should approach Google's ventures. Everything must be considered case by case and with an eye on particulars. "Is Google a monopoly?" is the wrong question to ask. Instead, we should begin by examining what Google actually does and how that compares to what competitors do or might do in the future. That approach will give us a better sense of what the Googlization of everything means and what has already been done about it.

THE SEARCH FOR A BETTER SEARCH

There is a broad consensus that Web search is still in a very pedestrian phase. Both Yahoo and Google generally work the same way, and neither offers consistently superior search results. People tend to choose one or the other platform based on other factors—habit, the default search service embedded in a browser, their choice of e-mail client, appearance, or speed.[16] At most search-engine companies, the computers tend to take the string of text that users type into a box and scour their vast indexes of copies of Web pages for matches. Among the matches, each page is ranked instantly by a system that judges "relevance." Google calls its ranking system PageRank: links rise to the top of the list of search results by attracting a large number of incoming links from other pages. The more significant or highly ranked a recommending page is, the more weight a link from it carries within the PageRank scoring system.[17] Each website copied into Google's servers thus carries with it a set of relative scores instantly calculated to place it in a particular place on a results page, and this ranking is presumed to reflect its relevance to the search query. Relevance thus tends to mean something akin to value, but it is a relative and contingent value, because relevance is also calculated in a way that is specific not just to the search itself but also to the search history of the user. For this reason, most Web search companies retain records of previous searches and note the geographic location of the user.

While this approach is standard, and works fairly well in most situations for most users, a number of search-engine companies have been working furiously to deepen the "thinking" that computers do when queried. Since 2008, we have seen the debut of a number of new search engines that offer a different way of searching and depend heavily on the ability to understand the context and purpose of the search query. And Google, understandably, refines and alters its search principles with regularity.

Cuil, which debuted ignominiously in 2008, was founded by a group of former Google employees. Its launch was marred by too much publicity and attention. The first users found the system terribly slow and fragile. Cuil boasts of searching a larger index of sources than either Google or Microsoft's search engine, Bing. It also claims to be able to conduct rudimentary semantic analyses of the potential results pages to assess relevance better than the popularity method of PageRank. By the summer of 2009, Cuil delivered consistently good results to basic queries, but no one seemed to notice. Most importantly, Cuil pledged not to collect user data via logs or cookies, the small files with identifying information that Google and other search engines leave in every user's Web browser, because it is more interested in what the potential results pages mean than what the user might think about. Cuil is a clever and innovative search service that has suffered from terrible business and public-relations decisions.[18]

In early 2009, the eccentric entrepreneur and scientist Stephan Wolfram released what he called a "computational knowledge engine," Wolfram Alpha. By staging a series of small-scale demonstrations for the most elite Web thinkers in the United States, Wolfram was able to seed curiosity and attract attention for his service. Unlike a commercial search engine, Alpha is not so much designed to find pages and videos on the Web as to answer research questions by mining publicly available data sets. It does not even attempt to index Web sites. Its utility to users and advertisers, therefore, is narrow. But as a concept in knowledge management and discovery, it is potentially revolutionary. If you ask Alpha, "How many atoms are in a molecule of ammonia?" it will tell you the answer. It finds facts. It even generates facts, in a sense, by computing new information from different, distinct data sets. Wolfram Alpha is not intended to compete with Google in any way or in any market (although Google's Web search can answer the same question by directing users to the top link: a page from Yahoo Answers!). However, if it succeeds, Alpha will remove a small set of scientific queries from the mass of Google searches. Google will hardly notice—unless it decides to adopt elements of Alpha technology for its own services. Wolfram Alpha is certain to serve as a useful experiment in the development of machine-based knowledge development. But it's not for shopping.[19] It won't have anything like Google's effect on people worldwide, and it, too, is designed to remain a clever resource but never to become a major player in general information or Web searching.

Currently, the major search engines do not "read" the query for meaning. They are purely navigational: they point. However, all the big search companies (and most of the small ones, as well) are working on what is known in the industry as "semantic search," searches that take account of the contextual meaning of the search terms. For example, in 2001, if a user typed "What is the capital of Norway?" into Google, the results would have been a set of pages that included the string of text

"What is the capital of Norway?" By contrast, a semantic search engine that reads what computer scientists and linguists call "natural language" can understand the patterns of human diction well enough to predict that a user expects the result of this search to be the answer to the question, not a set of pages asking the same question. To accomplish the goal of generating a natural-language or semantic search system, search companies need two things: brilliant thinkers in the areas of linguistics, logic, and computer science, and massive collections of human-produced language on which computers can conduct complex statistical analysis. Many companies have the former. Only Google, Yahoo, and Microsoft have the latter. Of those, Google leads the pack.

It's no accident that Google has enthusiastically scanned and "read" millions of books from some of the world's largest libraries. It wants to collect enough examples of grammar and diction in enough languages from enough places to generate the algorithms that can conduct natural-language searches. Google already deploys some elements of semantic analysis in its search process. PageRank is no longer flat and democratic. When I typed "What is the capital of Norway?" into Google in August 2010, the top result was "Oslo" from the Web Definitions site hosted by Princeton University. The second result was "Oslo" from Wikipedia.

One search company is trying to combine the two approaches, blending semantic search with community-based assessment of the quality of sources. By those standards, Hakia should be the best search engine in the world. Hakia specializes in medical information, and it invited medical professionals to help assess the value and validity of potential result sites. The results, however, are not clearly superior to Google's. Hakia does place medical journal results higher in many searches.[20] But a search for "IT band" on Google and Hakia conducted in July 2009 yielded excellent results on Google and inappropriate results on Hakia. Google directed me to sites such as the Mayo Clinic's orthopedic pages, where I leaned about the malady known clinically as iliotibial band syndrome, which involves chronic tightness and pain in a band of connective tissue that runs from the hip to the knee. Hakia, supposedly specializing in medical searches, directed me to the Wikipedia site for the Band, the musical group that first gained international acclaim by backing up Bob

Dylan in 1965 and 1966 and went on to deliver some of the greatest American music until it broke up in 1976.[21]

While Yahoo struggles to keep itself in the game, the two behemoths in the search-engine competition, Google and Microsoft, continue to battle each other, not just in the search-engine field, but increasingly across the whole domain of computer software and online services. In hopes of keeping Google off its guard, in June 2009 Microsoft released Bing, developed in a partnership with Yahoo, which is a completely revised version of its Live Search engine. To differentiate itself from Google, Microsoft has advertised Bing as a "decision engine" as opposed to a search engine. It specializes in searches about travel, shopping, health, and local knowledge. In other words, while Wolfram Alpha is experimenting with ways to peel off some searches from Google that concern factual data, Microsoft hopes to attract consumers. The advertisements Microsoft ran ridiculed Google for offering too much information when users just want to buy stuff. Early on, Bing seemed able to pry some users away from Yahoo but posed no major threat to Google in the U.S. search market.[22]

In July 2009, just after Microsoft announced Bing in an attempt to force Google to refocus on its core moneymaking activity—Web searches and the advertising they generate—Google countered by announcing the development of a light, clean operating system that would run on a small, cheap computer, a netbook. This operating system, to be known as Chrome OS (just like the Web browser Chrome), would simply run a browser—like Chrome, for instance. It would facilitate Web-based services, thus pushing more users away from bulky, expensive, poorly designed programs such as Microsoft Windows and Office and toward programs that operate via the Web ("in the cloud"), such as Google Docs. Realistically, Google's initiative is no short-term or direct threat to Microsoft's dominance in the personal computer software market. But over time it could chip away at new markets in the developing world that are much more price sensitive and whose consumers are interested in connectivity rather than processing power.

All these developments have occurred as part of the dance between these two behemoths. Among the arenas where that dance takes place are the law courts and the halls of regulatory agencies. Microsoft suffered some major legal hits in 2000 when regulators in the United States and Europe cracked down on its abusive practices that had limited competition in the Web browser market and threatened to lock down Microsoft's advantages in a number of markets. By 2008, Microsoft was pushing for regulators to rein in Google's ambitions and initiatives. Microsoft's complaints were a key element in scrapping the proposed Google-Yahoo collaboration on Web advertising in 2008.[23]

Bing did not threaten Google's core revenues. Chrome will not threaten Microsoft's core revenues. But in the event that something changes in the world and one firm or the other undergoes a serious change in structure or personnel (because of pressure from new firms, consumer uproar, or government actions), the other would be poised to capitalize on the shift.

Among the most interesting responses to Google's dominance of search in Europe and North America was Quero. Funded in 2005 by a partnership between the governments of France and Germany, and with the support of the European Union, Quero was intended to correct for the perceived American cultural bias inherent in Google. Underfunded, slow to develop, and unable to resolve disputes between France and Germany over Quero's scope and role, the project died in 2007. As of 2010, Google is more popular than ever among European Web users.

None of these new search initiatives are compelling enough to wrest major portions of the search market away from Google, which is just so good at what it does, and clearly getting better every day. Even a slightly better service, result set, or interface design makes almost no difference to users. Google is now the comfortable choice for most users, and its array of services makes it undeniably useful. By default, it's easier to stay in the Google universe. One must consciously act to move beyond it (although, as I discuss in chapter 4, Google's dominance does not extend to some of the largest and most interesting markets in the world: Japan, South Korea, Russia, and China). Ultimately, Google's overall dominance matters chiefly if we are concerned with the intellectual and cultural health of the Web. And if we are worried about the economic effects of Googlization, we must follow the money. Users have no stake in questions of market share. Firms that advertise on the Web, however, do.

ADVERTISING

At least in terms of revenue generation, Google's core business isn't facilitating searches, it's selling advertising space—or rather, selling our attention to advertisers and managing both the price it charges for access to our attention and the relative visibility of those advertisements. In this field, Google is more than successful: it is simply brilliant.

In the era before Google, firms created products that they sold to customers by means of advertising that conveyed information to potential buyers. Google has completely reconfigured this model. Its own product, as I have said, is in fact the attention and loyalty of its users. While Google provides users with the information that they seek, seemingly for free, it collects the gigabytes of personal information and creative content that millions of Google users provide for free to the Web every day and sells this information to advertisers of millions of products and services. Through its major advertising program, AdWords, Google runs an instant auction among advertisers to determine which one is placed highest on the list of ads that run across the top or down the right-hand column of the search results page.

Using Google is far from free.[24] Users incur up-front, sunken costs (computer hardware) and regular utility costs (Internet service), but Google doesn't profit from these costs. Google's real customers are the advertisers who pay Google to compete in an auction to rise to the top of a list of "sponsored results" that frame the "organic results" of each search. Content creators have passively allowed Google access to their sites for the privilege of being indexed, linked, and ranked. The data on who cares about which of these sites is accumulated, and access to those potential consumers is sold to advertisers at a profit.

It's here that some troubling effects of the Googlization of everything start to become apparent, and where existing efforts to deal with those problems have fallen short. If there is one market in which Google has an inordinate share and exercises alarming power, it is Web-based advertising. In 2008 Google earned more than $21 billion (97 percent of its revenue) from online advertisements. In contrast, Microsoft lost $1.2 billion in its online advertising business. Google gives away most of its services to users for free in exchange for their attention. Microsoft, by contrast, leases software to consumers so successfully that it has been among the fifty wealthiest corporations in the world for most of the past fifteen years. Viewed in these terms, it's inaccurate to consider Microsoft as even being in the same business as Google. The parties most concerned about Google's dominance in the field of advertising on search engines are not Google's ostensible competitors like Microsoft, but the companies that buy slots to run the small bits of text that sit to the right and just above the search results on most queries—the advertisers themselves.

Google did not invent contextual advertising on the Web, but it certainly mastered it. A long-gone search-engine company called GoTo .com developed a way to link search results to advertisements in 1998.[25] By the time Google decided to adopt that practice in 2002, it had settled on an ingenious way to sell the best positions around a search term: an instant auction. If a user types "shoes" into a Google search box, Google's computers instantly solicit bids from shoe vendors. The highest bidder—the firm that offers the most money per click, with a clear ceiling of maximum clicks it is willing to pay for—gets top placement.[26]

This formula often has served the interests of small firms better than large firms. Large firms can afford to waste money on advertising. Small firms must target their ads as carefully as possible. They don't need to scream at millions of people that they should be buying some brand of weak beer. They need to attract the attention of potential consumers who have expressed interest in, say, Bavaria. For this reason, Google needs to understand how patterns of searches indicate behaviors. If Google can customize the placement of ads, giving a user results listing only local shoe stores or only Bavarian lager, then it can generate more clicks per advertisement. This maximizes revenue without necessarily pushing a small firm out of the advertising market or out of business. Google takes its money in small increments millions of times per day rather than by using the network TV model of taking millions of dollars a few times per day. In addition, Google can demonstrate to firms that these advertisements do indeed attract interested customers. There is no such clear feedback with expensive broadcast advertisements.[27]

Google's method of generating and selling advertisement placement is brilliant. It uses an unusual auction system that ensures bidders do not overpay for their winning bids. The bidding occurs dynamically and instantly on the initiation of any search. The results—the order in which ad links get placed on the results page—are determined by a number of factors, including the preferences and Web habits of the individual user or population of users in the general area (thus allowing local results to show up). Google does not charge the winning bidder the amount it bid, but instead the amount of the second-place bid, so that bidders need not fear placing a needlessly high "sucker" bid; it thereby helps small firms compete with large ones. And earning the top place in a search for a term like "shoes" or "cars" is in part determined by the "quality" of the bidder's Web page as well as the amount of the bid. In other words, Google ensures that firms bidding on terms such as "shoes" and "cars" actually offer shoes and cars. Thus customers do not fall victim to "bait-and-switch" tactics and lose trust in Google's advertisements. This system not only enhances consumer satisfaction with Google's service but also, as I state above, helps keep the Web clean. If a firm's site does not say what it means and mean what it says, or if it installs malicious code onto users' computers, or if it is just ugly and complicated, Google will not reward that site with revenue, no matter how high the bid. This system has generally kept firms happy, consumers happy, and Google's stockholders very happy.[28]

Google has not abused its market position in online advertising in any obvious way. It has, however, kept raising the minimum bid levels for many popular search terms. Although Google's contextual advertising and instant auctions often serve the interests of small firms, its freedom to set such rates at any level it desires allows it to crowd out some of the small firms that have grown to depend on Google for their most valuable advertising outlets—including small firms that are Google's potential competitors. That's mean, but it's not illegal. If Google's advertising dominance and revenues are a legal problem at all, it's because of a touchy issue called cross-subsidization.

Google can use its prominence in people's lives—the network effect—and its surplus revenues to support its other ventures—its online document business, for example, which is likely to lose trivial money for the company. This process is not yet a direct threat to Microsoft, which can withstand a few thousand customers sneaking off to the "cloud" instead of using Word on their own laptops. But it poses a serious threat to small, creative companies that offer Web-based word processors, such as Zoho, Thinkfree, Writely, and Ajaxwrite.

When I asked the *New Yorker* writer Susan Orlean why she uses Google Docs to compose her work, she replied that she found the cloud comforting. "I was starting a new book, working on two or three different computers, and finding it maddening to have different versions of work on each one, trying to remember which was the latest, etc.," Orlean wrote to me. "I happened to look at Google Docs and realized it would keep the work synced on all computers, so I thought I would give it a try. I also liked that it was so simple and clean—more like a piece of typing paper than a fancy program." When I asked her if she considered using Zoho, which is a superior service, she responded, "No, I haven't, and I trusted Google Docs because I figured it would be around for a long time, where smaller services might disappear (along with my documents)."[29]

If Google uses its profitable ventures to subsidize those activities destined to lose money, and if that practice kills off innovative potential competitors like Zoho, Google has crossed the line into shaky legal territory. This is essentially what Microsoft did in the 1990s when it used its dominance in desktop software to subsidize and promote its Internet Explorer Web browser. Microsoft managed to kill off several innovative competitors, including Netscape, the original commercial browser. The only remaining major competitors for Explorer were Apple's Safari (also subsidized by Apple's profitable ventures) and Firefox, an open-source product released by the Mozilla Foundation. Explorer was for a long time the default browser on more than 70 percent of the computers in the world.[30] Although it has been displaced by Firefox in recent years, Explorer is still installed along with Microsoft Windows, the operating system of choice for more than 90 percent of the world's personal computers.

Competition, both fair and unfair, is but one point of friction between Google and other powerful interests. Increasingly, Google is the target of attacks from firms that provide content to the Web, largely because they are failing to make much money from the Web and Google makes so much.

THE FREE RIDE

Whenever we write blog entries, post reviews of products, upload photos, or make short videos for viewing by anyone who is using the Web, Google finds them. And it copies whatever it finds. All search engines must make a "cache" copy of material they find so that their computers can conduct a search. Then, when others search for content relating to their search queries, Google places revenue-generating advertisements on the margins of the search results through its Ad Words auction program, described above. In a sense, we could say Google is taking a free ride on the creative content of billions of content creators. But the ride is not free at all. Even though we don't ever negotiate terms of a contract, we essentially agree (by not opting out or actively disagreeing) that search engines may copy our content and make money from the process of judging, ranking, and connecting people to it in exchange for the privilege of our content being found. After all, why would we put content up on the Web if we did not want people to find it? And clearly, opting out of all search engines (there is no simple way to opt out of one or two search engines but not others) is infeasible. So although we get a pretty good deal out of the relationship, it is hardly a fairly negotiated arrangement. But we have little to complain about. Google invests billions in its techniques and technologies to make the Web a reasonable and navigable place. So if we are in the business of trying to get people to notice our work on the Web, we should probably be grateful that Google treats us as well as it does.

Besides, what is so free about a free ride anyway? In basic economic terms, a free rider consumes more than a fair share of limited resources or shoulders too little of the cost of a product or service.[31] Economists consider free riders a problem because their presence can lead to under-production or excessive use of a public resource. If most people in the United Kingdom pay their television tax for over-the-air broadcast-ing, but a few watch without paying the tax, then the norm of paying for the tax could break down, and more people might be encour-aged to be scofflaws. If too many people jump the turnstiles on the Lisbon underground, then too few fare payers will bear the burden of supporting the service. If free riding becomes the norm, the entire system could break down. If a labor union succeeds in securing a wage hike or benefit for all the employees of a firm, but some employees refuse to join the union and pay dues, they are riding for free on the efforts of the union.[32]

Another way of looking at a free rider problem, dealing with private firm behavior rather than unions, public goods, or public resources, is the argument that when firms provide services to the public that add to costs (such as a telephone help line), yet retailers sell the item below the sug-gested retail price, the manufacturer fails to benefit from providing the service while incurring the entire cost. This argument led to the legaliza-tion of the practice of letting manufacturers establish minimum prices for their products, even if such restrictions kept prices artificially high and limited competition. We see these arguments employed today in efforts by manufacturers such as book publishers trying to keep Amazon from offering or advertising extremely low prices for their goods.[33]

So what does Google have to do with any of this? Not as much as some would assume. Our lives are full of goods and services that are built to enhance the value of other goods and services. Other goods we buy are generic replacements for parts of other goods, such as lightbulbs, universal remote controls for televisions, or replacement batteries for automobiles. In many of the cases in which Google has been accused of riding for free on the investment of others, Google is in fact just offering a cheaper and more effective replacement for part of the original service. But because of the state-granted monopoly that we call copyright, the role Google plays in the information world is nowhere as simple as the role that cheap lightbulbs play in the electric appliance economy.

Although no court has taken the argument seriously enough to endanger Google's core business, a growing number of firms have started voicing complaints that Google rides for free on the creative work and investment of others. This argument seems futile for a number of reasons, not least of which is the fact that Google has strong legal grounds (at least within the United States) to do just about everything it does with online content (but not, as I show later, with stuff that resides in the real world). One landmark U.S. case in search-engine law in 2003 set a good precedent that search engines could—in fact must—make copies of others' work to ensure that the Web functions well for everyone.[34] And the American copyright concept of fair use generally protects anyone who wishes to copy and distribute small portions of copyrighted works as long as the purpose of the distribution fulfills some role that enhances the public good, such as education, informing the public about current events or debates, or creating highly transformative work out of the raw materials of existing expressions. So when Google scans someone else's site, it can feel confident in its practice of excerpting a small slice of descriptive text from the site to help users decide whether it is relevant to their search.[35]

The story is quite different in much of Europe. In 2007 a Belgian newspaper trade organization won a suit against Google for incorporating its clients' content in searches on Google News. Because Europe does not have a flexible fair-use provision in its copyright laws, European courts consider different and much more clearly defined factors when determining whether a party has infringed on the rights of another. Since that time, Google has entered into partnerships with some European news organizations, essentially giving them preferential treatment over American sources that have the crude option of being searchable or not by the major Google services.[36]

None of these arrangements have stopped media from complaining. The media baron Rupert Murdoch has blustered about Google's ability to monetize the Web in general and Murdoch's News Corporation in particular. "Should we be allowing Google to steal all our copyrights?"

Murdoch said in April 2009.[37] In a speech in June 2009, the *Wall Street Journal*'s publisher, Les Hinton, proclaimed, "There is a charitable view of the history of Google. [It] didn't actually begin life in a cave as a digital vampire per se. The charitable view of Google is that the news business itself fed Google's taste for this kind of blood." Hinton went on to complain that the news business had made a mistake by offering its content for free over the Web, and thus "gave Google's fangs a great place to bite. We will never know what might have happened had newspapers taken a different approach."[38] And Robert Thomson, the editor in chief of the *Wall Street Journal*, went even farther by comparing Google to a tapeworm. "There is a collective consciousness among content creators that they are bearing the costs and that others are reaping some of the revenues—inevitably that profound contradiction will be a catalyst for action and the moment is nigh," he told an Australian newspaper in April 2009. "There is no doubt that certain websites are best described as parasites or tech tapeworms in the intestines of the Internet."[39]

By the autumn of 2009, Murdoch had grown so alarmed at the decline in advertising revenues of his publications and the continued growth of Google's revenue even during a crippling global recession that he threatened to block Google from scanning stories from his prize properties, the *Sun*, the *Times* of London, and the *Wall Street Journal*, and begin charging for access to all of News Corporation's online content. By early 2010 he had done none of those things. But his anger and accusations of free riding set the tone for debates over the relationship between Google and news sources.[40]

Google has some simple rejoinders to the complaints of Murdoch and others in the journalism field. First and foremost, Google drives traffic to quality sites, although the amount of that traffic is a matter of some dispute. The *Wall Street Journal* is a quality site. Its readers, and Web readers in general, have approved of its content by linking to its articles despite the fact that they have always sat behind a paywall, largely inaccessible to those without a subscription to the paper. Second, the fact that Google makes ad revenue off search results for a subject does not necessarily undermine the value of the site itself on the advertising market. There is no zero-sum game going on here. Although it's true that Google presents a potentially cheaper and more effective way for firms to purchase advertising space, that is true regardless of whether Google includes news results in its general searches (Google does not place ads on the Google News front page but does so on the first page of search results). In the meantime, Google officials have been working with news organizations to figure out ways to generate new interfaces that would privilege "mainstream" content over the noise generated by blogs and aggregation sites such as Huffington Post.[41]

It is these secondary sites, not Google News or Google Web Search, that pose the real problem for news organizations, and potentially for Google. Many blogs reuse material from mainstream commercial sites, often copying most or all of the text of a news article in a blog post. And many blogs generate revenue through a different Google advertising placement service, AdSense (which is distinct from AdWords, described above). This service allows bloggers and other Web publishers to earn money from click-through ads placed on their sites by Google. Google takes the context of the content on the site into account when placing ads. So a blogger who has ridden for free on content from the *Wall Street Journal* could profit from readers who chose to read the story on the blog instead of the *Journal*'s website and clicked an ad on the blog page.[42] If there is any substantial free riding on news content going on in the Google universe, it is through these aggregators and Google AdSense. Still, that seems a trivial problem compared to those that the American and European journalism industries have been facing since the global recession started in 2007.[43]

If Murdoch has a valid point at all in his complaints about Google, it is a minor one. The process of scanning a news site to pick a story to read exposes readers to advertisements. A particular news story might interest the reader and solicit a click. A particular advertisement might do the same. There is a chance that no stories and no advertisements would warrant a click. But at least if a reader is viewing the official site of a news organization, that organization has a chance to profit from that reader's attention and curiosity. If we assume that most readers ignore most news stories, then the rare and selective clicks from Google Web Search or Google News to a specific story on a news site are worth something to the reader, but possibly less than the scanning time that the reader spent on Google. Murdoch assumes that if Google did not offer links to news content, then readers hungry for his company's work would spend more time on official sites, giving those sites a better chance to attract a click on an advertisement. Whether this assumption is correct is an empirical question that no one has fully explored. In the meantime, this battle remains one of bluster and legal technicalities. Murdoch believes the world works one way. Google believes the world works another way. Murdoch is losing money. Google is making money. There is not much chance that under current conditions we will be able to design a system that supplies citizens with the knowledge they seek, consumers with the content they desire, and firms with the revenue they need. The intransigence and arrogance of the parties involved do not help.

In the meantime, and contrary to its Murdoch-inspired public image as an insurgent force against mainstream news, Google has been working furiously on a system that would combine the efficiency of news search with the depth and professional quality of serious journalism. The company has a team of engineers working with major news organizations such as the *Washington Post,* the *New York Times,* and the Associated Press to experiment with better ways to present serious journalism coherently and systematically, so that quality journalism does not get buried among the detritus of a million shoddy Web pages that share search terms. Google is essentially bending its news-search and indexing services to favor established, commercial sources in hopes of keeping the Web filled with quality content. What's good for the Web, after all, is good for Google. So clearly, Google's future role in the journalism industry will be far more complex—and perhaps more positive—than Murdoch's shallow accusations of free riding would indicate.[44]

Viacom is the most notorious accuser of Google as a free rider. The video production company, which owns MTV, Nickelodeon, and Comedy Central, among many other major video services, objected to the fact that millions of fans of its programs had the habit of taking bits of those shows and putting them up on YouTube. Digital copyright law in the United States is clear on these matters: the service provider has no legal obligation to block copyrighted content from appearing on the Internet if it's put there by a user, a third party. An Internet service provider is simply required to remove the content on receiving a notice of its existence. That way, providers don't have to spend resources inefficiently filtering and blocking the actions of their users. Congress decided to insulate them from liability for the damage that their users do, much as phone companies cannot be held responsible for crimes planned or executed using the phone. So the burden of enforcement, according to a law that Viacom helped write back in 1998, rests on the copyright owner to defend its own interests. Viacom no longer likes this policy, as the burden of scrubbing YouTube of Viacom content quickly became expensive. So in 2007 Viacom filed suit against Google asking for $1 billion in damages. In early 2010 Google prevailed in a court ruling. So for now, Google and other Internet companies may be secure in the belief that they are not responsible for the copyright infringement their users might commit within the United States.[45]

The political significance of the case is clear, regardless of Google's victory in court: even though YouTube itself loses money, Google overall makes money. Therefore, Google is a source of Viacom's anxiety. Google does, in fact, try to police the content of YouTube, even though the law does not require it to do so. In fact, Google regulates YouTube more heavily than it regulates the Web in general, largely because of the more immediate threats to its reputation and the potential to offend millions of users with violent, hateful, or sexually frank videos.

YOUTUBE TROUBLE

Since about 2002, every segment of the traditional media industries has apparently been losing money—or at least making less money than before. Yet Google has succeeded spectacularly. This fact has generated a significant sense of envy among media industry leaders and has led to many outbursts and frictions. Interestingly, Google's power over the media phenomenon of the first decade of the twenty-first century—YouTube—has challenged many of the core beliefs and values of

Google itself. If the stakes are high for governing the Web in general—a mostly textual collection of pages that are hosted beyond Google's control—they are enormous for running the most important source of visual entertainment and information in the world. YouTube is where politics and culture happen online. Video is uploaded at a rate of ten hours of content per minute and consumed at a rate of 200 million videos per day worldwide.[46] YouTube videos produced by Barack Obama's supporters generated more passion and interest than his official election campaign. YouTube is where global terrorists try to recruit followers and boast of their gruesome actions. It's where serious academic lectures and goofy home videos intermingle. It's where dogs ride skateboards. And while you and I create and donate the content, Google hosts it on its servers and acts as publisher of all this potentially litigious and controversial material.

Ever since Google purchased YouTube in 2006, when the video service was just over a year old and already a major sensation on the Web, YouTube has changed Google, and Google has changed YouTube. YouTube has become the central battlefield in the struggle to define the terms and norms of digital communication. YouTube is where Google most clearly governs, and not always gently. As YouTube grows in cultural and political importance every week, we hear more stories of important video clips coming down. It's understandable when YouTube removes a clip after a music or film company sends a "notice and take-down" letter to YouTube complaining that a user-posted video contains its copyrighted material and thus possibly infringes on copyright, but when someone demands the removal of clips simply because of their political content, that's a different problem. Here is an example in which copyright acts as an instrument of political censorship: U.S. representative Heather Wilson (R-New Mexico) was running for reelection in a close race in 2006. Back in the mid-1990s, she chaired the New Mexico Department of Children, Youth, and Families. Her husband was being investigated about accusations that he had been sexually involved with a minor, and one of the first things she did as head of the department was remove his file. Soon, however, people across New Mexico found out about the cover-up. A political blogger in New Mexico posted on

YouTube a news clip of Wilson and others discussing it. But New Mexico voters could not view the clip for long: the TV station invoked the "notice and takedown" provisions of the Digital Millennium Copyright Act to require YouTube to remove the video clip. Any of my media studies students could explain why posting a news clip of a public official under scrutiny and up for reelection is considered fair use under U.S. copyright law: it constitutes an allowable use of copyrighted material for the purpose of news and commentary. But when it comes to the Web, the copyright act respects fair use only as an afterthought, long after the provider has removed the content. The clip came down, and Wilson was reelected.[47]

In another blatantly political example, the radical right-wing American columnist Michelle Malkin posted a video of a slideshow she had spliced together showing the consequences of violence by Muslim extremists. For some reason, the editors at YouTube judged it inappropriate. When Malkin asked YouTube officials to explain the their reasoning, especially in light of the fact that YouTube is full of clips that seem to glorify violence against American troops, she got no response. Malkin started a conservative YouTube group to protest the removal, and soon *that* group was flagged by users who dislike Malkin's politics for having "inappropriate" content.

The Malkin story is troubling and revealing on a number of levels. One of the clever things about YouTube is that it uses its members to police its content. Thus a virtual community could, in theory, enforce something like community norms. However, YouTube has no mechanism to establish what those standards or norms should be, and reaching a consensus among billions of viewers would be impossible. So YouTube employees make these decisions internally to minimize controversy. Current YouTube policies make sure that sexually explicit content rarely comes up in a YouTube search, and that's nice: YouTube is one of the few places on the Web where you can be confident that people won't appear naked uninvited on your computer screen. But such broad policies effectively invite flame wars and flag wars, in which competing political activists flag the other sides' videos as inappropriate. That is what seems to have happened in the Malkin controversy.

I watched Malkin's video on a competing site. It's pretty dumb and simplistic, consisting merely of images of victims of violent extremists, spliced with some of the controversial Danish cartoons of Mohammed. If all dumb and simplistic material were considered inappropriate for YouTube, far fewer videos would be posted there. In her writing, Malkin recklessly associates the deeds of a handful of marginal, murderous thugs with the sincere and humane faith of more than a billion followers. She spreads bigotry on her blog (to which Google's Web Search links) and her books (which Google offers on Google Books). But that does not mean that this particular video is bigoted: it's not. But because it's by Malkin, it's a target. Author-based rather than content-based editing is bad policy. The Web should always be the sort of place where you can find troubling and challenging material. It should accommodate stuff too controversial for the mainstream media. Because YouTube is a commercial enterprise, it has no obligation to present everything or to protect anything. But as it folds itself into the pervasive entity known as Google—which increasingly filters the Web for us—we need to find ways to pressure it to be more inclusive and less sensitive.[48]

MARKET FAILURES AND PUBLIC FAILURES

Google walked into its regulatory role out of opportunity and necessity. The Internet in the late twentieth century was too global, too messy, and too gestational to justify national or international regulation.[49] Some illiberal states, such as the People's Republic of China, chose to step in and aggressively perform those regulatory duties either through direct action or through proxies in the quasi-private sector.[50]

In the more liberal world of the United States and—to a lesser extent—Europe, a presumption that market forces can best solve problems and build structures so dominated political debate from about 1981 onward that even considering the possibility of state involvement in something so delicate and new as the Internet was implausible.[51] After the recent collapse of the corrupt and disastrous command-and-control economies of Eastern Europe, it was difficult to propose a way of doing things that fell between the poles of triumphant market fundamentalism and incompetent, overbearing state control. Of course the market had survived and thrived. There seemed to be no other mechanism that could deliver positive results to a diverse, connected world.[52] The notion of gentle, creative state involvement to guide processes toward the public good was impossible to imagine, let alone propose.

This vision was known as neoliberalism. Although Ronald Reagan and Margaret Thatcher championed it, Bill Clinton and Tony Blair mastered it. It had its roots in two prominent ideologies: techno-fundamentalism, an optimistic belief in the power of technology to solve problems (which I describe fully in chapter 3), and market fundamentalism, the notion that most problems are better (at least more efficiently) solved by the actions of private parties rather than by state oversight or investment.[53] And it was not just a British and American concept. It was deployed from Hong Kong to Singapore, Chile, and Estonia.[54] Neoliberalism went beyond simple libertarianism. There was, and is, substantial state subsidy and support for firms that promulgated the neoliberal model and supported its political champions. But in the end the private sector calls the shots and apportions (or hoards) resources, as the instruments once used to rein in the excesses of firms have been systematically dismantled.[55] Neoliberalism may have had its purest champions in the last two decades of the twentieth century. But it's still with us, and harming us, today.[56]

Our dependence on Google is the result of an elaborate political fraud, but it is far from the most pernicious result of that fraud. Google has deftly capitalized on a thirty-year tradition of "public failure," chiefly in the United States but in much of the rest of the world as well. Public failure is the mirror image of market failure. Markets fail when they can't organize to supply an essential public good, such as education, or have no incentive to prevent a clear harm to the public, such as pollution. Market failure is the chief justification for public intervention.[57] For instance, market actors don't envision sufficient financial returns to justify investing in the production of children's educational television, folk festivals, or opera. If a society wishes to enjoy the benefits of such productions, then it must subsidize them with public funds. The U.S.

government justified the creation of the Corporation for Public Broadcasting in 1967 to correct for precisely these market failures.[58]

Public failure, in contrast, occurs when instruments of the state cannot satisfy public needs and deliver services effectively. This failure occurs not necessarily because the state is the inappropriate agent to solve a particular problem (although there are plenty of areas in which state service is inefficient and counterproductive); it may occur when the public sector has been intentionally dismantled, degraded, or underfunded, while expectations for its performance remain high. Examples of public failures in the United States include military operations, prisons, health-care coverage, and schooling. The public institutions that were supposed to provide these services were prevented from doing so. Private actors filled the vacuum, often failing spectacularly as well and costing the public more than the institutions they displaced. In such circumstances, the failure of public institutions gives rise to the circular logic that dominates political debate. Public institutions can fail; public institutions need tax revenue; therefore we must reduce the support for public institutions. The resulting failures then supply more anecdotes supporting the view that public institutions fail by design rather than by political choice.

The most lucid example of public failure in recent years involves the role of private firms in the relief efforts after Hurricane Katrina hit the southern coast of the United States in 2005. After the hurricane wiped out large sections of New Orleans and much of coastal Louisiana and Mississippi, state and federal relief efforts were slow and ineffective. Officials had not planned for massive evacuations and medical relief, despite ample warnings. In addition, poor engineering and maintenance and years of general underfunding and neglect had left much of New Orleans vulnerable to breeches in the essential levees intended to protect the city from high water. Under President Bill Clinton in the 1990s, the Federal Emergency Management Agency (FEMA) directorship had been raised to a cabinet-level position and had been held by an acknowledged expert in disaster management. Every major disaster in those years was handled deftly. Once President George W. Bush assumed control, he appointed as head of the agency former campaign staffers who had no training or experience in disaster relief. In addition,

Bush moved FEMA out of the cabinet and into another new agency, the Department of Homeland Security. The failures of FEMA to help people stranded and left homeless are well documented and deeply troubling. Ultimately, 1,836 people lost their lives in the hurricane and subsequent floods. More than 60,000 people were stranded in New Orleans during the flooding. Bush publicly commended the director of FEMA for the job he was doing, even in the face of his obvious ineptitude. The public sector failed, and it failed by design.[59]

In contrast, the American department store company Walmart managed to use its wealth, inventory, distribution networks, and logistical expertise to deliver water and supplies where FEMA could not.[60] The American private sector in general greatly assisted many thousands of people by donating labor and funds to the relief and reconstruction effort, even though these efforts were often poorly coordinated. As a result, market fundamentalists used the designed failure of the public sector to argue that it should be structured to do less in future emergencies.[61] Such arguments occur in other areas of public policy as well, as citizens in the United States witnessed during the efforts to pass an economic stimulus package and comprehensive health-care reform legislation in 2009. The very hint of government involvement was enough to disrupt rational debate over policy.

Public failure has had two perverse effects on politics and policy. First, it has corroded faith in state institutions, effectively precluding arguments for their extension or preservation (in the United States, anyway). For example, President Barack Obama apparently considered that proposing a Canadian-style, single-payer health-care system would be completely unpalatable to the American public and powerful health-care interests. So he quickly and publicly dismissed the idea early in 2009, reversing years of endorsing such a system's proven success in Canada and many other places.[62] In the United States any suggestion of regulation or public investment must be couched in the language of the market if it is to be taken seriously.

The second pernicious result of public failure is the rise of assertions of "corporate responsibility." As the state has retreated from responsibility to protect common resources, ensure access to opportunities, enforce worker and environmental protection, and provide for the health and general welfare of citizens, private actors have rushed in to claim the moral high ground in the marketplace. So, for instance, instead of insisting that farms grow safe food under environmentally sound conditions, we satisfy our guilt and concerns by patronizing stores like Whole Foods and celebrating the wide availability of organic products. Thus food that keeps people healthy and the earth livable remains available only to the well informed and affluent.

Because market fundamentalism declares that consumers have "choice" in the market, doing little or no harm becomes just another tactic by which vendors exploit a niche market. Consumers have become depoliticized, unable to see that personal choices to buy Timberland shoes (not made in sweatshops by children) and Body Shop cosmetics (not tested on animals) make no difference at all to the children and animals that suffer supplying the bulk of similar, less sensitively manufactured products to the vast majority of the world's consumers. Feeling good about our own choices is enough. And instead of organizing, lobbying, and campaigning for better rules and regulations to ensure safe toys and cars for people everywhere, we rely on expressions of disgruntlement as a weak proxy for real political action. Starting or joining a Facebook protest group suffices for many as political action.

Since the 1980s, firms in the United States and Western Europe have found it useful to represent themselves as socially responsible. As states have retreated from their roles as protectors of the commons and mitigators of market failures, firms have found that trumpeting certain policies and positions puts them at an advantage in competitive markets, especially for consumer goods and services.[63]

The problem, however, is that corporate responsibility is toothless. Corporations do—and should do—what is in the interests of their shareholders, and nothing more.[64] We become aware of the voluntary benevolence of certain firms only when it is in their interest to make that benevolence known.

The principal reason why the idea of corporate responsibility appeals to us is that for thirty years, we have retreated from any sense of *public* responsibility—any willingness to talk about, identify, and pursue the public good. In the absence of the political will to employ state power to push all firms toward responsible behavior, the purported responsibility of one firm is quickly neutralized by the irresponsibility of the rest. Because we have failed at politics, we now rely on marketing to make our world better. That reliance is the height of collective civic irresponsibility. It's a meaningless pose.

Google has taken advantage of both of these externalities. It has stepped into voids better filled by the public sector, which can forge consensus and protect long-term public interests instead of immediate commercial interests. The Google Books project, as I show in chapter 5, is the best example of this tendency. Google has used such undertakings to its advantage by generating a tremendous amount of goodwill and pushing a strong ethic of corporate responsibility. This in turn retards efforts to propose even mild and modest regulations on the firm to protect users' privacy and ensure competition in the Web advertising world. After all, if you can't trust Google to do something well and ethically, whom can you trust?[65]

WHO'S REGULATING WHOM?

The ways we talk about markets and regulation have become impoverished in recent decades. In June 2009, the radio journalist Brian Lehrer asked Eric Schmidt about the potential for the regulation of Google. "I use Google all day every day like a lot of people in this room," Lehrer said to Schmidt after Schmidt had given a talk at the 2009 Aspen Ideas Festival. "But is there ever a point at which Google becomes so big that it's kind of scary and needs to be regulated as a public utility?" The room filled with laughter before Schmidt could respond. So Lehrer, a knowledgeable and experienced interviewer continued: "We kind of reached that with Microsoft in the '90s, some of the same discussions. When you're aggregating all of the contents of books, when Google News is the place that people go for news content instead of the sites— *New York Times* and everything else that you are aggregating—and you know some in traditional media are upset with you for that.

Seriously, literally, is there a point where you need to be regulated as a public utility?"

"You'll be surprised that my answer is no," Schmidt responded. "Would you prefer to have the government running innovative companies or would you rather have the private sector running them? There are models and there are countries where in fact the government does try to do that, and I think the American model works better."

Lehrer interjected: "But Eric, if I could jump in, I would expect a more sophisticated answer from you. As we saw with the banks, it's not a question of Soviet-style communism or free-market capitalism. Banks needed smart regulation that they didn't have—as I think you were just saying. Is it possible that information is in the same boat?"

Schmidt started again:

> Well, again. My answer would be no. Perhaps I should expand on my answer: Google plays an important role in information. And the reason you are asking that question is because information is important to all of us. We run Google based on a set of values and principles. And we work very, very hard to make sure people know what they are. . . . Companies are defined by the values that they were founded with and that they operate with today. So if you are concerned about the need for regulation of Google's role, part of my answer would be that—independent of my leadership and the founders' leadership and so forth, the company's formed in a certain way. A thing that you should be worried about is that a combination of special interests plus unintended regulation could in fact prevent the kind of consumer benefits that we push so hard to do. Part of the other pushback that I would offer is that the things that we do are available to others. . . . We haven't largely prevented people from doing their own thing.[66]

Of course Google is regulated, and Schmidt knows it. Google spends millions of dollars every year ensuring it adheres to copyright, patent, antitrust, financial disclosure, and national security regulations. Google is promoting stronger regulations to keep the Internet "neutral," so that Internet service providers such as telecommunication companies cannot extort payments to deliver particular content at a more profitable rate. But we have become so allergic to the notion of regulation that we assume brilliant companies just arise because of the boldness and vision of investors and the talents of inventors. We actually think there is such a thing as a free market, and that we can liberate private firms and people from government influence. We forget that every modern corporation—especially every Internet business—was built on or with public resources. And every party that does business conforms to obvious policy restrictions. But Schmidt, who understands the state of political rhetoric in the United States, knew how to tease laughter out of the audience, and he understood that positing "regulation" as a choice of oppression over freedom would resonate.

Schmidt also knew that his best rejoinder to concerns about Google's enormous power was to remind people of Google's internal code of ethical conduct: "Don't be evil." Oddly, Schmidt asserts, without evidence or explanation, that this ethic would survive at the company regardless of who ran it and how far into the future we might look. Like so much else about Google's public image, this is a matter of faith. Last, Schmidt asserted that Google was careful to avoid locking in content or locking out competition through computer code or restrictive contracts: in other words, it does not behave like Microsoft. If market entry is open de jure, on paper, then that should satisfy doubters, Schmidt argued. It is easy to elide the fact that real competition in many of Google's successful areas of business such as search and advertising is almost impossible to imagine.

So if we push past the idealistic rhetoric of Google's officials, we can see that the proper question is whether Google—or the knowledge ecosystem in general—is appropriately regulated. In some areas, Google might be regulated too lightly. In others, it might be overly or improperly regulated. There is no general notion of regulation that can apply to such a complex company involved in so many different areas of life and commerce. Sadly, we seem incapable of holding a reasonable debate on this topic because raising the question seems to violate the current standards of polite political discourse.

Google's ventures can be arranged into three large categories of responsibility. By that I mean that Google has at least three ways of hosting content, each of which grants the company a different level of control over the content. Each category of responsibility demands a different level of regulation. The first category is what I call "scan and link." Google Web Search is the best example of this. Google does not host the relevant content. Content sits on servers around the world run and owned by others. Google merely sends its spiders (a small program that "crawls" around the Internet, following hyperlinks from one file to another) out to find and copy the content onto its own servers so that it can supply links to the original content via Web Search. In this case, Google bears minimal responsibility for the content. If it links to illegal or controversial material, Google may remove the link, as in the standard "notice and takedown" process that governs much behavior on the Web, including copyright infringement in many places. In most areas of U.S. law, search companies are generally not held liable for the existence of the content on some third-party server. But in most other countries, including those in Western Europe, search engines are held at least minimally responsible for the links they provide. In France and Germany, for instance, Google must actively block anti-Semitic and other hate-filled sites. In less liberal countries such as Egypt, India, and Thailand, Google actively removes links to content that offends the state. But generally, Google has little responsibility for content hosted by others, and thus its search activities demand the lightest level of regulation.

The second category is what I call "host and serve." Blogger and YouTube are the best examples of this. In these cases, Google invites users to create and upload content to Google's own servers. As in the Viacom case, Google certainly bears some responsibility for the nature of the content it holds on its own servers. In February 2010 a court in Italy convicted three Google executives of failing to remove an offensive video that showed an autistic teenager being bullied by rowdy youths. Despite hundreds of comments on the page objecting to the content, Google was not made aware of its existence until two months after its posting, when Italian police requested its removal. Google has tried to argue that it should be held to the same level of responsibility for this content that it would have for a link to a third-party site. And there was much confusion in European law over what constitutes "notice." In early 2010 an Italian judge ruled in a manner out of step with most European understandings of how notice and regulation should work in matters of privacy violations. Relying on bizarre reasoning, Judge Oscar Magi concluded that Google's position as a profit-making venture limited its exemption from liability. Nonetheless, it's clear that in situations in which Google solicits and hosts content—as with YouTube—it bears a higher level of responsibility and is likely to attract more litigation and regulation as a result.[67]

The areas in which Google has faced the strongest protest world-wide just happen to be those ventures in which Google has the greatest responsibility for content, what I call "scan and serve." In these activities, Google scours the real world, renders real things into digital form, and offers them as part of the Google experience. The two best examples are Google Books, which has generated objections and lawsuits from authors and publishers around the world, and Google Street View, which has sparked actual street protests and government actions. In Street View, Google staff take cameras out around the globe to capture images of specific locations that can be used to enhance Google's services, such as its map feature. In doing so, Google's cameras also capture images of individuals and their property. In this case, Google bears great responsibility for creating the digital content as well as hosting and delivering it to Web users. And thus these actions justify the highest level of regulatory scrutiny.

Although its various services thus incur differing levels of responsibility, Google insists on being regulated at the lowest level, specifying a one-size-fits-all prescription to regulate its complex interactions with real human beings and their diverse needs. In response to every single complaint about its behavior, Google officials answer that they are happy to take down offensive or troublesome content if someone merely takes the initiative to inform the company. It does not want to be held responsible for policing its own collections, even those collections that would not exist at all if Google did not aggregate or create them. Through its remarkable cultural power, Google has managed to keep much regulatory action at bay around the world.

In fact, Google seems poised to try to mold regulations in its favor in several important areas. In the United States there are signs that the current government has established a close relationship with Google.

During his presidential campaign in 2008, Barack Obama made it clear that he has strong ties with Google's leaders, employees, and technologies. Obama visited Google headquarters in the summer of 2004 and again in November 2007, when he announced his "innovation agenda."[68] Most of Obama's campaign speeches were released on YouTube. Eric Schmidt endorsed Obama and traveled with him in the fall of 2008. Once elected, Obama's transition team continued to use YouTube as its video platform of choice for reaching a broad audience. This relationship raised many questions and criticisms by privacy and consumer advocates, because Obama seemed to favor the Google-sponsored platform over other commercial sites or open-source alternatives. All of this occurred just as Google came under intense scrutiny for its data-retention policies and the extent to which it controls the market in Web advertising. Having a close friend in the White House could make a difference if Google gets into trouble with either U.S. or European officials.[69]

Another troubling example occurred in the summer of 2010, when Google abandoned its long-standing pledge to support open, nondiscriminatory, "neutral" digital communication networks in the United States. In July, the U.S. Federal Communications Commission failed to forge a compromise between Internet companies that support a "neutral" Internet and telecommunications companies, such as Comcast and AT&T, that would like to control the speeds at which certain data flows over their segments of the networks. Google stepped in where regulators had stalled to forge an agreement with Verizon in hopes of establishing a template for policy—or at least a framework for private agreements among firms. The result was that Google continued to claim it stood for the public interest—and an open, "classic" Internet—while dealing away significant control over mobile data channels and many future areas of growth. Significantly, Google's agreement would bar the FCC from making new rules governing data flow over networks, thus effectively privatizing policy.[70] All of these developments speak to the complex and changing relationship that Google, the chief regulator of the Web, has with the United States government, one of the chief regulators of commerce around the world.

Over and above these particular ways that Google dominates the nature and function of the World Wide Web, it has a greater, albeit more subtle governance effect.[71] Mostly by example, the company manages to spread the "Google way" of doing things. It executes a sort of soft power over not just the content of the Web but also users' expectations and habits when dealing with it. Google trains us to think as good Googlers, and it influences other companies to mimic or exceed the core techniques and values of Google. In addition, Google's success at doing what it does enhances and exploits a particular ideology: techno-fundamentalism. This soft-power mode of governance, one that depends so heavily on the blind faith we place in Google, is the subject of the next three chapters.

TWO GOOGLE'S WAYS AND MEANS

FAITH IN APTITUDE AND TECHNOLOGY

The American comedian Louis C.K. tells a story that illustrates the constant ratcheting up of expectations for newness, "nowness," speed, and convenience. He was traveling on an airplane in early 2009, C.K. told the television host Conan O'Brien, when the flight attendant announced that his flight offered a new feature that airlines had been working to install for some years: in-flight access to the Internet. "It's fast and I'm watching YouTube clips," C.K. said. "It's amazing. I'm on an airplane! Then it breaks down and they apologize that the Internet is not working. The guy next to me goes, 'Pphhhhhh. This is bullshit.' Like how quickly the world owes him something he knew existed only 10 seconds ago."[1] C.K.'s point is that when we become habituated to the amazing technological achievements of recent years, we forget to be thrilled and amazed. We lose our sense of wonder. We take brilliance for granted, and so we

51

ignore the human elements of fortitude, creativity, and intelligence that underlie so many tools we use every day. The dynamic of consumer expectations has been running at such high speeds for so many years that we become frustrated with devices and services (such as slow computer processors and Internet access) that did not even exist a few years ago.

This constant, insatiable hunger is sharpened by constant pressure on firms to expand markets and revenue, as well as by a widespread lack of historical perspective on technological change. But at its root is the black box of technological design. Although consumers and citizens are invited to be dazzled by the interface, the results, and the convenience of a technology, they are rarely invited in to view how it works. Because we cannot see inside the box, it's difficult to appreciate the craft, skill, risk, and brilliance of devices as common as an iPod or a continuously variable transmission in an automobile.

This chapter examines some of the cultural assumptions that underlie the enthusiastic reception of Google and our willingness to trust the company with information about us. First, the chapter examines how we discovered and celebrated Google in its early years and the values that it built on to earn our trust. Then it explores the values that have characterized Google's practices and people.

Google's first brilliant innovation was, of course, its search algorithm. Its second was the auction system for placing advertisements, which generates tremendous revenue for the company. But a close third is the way that Google measures us and builds its systems and services to indulge our desires and weaknesses. Google works for us because it seems to read our minds—and, in a way, it does. It guesses what you might want to see based on requests that you and others like you have already expressed. You can type a vague term into the search query box, not knowing exactly how to phrase your desire, and Google will most likely return a remarkably appropriate list of things you might want. Moreover, Google conditions us to accept and believe that that list does in fact deliver what we want. The suggestive power of Google Web Search, made explicit by the drop-down list of choices that appears when we start typing, is the magic that hooks us. In many ways Google has measured and understood us better than we have assessed ourselves.

Google works so well, so simply, and so fast that it inspires trust and faith in its users. As the science fiction writer Arthur C. Clarke famously wrote, "Any sufficiently advanced technology is indistinguishable from magic."[2] And of course trust in magic, or suspension of disbelief, is a central part of the process of embracing the deific. That's why so much of what we say and write about the experience of Google sounds vaguely religious. It sure looks like magic from this desk chair. I send a string of text out into the ether, and less than a second later the glowing screen in front of me offers a list of answers. It's not quite an abundance; that would be overwhelming. It's a manageable set of choices—just enough to give me a sense of autonomy over my next move but not too many to paralyze me. If I am shopping for shoes, there is little spiritual about the process. But if I am searching for connection, affirmation, guidance, even directions, the interactions I have with this semi-intelligent system (and all the intelligent beings to whom it can connect) can verge on the spiritual. If I am seeking something meaningful, Google seems to help me find meaning.

If you are a lonely Muslim boy growing up in Berlin, offended by the spiritual poverty and sexual depravity you perceive around you, then Google can connect you with a community that understands. If you are gay young woman growing up in a suburb of Salt Lake City, Utah, Google could be the first place you go to seek affirmation and advice. If you are a commodities trader in the City of London, you might feel a rush of adrenaline and testosterone as you use Google to sift through business news and rumors. We all Google our various gods, no matter what we worship or how worthy those gods are of our devotion. And now we expect nothing less than a meaningful response. Google's success is a function of our collective cultural weaknesses, and it in turn encourages them by ratcheting up our expectations.

As Google vice president Marissa Mayer explained during her 2008 keynote speech at a software developers' conference, one of the most significant things that Google discovered in its early user studies was that speed mattered more than anything else in generating a "positive user experience." This fact has driven Google to push the Internet industry for faster broadband service, create faster-running Web applications, and invest in an expensive, complicated, and powerful infrastructure to conduct Google's core activity: copying and searching the World Wide Web. "Users really care about speed," Mayer told developers. "They respond to speed. As the web gets faster, as Google gets faster, people search more."[3] More searching yields more advertising links displayed, more advertising links clicked, and more revenue for Google's advertising clients and Google itself. Users clearly reward the speed and the quality of search results.

Under the hood, Google runs an astounding set of machines and brilliant code. Mayer explained that every time someone types a simple query into the empty search box on the blank Google home page, that query fires up between 700 and 1,000 separate computers in several huge data centers around the United States. These computers generate 5 million search results by scanning indexes and previous search queries in a mere .16 seconds.[4]

To Google users, this amazing process is invisible. Making users wise to its power is not a priority of the company: quite the opposite. "It's very, very complicated technology, but behind a very simple interface," Mayer said. "We think that that's the best way to do things. Our users don't need to understand how complicated the technology and the development work that happens behind this is. What they do need to understand is that they can just go to a box, type what they want, and get answers."[5]

If Google users were to understand or appreciate the scale and complexity of Google's operation, their expectations for magical results might be tempered, their appreciation for human work and ingenuity bolstered, and their abilities to use the tools enhanced. Such changes would not benefit Google now, as it has bet the future of the company on being bigger, faster, better, and more embedded in the constant collective consciousness of human beings than any commercial firm in history. And by promoting its operations as almost magical, Google is not doing anything wrong. Its apparent omnipresence and omnipotence are merely functions of its abilities to capitalize on our weaknesses and desires, cravings, and curiosities.

Faith in Google is dangerous because it increases our appetite for goods, services, information, amusement, distraction, and efficiency. We are addicted to speed and convenience for the sake of speed and convenience. Google rewards us for our desires for immediate gratification at no apparent cost to us. There is nothing wrong with immediate gratification per se; it's certainly better than no gratification. Immediacy should not, however, be an end in itself. And providing immediate gratification draped in a cloak of corporate benevolence is bad faith.

THE TECHNO-FUNDAMENTALIST ESCHATOLOGY

Google spreads an eschatological ideology: a belief in fulfillment of prophecy. Those who profess eschatologies are uninterested in origin stories or accounts of miracles: instead, they look ahead. Eschatology is the study of the ultimate destiny of humanity. For Google, that destiny involves the organization and universal accessibility of the world's information. The road to that destiny is paved with the ideal expressions of techno-fundamentalism. Google believes that the constant application of advanced information technologies—algorithms, computer code, high-speed networks, and massively powerful servers—will solve many, if not all, human problems.

No firm operates independently of the culture in which it operates. Industry does not drive history any more than history drives industry. To grasp the full significance of a particular firm or institution, we must consider its place in culture and society—the work it does and the beliefs that value and enable that work. Google is both a product of early twenty-first-century American culture and an influence on global culture.

LIFE BEFORE GOOGLE

Google may be sui generis, but before Google, a number of search engines competed for business in the field. Each of them conducted indexing and searching a bit differently. Like Google, they all originated from a rich academic field devoted to information coding and retrieval, one that lies at the intersection of computer science, linguistics, and library and information studies. It remains an exciting intellectual field. But the late-1990s market gurus of Silicon Valley did not necessarily see search as the key to riches. They saw it as an ancillary feature designed to hold customers' attention, along with all the other services and content that crowded pages such as Yahoo and Excite.[6] Early news coverage of Google generally folded the company in with other search companies launched around the same time. Rarely did a technology or business journalist declare that there was anything remarkable or distinct about Google, even though the simple act of using it demonstrated Google's superiority almost instantly.

Business Week first took note of Google in September 1998. In a brief entry about how search engines work and the challenge of assessing the quality of their results, its editors wrote: "There's another ranking system that may be even better for managers. Google (http://google.stanford.edu/) rates Web sites by the number of other sites linked to them. The rankings, in other words, are determined not by surfers, but by Webmasters who presumably took time to evaluate a site before setting up a link to it. It's an adaptation of the time-honored practice of assessing scientific papers by the number of citations they've gotten in other papers."[7]

It's notable that the link to Google given in that article was within the Stanford University computer system. This is the earliest reference I could find to the search engine that ten years later would dominate the Web experience in most of the world. The *Press* of Christchurch, New Zealand, mentioned Google as a new idea for Web search in December 1998. By then, the URL already stood alone as www.google.com.[8] *USA Today* also listed Google in a brief about interesting websites in December 1998.[9] Business and computer publications with specialized circulations started mentioning Google in mid-1999. The *New York Times* apparently did not consider Google important enough to write about until its columnist Max Frankel mentioned Google among a list of search engines in November 1999.[10]

The first serious consideration of Google by the *New York Times*, the leading American newspaper, was a de facto endorsement by the technology writer Peter Lewis in September 1999. "Until recently my favorite search engines were Hotbot (www.hotbot.com) and Alta Vista (www .altavista.com)," Lewis wrote. "Hotbot is useful for finding popular Web sites, and AltaVista is good at ferreting out obscure information. Alta Vista in particular returns a bazillion potential hits when it is asked to scour the Net for a word or phrase. But the larger the World Wide Web becomes, the more important it becomes for search engines to return fewer results, not more. Few people have time to click through 70,482 query matches hoping that the one they want, the most relevant one, is in there somewhere. The engines not only have to be smarter, but also faster." Lewis noted that "several search engines introduced recently deserve serious consideration, including the revamped version of MSN .com Search (msn.com), introduced by the Microsoft Network last week, and AOL.com Search (aol.com), to be introduced by America Online next week. But if you are searching for the next generation in search technologies, look for Gurunet and Google."[11]

Gurunet did not last long after Lewis wrote about it, and he offered only qualified interest in its methods. He was smitten with Google, however. At the moment when the president of the United States was enmeshed in a tawdry scandal involving sex with a White House intern, Lewis found that Google filtered for relevance effectively enough to avoid pornographic sites when searching for terms such as "Bill Clinton" and, more important, "sex." As Lewis wrote,

> What Google does do, however, is to come up with a list that starts with a guide to marriage and sex, not the long string of pornographic sites that would pop up in the search listings of most other engines. Many disreputable Web site operators attempt to fool search engines by salting their pages with bogus key words in an attempt to lure unsuspecting users. Google does not ogle. Instead, Google determines the relevance or importance of a page in part by measuring how many other sites have links to it. That technique enables Google to rank even those sites that it has not visited. Many Web sites do not allow search engines to catalogue their content, but they may hold the information a searcher wants.

Unlike other search engines, Lewis wrote, "Google . . . takes into account the importance, measured in popularity, of the sites that are linking to the page. Links from popular sites are given more weight than links from obscure sites. If a lot of important sites establish links with the page, the reasoning goes, it must be important too. It is the cyber-age variant on the common wisdom that the best roadside diners are the ones with all the big trucks parked outside." Once the *New York Times* parked its truck outside Google and explained the virtues of PageRank to the elites of America, it was impossible to stop Google's proliferation.[12]

Still, through its early years of rapid growth, Google never advertised on television or in standard print media (although it did purchase a gratuitous, albeit clever, advertisement during the Super Bowl in 2010). Its growth in popularity was in part sparked by glowing reviews among technology writers, but the most significant factor in its growth was word-of-mouth recommendation. Most of us discovered Google because it worked for our friends. It took a mess and put it in order. It took a frustrating task and made it simple. And it seemed so unassuming about the whole matter.

This is a story of commercial success rarely seen in business history. The business was all about leveraging technology and science. Those, after all, were what lay behind Google's mission, however humanistic its statement might be: "To organize the world's information and make it universally accessible and useful." The larger question that we need to ponder, however, is why we all welcomed such an enterprise with open arms and why we have unreflectively trusted it with such massive amounts of our personal information and with control over our access to knowledge.

"TRUST BIAS" AND THE PRAGMATISM OF PAGERANK

Questions of trust and control are not merely matters of abstract speculation. The core practices of Google—the massive accumulation of data on consumer and citizen preferences, the ability to accurately and precisely target small advertisements for small services for a small fee billions of times per day, and the appearance of offering access to information for no monetary cost—could soon be dominant modes of information commerce.[13] Google has already forced big media companies and mobile-phone services to alter their expectations and services. Soon other companies will no doubt try to mimic Google's style, philosophy, and moves.[14]

We trust Google with our personal information and preferences and with our access to knowledge because we trust technology that satisfies our prejudices. We want fast access to relevant and reliable information. Google has ascended to great heights in twelve short years by emphasizing three characteristics of its technology that build trust among users: speed, "precise comprehensiveness," and honesty. On one level—that of simple practicality—we trust Google because, compared with the alternatives, it indeed works fast, produces information that usually seems relevant, and, as a result, seems trustworthy.

Precise comprehensiveness is the term I give to the list of results that appears to be clear and ranked in order of relevance. If a number of users doing the same search click on the third result instead of the first, then, over time, Google will raise the rank of that result. Google Web Search presents us with a linear pattern of display—the ordered list—that offers a sense of precision. The impression of comprehensiveness derives from the declarations of (largely useless) abundance that Google offers along the top of each search results page, such as "Results 1–10 of about 481,000,000 for God." The sense of precision derives from the short list of ten results returned on the first page.

Users thus believe that Google's rankings are honest expressions of probable importance and relevance. They demonstrate a "trust bias" when selecting one of these links to click: they inherently trust Google's algorithmic judgment about which links are appropriate for them.[15] This trust bias is reinforced by the fact that most people who use Google do so in a very unsophisticated way while nonetheless expressing a high level of confidence about their own skills at navigating a search system.[16]

Whether or not users know the company's motto, "Don't be evil," this trust bias reflects a faith, avowed or latent, in Google's corporate ethos.

I examine this faith at greater length in the next chapter. Users believe in Google's honesty regardless of whether they understand the way its core algorithm, PageRank, chooses what to display and how to rank links. Users trust Google to make choices for them, or at least to guide them toward a few choices that attract the most attention.[17] Needless to say, appearing on the first page of results is of paramount importance for firms competing for attention and sales.[18]

Despite a shallow understanding of how search engines work, Web users express deep satisfaction with them. Only 19 percent express a lack of trust in search engines. More than 68 percent of Web search users report that they consider search engines to be fair and unbiased. About 44 percent of those surveyed by the Pew Internet and American Life Project in 2005 said they use only one search engine, and 48 percent use only two or three. Only 38 percent said they were aware of the distinction between the sponsored advertising links that Google and other search services offer and the algorithmically generated "organic" results that dominate the page. Only one in six search users could testify that they can always tell the difference between the sponsored links and the generated results.[19]

Thus Google is inherently conservative in its effects on the information world: winners keep winning, unless Google changes the rules of the system or intervenes with human judgment.[20] By favoring the majority or the consensus among search sites, Google Web Search results also favor the comfortable middle ground of controversial subjects.[21]

THE PRAGMATIC THEORY OF SEARCH

Our trust in Google is pragmatic in more than just the ordinary sense of the term, however. We believe that a consensus about what's important, arrived at by apparently democratic means, is probably trustworthy. Google's method of relying on the collective and active judgment of millions of Web users seems in the abstract to realize one of the most influential theories of epistemology: American pragmatism. As Charles Sanders Peirce and William James developed it in the 1890s and Richard

Rorty refined it almost century later, the pragmatic theory of truth states that truth is generated through a process of experimentation, discovery, feedback, and consensus.[22] The true statement is therefore one that works in the world, James would say. It conforms to experience and observation, yet is under constant pressure of revision, as Peirce explained.[23] Truth is not attached to a thing in the world per se, but to our experiences of that thing and to our conversation about and collective understanding of it. People and peoples can disagree over what is true, and that disagreement is a part of the process of lurching toward truth.

Thus truth is not merely a thoughtful reflection of reality. It's different for everyone, depending on differences of perspective and experience. What is true about a clock is different for a clockmaker than for a person who merely knows how to tell time, James explained. "The truth of an idea is not a stagnant property inherent in it," James wrote. "Truth happens to an idea. It becomes true, is made true by events. Its verity is in fact an event, a process: the process namely of its verifying itself, its veri-fication."[24]

James's focus on the dynamism of truth—what Rorty later called "contingency"—is embodied in Google PageRank.[25] Rank is assigned to a site through a dynamic process of verification by communal affirmation. The instrument of that affirmation is the hyperlink. The secondary instrument is the click on the hyperlink. The field in which the affirmations are transformed into contingent, temporary judgments of relevance or, as James might say, truth, is the PageRank algorithm. And this is the brilliance of PageRank and Google's Web Search system in general: how else would one make sense of something as dynamic and messy as the World Wide Web? Just as pragmatism helps us understand what we mean when we say something in the world is "true" or that we "believe" something, Google sifts through an enormous array of documents and orders them in a way that reflects a rough—very rough—consensus among Web users. However, pragmatism also helps us understand that the contingency of truth and value demands that we interrogate the biases and flaws in our collective judgments and the language we use to describe what is true and valuable.

When James described and defined truth, he did not consider that some people would have more power to influence the consensus than others do. He was not a sociologist or political scientist of truth: he was a philosopher. But we can't unquestioningly accept the assumption of neutrality and equality, the belief that Google ranks are generated fairly by a large, disinterested collection of "users" who feed Google enough information to generate a rough and neutral consensus. We need to pay attention to power—to biases—in the system.[26]

All information technologies favor some content or users over others. One cannot design a neutral system. To use technologies wisely, we need to grasp the nature of biases and adjust expectations to accommodate or correct for them. So a declaration or description of bias is not an indictment of a system or a firm. A bias is not necessarily bad: it is necessary. A search system cannot rank and choose information without some criteria on which to do so. The Google search algorithms are built to favor certain types of content over others, and to reward the accumulation of acts and behaviors of users. So the biases are rarely direct and obvious.[27]

It's essential to grasp some of the major biases inherent in Google's Web Search. First of all, no search engine indexes everything. All of them make choices based on characteristics of a page. They try to exclude sites that match computer-generated profiles of junk pages intended to manipulate users, computers, or search engines themselves. And as we will see, sometimes search engines such as Google impose human editorial judgment on indexes and results if the search results are troublesome or potentially illegal.[28]

More important, not all hyperlinks are created equal. Many, perhaps most, are "votes" of support or affirmation. Many hyperlinks are votes of derision, generated by a critic to point to flaws, falsehoods, or weaknesses. Still others exist for purely functional purposes, such as to enable the downloading of a file.[29] And not every page creator employs links the same way or to the same extent. There is an ethic of link reciprocation among bloggers, for example, by which one blogger will link to another's page when she refers to or discusses it. Links are a sort of currency on the Web because those who make Web pages usually understand that

Google rewards them, but no such ethic exists generally among commercial sites. By relying on PageRank, Google has historically favored highly motivated and Web-savvy interests over truly popular, important, or valid interests. Being popular or important on the Web is not the same as being popular or important in the real world. Google tilts toward the geeky and Webby, as well as toward the new and loud.

For example, if you search for "God" on Google Web Search, as I did on July 15, 2009, from my home in Virginia, you could receive a set of listings that reflect the peculiar biases of PageRank. The Wikipedia page for "God" ranks highest. That's interesting for a number of reasons. Sometime in 2006, Wikipedia pages began ranking very high in many Web searches on Google. This could be a result of Wikipedia's widespread use and good reputation for usefulness, if not accuracy and comprehensiveness. It is just as likely, however, that Google's engineers decided around that time that for searches on controversial or emotionally charged topics, it was wise to hand off the responsibility of expressing and describing such a concept to a community that has already worked out norms and processes for mediating differences of opinion.[30] Wikipedia serves Google well in that way. In turn, Google serves Wikipedia well, because the editing standards for inclusion in Wikipedia depend on an entry's relevance; and relevance, circularly, depends on how prominently Google presents that subject.[31] Google could have presented another authoritative source about the idea of God. However, the synergy between Google and Wikipedia seems strong enough that it's unlikely any reference source could unseat Wikipedia.[32] Still, Wikipedia, like Google, is biased toward the digital. Any person or concept showing up frequently in the pages of *Wired* magazine is likely to enjoy prominence in both Wikipedia and Google results.[33]

That set of results for "God" reveals other biases inherent in Google Web Search. The second result I generated is for something called "God .com," sponsored by the Evangelical Media Group. It promises to recommend books that can answer questions such as "Why are there so many religions and which one is right?" In rural Virginia, this might be one of the more "relevant" results, because it clearly serves evangelical

Protestant Christianity, which is the most significant religious community here. The page for God.com is free of clutter, and it must have many
highly popular referrals. It's thus well suited to Google's standards for
inclusion and high scoring with PageRank. But one would hope that
in Cairo or Venice a different result would end up second behind
Wikipedia's entry for "God."

The first page of my search results shows a limited range of sites,
considering the wide array of possible references to "God" in the world.
It includes a video of John Lennon singing his song "God" (a search
for "Mother" also links to a video of the Lennon song of that name,
however—above a link to Mother brand polishes and waxes). There are
links to a number of atheistic sites, as well as a link to the Twitter feed of
someone who calls himself "God." There are no links to Islamic, Hindu,
or Jewish sites, or even to Catholic sources. Here in Virginia, we are led
to believe that the answers about God come from Wikipedia, evangelical
Christianity, atheist sites, and John Lennon.

HUMANS IN THE MACHINE

Despite the pragmatic devotion to the technological virtues of speed, precision, comprehensiveness, and honesty in computer-generated results,
and despite our pragmatic faith in truth arrived at by process and consensus, the local apparently matters more than the global in Web search.
In addition, because of some awkward results, Google has on occasion
intervened to impose human judgment from within the system, rather
than rely on the slow-changing collective judgment of the users. Google's
general response to complaints about the content of particular sites, even
if the sites are offensive, untrue, or dangerous, is to refer the complainer
to the author or Internet service provider of the offending site. However,
the attention generated by the results for some searches has pushed
Google to intervene.[34]

Google intervened, for instance, in April 2004, when the home page
of an anti-Semitic site called Jew Watch displaced the Wikipedia entry
for "Jew" as the top result for that search on Google.[35] It also took action

when results for the search "Holocaust" or "Jew" generated high first-page results for sites denying that the slaughter of more than six million Jews during World War II ever happened. In the United States, Google has no legal obligation to remove hateful, bigoted material. In places such as Germany and France, however, it does. When the Anti-Defamation League in the United States complained about the results for "Jew", Google responded at first by posting an explanation of how its search engine works and a pledge to honor the alleged neutrality of its algorithms. An updated version of that notice is still appended to the search-result page for "Jew":

> A site's ranking in Google's search results relies heavily on computer algorithms using thousands of factors to calculate a page's relevance to a given query. Sometimes subtleties of language cause anomalies to appear that cannot be predicted. A search for "Jew" brings up one such unexpected result. If you use Google to search for "Judaism," "Jewish" or "Jewish people," the results are informative and relevant. . . . The beliefs and preferences of those who work at Google, as well as the opinions of the general public, do not determine or impact our search results. Individual citizens and public interest groups do periodically urge us to remove particular links or otherwise adjust search results. Although Google reserves the right to address such requests individually, Google views the comprehensiveness of our search results as an extremely important priority. Accordingly, we do not remove a page from our search results simply because its content is unpopular or because we receive complaints concerning it.[36]

Once Google explained itself to the Anti-Defamation League, the organization posted a notice that it accepted Google's apology and assured its members that Google was not responsible for the results because they were purely "computer-generated," as if that absolved humans of responsibility. The Anti-Defamation League even praised Google for announcing that the company would find a way to mark offensive material in the future. (I see no evidence that it has done so, even five years later.)[37] This is odd, because the American Anti-Defamation League ignores the fact that Google.de, the German version of Google Web Search, generates no anti-Semitic results in a search for "Juden". And searching for "Jew" on Google.de generates a series of English results without listing Jew Watch. The results, in other words, are clearly within Google's control. Google just chooses not to intervene so directly for searches done in the United States.

In the wake of the public controversy, those who sought to scrub the anti-Semitic sites from Google rankings posted pages on the Web linking to Wikipedia and to other, more legitimate and accurate sources of information about Judaism and the Jewish people. They hoped to flood the PageRank system with their preferred links, thus moving Jew Watch lower. The small number of supporters of the anti-Semitic site Jew Watch did the same. One would think that this process would enable the forces of light to triumph over the forces of darkness. However, because Google's computers are sensitive to the strategies known professionally as search-engine optimization and colloquially as "Google bombing," the anti-Semitic site retained its high ranking, although it lost the top place.[38] Over time, the top two results for "Jew" in the United States on Google .com have frozen such that Wikipedia remains at the top (as of August 2010, from Charlottesville, Virginia) and Jew Watch remains second. The current first-page results include more recent sources, revealing Google's desire to present the current as relevant. Near the bottom of my search results for "Jew" was a video of the parody artist Sacha Baron Cohen performing "Throw the Jew down the Well" as his character Borat.

So human intervention in Google search results occurs when Google wants it to—or when it is compelled by law to intervene. Most often, if Google wants a different set of results to appear in a particular context, it adjusts its algorithm to create a general change in the system, rather than bluntly editing the index or the results. However, three years after the controversy over search results for "Jew", Google quietly changed its "Explanation of Our Search Results" page. Where it used to read "A site's ranking in Google's search results is automatically determined by computer algorithms using thousands of factors to calculate a page's relevance to a given query," it became in May 2007 "A site's ranking in Google's search results relies heavily on computer algorithms using thousands of factors to calculate a page's relevance to a given query." So Google dropped the word *automatically,* the very term that got it off the hook with the Anti-Defamation League.

By 2007, Google had folded human intervention into page ranking in a number of subtle ways. It now employs a team of human "quality raters" to evaluate search results and report the results back to those who tweak the algorithm.[39] And by 2009, Google's registered users (those who use other Google services such as Gmail, Google Books, and Blogger) were empowered to add or delete sites from particular search results, thus giving the search quality team very specific guidance about pages.[40] This process allows registered users to exercise disproportionate influence over the search results that others see. These are "super citizens" of the Web. Their opinions matter more to Google than those of unregistered users.

Google also takes action in cases of egregious abuses of Web etiquette. If a search term consistently generates inappropriate results, such as pornography sites for search terms unrelated to sexual matters, Google will intervene immediately and punish the pornographic site for rigging its page rank. It will do the same if it suspects that a site has faked the number of incoming links. So the human element in Google's search business is present and perhaps growing. It's important to look critically at the people who are making these decisions and the cultural backgrounds from which they have emerged. They are, as might be expected, by and large technicians and technocrats.

A "SOVIET OF TECHNICIANS" AT BURNING MAN

Google is built to support a technocratic way of working. Its founders, Larry Page and Sergey Brin, and most of its early employees are computer scientists by training. It has always been the sort of place where those devoted to solving some of the biggest challenges in logic, mathematics, and linguistics can find a supportive yet challenging environment.[41] It's the paradigm of the sort of practice that has emerged quickly over the past twenty years and that now dominates the scientific agenda in many fields: entrepreneurial science—the intersection of academic "pure" science and industrial technoscience.[42]

This technocratic mode of organization is anything but new. In *The Engineers and the Price System*, a book published in 1921 that fell into immediate obscurity, the iconoclastic economist Thorstein Veblen identified a new class of what we now call knowledge workers. In the late years of the American Industrial Revolution, Veblen saw that the increase in efficiency of the production and distribution of goods was creating tremendous wealth for the class that owned the means of production yet who were unable to do the mathematics necessary to understand the systems that enriched them. This situation would not stand for long, Veblen surmised. Unlike Karl Marx's unreliable proletariat, waiting to be sparked into revolutionary action by the sudden realization of historical exploitation, the engineering class might actually capture some of the wealth it created. In fact, engineers could work together to disrupt American industry and bring it down within a matter of weeks. No one else could do that, especially not laborers, who could always be replaced. Because there would always be a shortage of engineers, they had real social and economic power if they chose to use it. If the engineering class succeeded well enough, it could reengineer society, politics, and government as well as the firms themselves. In that event, Veblen argued, we might be ruled by a benevolent (or at least competent) "soviet of technicians."[43]

Google's position as both the dominant firm within its market and a model of how firms should behave in the world realizes Veblen's dream. And the ethos of the company meshes perfectly with one of the paradigmatic modern American values: merit conceived as technical competence. America, Walter Kirn writes, is run by "Aptocrats." These are people who excel at regimented procedures, such as standardized tests and other numerically quantifiable forms of achievement. They conform to highly structured expectations of excellence and clearly see every rung they must ascend on the ladder of success. "As defined by the institutions responsible for spotting and training America's brightest youth, this 'aptitude' is a curious quality," Kirn writes. "It doesn't reflect the knowledge in your head, let alone the wisdom in your soul, but some quotient of promise and raw mental agility thought to be crucial to academic success and, by extension, success in general. All of this makes for a self-fulfilling prophecy. The more aptitude that a young person displays, the more likely it is that she or he will have a chance to win the golden tickets—fine diplomas, elite appointments and so on—that permit you to lead the Aptocratic establishment and set the terms by which it operates."[44] Aptocracy, on which Kirn elaborates in his funny memoir, *Lost in the Meritocracy: The Undereducation of an Overachiever,* rewards a large measure of gumption in addition to its strata of otherwise "fair" technologies of assessment (test scores, diplomas, and certifications).

Google may be the perfect realization of Aptocracy. Google hires the best of the best from America's top university technological programs. Even those who work in marketing and sales must demonstrate aptitude via tests and gamelike interview questions.[45] This focus on standardized, predictable tasks as the measure of achievement is ostensibly fair. Success in America no longer depends so heavily on social status, ethnicity, or gender. Those things still matter, and once in a while a stunningly incompetent exception circumvents the Aptocracy and rises to power, as George W. Bush did. But the Aptocracy has transformed America largely for the better over the past forty years. It has also created the environment in which Google could gestate, grow, thrive, and dominate.[46]

Google shapes its products as well as its staff along Aptocratic ideological lines. In Web Search, a link ends up high on the first page of search results if it has qualified in a mathematically demonstrable way. It must satisfy a number of tests of viability and quality. If it appears to have too many attributes that statistically correlate with untrustworthy pages—if, for example, it contains spam links or obvious attempts to game Google's ranking system—the algorithm will downgrade the page or omit it from the index. A page must have been reviewed and elected by other sites through the affirmative technology of the hyperlink to achieve a high ranking. As with the Aptocracy, members of the Internet elite have more power to determine the standards of excellence in the next iteration of Web search results. The system is always learning, just as the Aptocracy is always adjusting to new inputs and influences among high achievers.

This reliance on technologies to measure aptitude is part of what Neil Postman identified in 1992 as technopoly, or rule by and for technology.

Postman was highly critical of what he saw as America's blind dependence on tools and its failure to apply critical thinking and deliberation.
If it's new and shiny, Postman lamented, people will adopt it. Soon, the
tools seem to set the priorities. They seem to demand more attention and
further refinement. And thus real life, or what Postman called "culture,"
is evacuated of all meaning. It's all about the tools.[47]

Postman committed the fallacy of assuming that technologies are
autonomous, that they have inordinate influence over our behaviors,
values, and expectations. He did not appreciate the extent to which
people influence and rework technologies.[48] Google understands this
better than Postman did. It's built to learn. It's designed to absorb influences, for better or worse. That's why the chief product the company
delivers to users, the search-results page with links and advertisements,
is contingent on the identity, history, and location of the user. The chief
product Google sells, users' attention, is also contingent. It changes all
the time because people's needs change and because people are fickle.
Google is designed to absorb and respond to culture as much as it influences culture.

However, it's a mistake to think of Google's social influence and social
role as purely a function of science and engineering. Google's social
milieu, the petri dish from which it sprang, is more than technological
or scientific. As the media historian Fred Turner demonstrates in *From
Counterculture to Cyberculture,* the ideology of Silicon Valley is rooted in
the practices and idealistic visions of 1960s counterculture. It's a peculiar
story: cultural anarchism melded with technologies developed for and
by the U.S. military, unleashed in the service of both commerce and
creativity, yet also accused of undermining both.[49]

Google, in particular, incorporates a twenty-first-century form of
countercultural hedonism in its corporate structure and everyday work
environment: the ethos of Burning Man. Burning Man is an annual festival held at the end of August in the Black Rock Desert in northern
Nevada. Thousands of people gather to camp and celebrate with music,
drugs, art, and digital technology. Turner highlights the fact that many
important players in the technological industries of Northern California regularly participate in Burning Man. For two weeks a year, Silicon

Valley's elite can immerse themselves in a grand network of human beings connecting for the sake of creating. "If the workers of the industrial factory found themselves laboring in an iron cage, the workers of many of today's post-industrial information firms often find themselves inhabiting a velvet goldmine: a workplace in which the pursuit of self-fulfillment, reputation, and community identity, of interpersonal relationships and intellectual pleasure, help to drive the production of new media goods," Turner writes.[50] Google's founders, Larry Page and Sergey Brin, have been regular Burning Man attendees since the 1990s. At the festival, Page and Brin would have encountered a radically decentralized social structure, one that facilitates creativity, collaboration, and experimentation with little or no "command and control." Burning Man, Turner concludes, is a distillation of the "cultural infrastructure" that nurtures Google, a spiritual manifestation of what Yochai Benkler calls "commons-based peer production."[51]

As the sociologist Dalton Conley has described, many of the most highly rewarded workers—those on the creative side of the technology industries—are either trapped in something like a velvet goldmine or struggling to get into one. They are decontextualized from their localities, overconnected to their mobile, cosmopolitan communities, and constantly striving to improve the speed and quality of those connections. They live in a place Conley calls "Elsewhere."[52] To use Turner's words, "the pursuit of self-fulfillment, reputation, and community identity, of interpersonal relationships and intellectual pleasure" helps drive the consumption of new media goods. The cycle of innovation and consumption is amplified by the deep cultural struggle to innovate and consume better, faster, and more than yesterday. That cycle is almost spiritual. It's not a cold, soulless process, nor a crass and cheap one. What drives people through the cycle is the real satisfaction of connecting with others over time and distance, valuable collaboration, and the potential for stunning creativity. Participating in the production, consumption, and use of the elements of digital culture creates a significant amount of joy and satisfaction. Moreover, the circulation of capital created by this process has generated tremendous wealth and opportunity, even if it has directly contributed to maldistributions of wealth.

And that's worth a lot, even if it also generates an insatiable demand for more.

THE PRACTICAL IDEALISTS

As I strolled through the Google campus in Mountain View, California, in the summer of 2008, I reflected on the monumental changes that this one company had brought into our lives. The "Googleplex" looks like a model business park. It's all glass, steel, and concrete. It's clean and well maintained. But it does not exude opulence or arrogance, as one might expect. Its buildings form a courtyard that is always filled with casually dressed people. Its workers drive a motley collection of Toyotas and Hondas, not the Mercedes-Benzes or BMWs one might expect in a parking lot of a company so wealthy. The campus is a collection of confusingly shaped and numbered stark glass buildings, unadorned and largely unassuming—just like the front page of Google itself.

With the exception of the full-scale replica of a *Tyrannosaurus rex* skeleton that dominates the ample courtyard, there is nothing to mark the place as eccentric. It's a nice place to work. Pleasant, smart people work there. Wandering amid shirtless volleyball players taking a break from long days and nights of coding, and lines of hungry young businesspeople waiting for a high-quality lunch buffet and enjoying ample on-site laundry and massage services, I kept wondering if these workers pondered how important they are to the daily lives of so many millions of people around the world. The decisions they make structure the patterns of discovery and communication in an increasing number of ways.

I wondered if those who do the thinking and building for Google thought, as I do, that Google is fast becoming the chief lens through which we see the world. In my exploration of Google over the past four years, I have at times considered it akin to the T-Rex that looms in its Mountain View courtyard, a fierce beast bent on devouring its neighbors in a single gulp. At other times, I have seen Google as a savior, a bold and powerful institution assuming an important role in our lives after thirty years of suffering because our public institutions retreat and atrophy, shrinking from challenges in favor of the timid management of resources. But I never saw Google as just another player. Clearly it has never settled for also-ran status in any project or market in which it has engaged. Wherever Google shows up, whatever Google touches, it changes.

Not surprisingly, those who work for Google tend not to share my concerns. Nor, impressively, do they share in the widespread veneration of the company. In fact, every Google employee I met offered a much more modest, utilitarian vision of the company's effects on the world than either its critics or its champions express. Google employees for the most part consider themselves to be engineers doing a job, solving a problem or two, generating or perfecting algorithms that make computers manipulate data. Some of the big thinkers at the company, such as Vint Cerf (often called the "father of the Internet"), see the process of mastering information search as a noble cause but still downplay Google's influence.[53]

Other major public voices of the company, such as Marissa Mayer, frequently describe the jobs Google is doing in matter-of-fact terms. Explaining in her 2008 speech why the iconic blank search screen, containing only an empty search box, a logo, and a copyright notice, emerged from a company so blessed with brilliant engineers and devoted to monumental tasks, she said, "It's sort of more about expedient solutions and much less about grand or broad design."[54]

Seen from the inside, then, Google is a place to get things done. The focus is on the pragmatic (in the broad sense) solving of some rather challenging problems. Googlers see their role and method as incremental, steady, benign, and optimistic. The vast resources at their disposal—cash, server farms, bandwidth, computer processing power, and a collection of brilliant minds—allow them to address big, long-term challenges such as artificial intelligence, real-language (as opposed to awkward keyword or text) search, and computer-generated language translation. If you get enough cool things done, they think, you can rock the world.

They're probably right. But if that's going to happen, it would be a good idea for us to think harder about our faith in the benevolence of those who will be doing the rocking, and especially about the basis for our own ready acquiescence in the Googlization of everything. After all, even if the ends of that process are something that may transform our lives in ways that we desire, there may be better means by which we can reach those ends.

TECHNO-FUNDAMENTALISM AND THE PUBLIC GOOD

Google makes much out of its commitment to benevolence. Google officials invoke its famous informal motto, "Don't be evil," to explain that the company is worthy of the "trust bias" of users when it enters sticky situations. It is devoted to "corporate responsibility," even if the judgment of what constitutes responsible behavior is not so easy to discern. On a page on its website titled "Corporate Information: Our Philosophy," Google explains the "ten things Google has found to be true." Number 6 on this list is "You can make money without doing evil." The text explains how Google makes money from positioning relevant and unobtrusive advertisements alongside search results. In addition, the page explains, the rank of a particular page in search results is never for sale.

The text says nothing about how Google has contributed to censorship in China or other oppressive countries, how much energy the company uses to run its elaborate system of server farms, or how it punishes certain companies with sudden and inexplicable downgrades in PageRank and others with higher minimum rates for advertising at auction. It says nothing about how Google treats its temporary contract workers or how much it charges employees to use on-site childcare.[55] It takes no account of the access Google provides to sexual content, weapon-making instructions, debilitating computer viruses, financial scams, or hate speech on the Web. It mentions none of the default settings for the retention of private information and preferences. It says nothing about the distractions, dependencies, and concentrations of power that Google and the Web have unleashed on the world.[56]

It says none of these things because the burden of dealing with the myriad potential harms to which Google and the Web contribute is just too great to shoulder. It's unreasonable to expect a company to confront such potential harms transparently and of its own volition. No company could exist if it did not do—or at least allow—some harm and impose some costs on other entities. Doing harm is not necessarily being evil, however. Google never promised to be comfortable and benign: it just promised not to be evil, whatever that means. If we want a large, successful, powerful, brilliant Web-search company to provide us with so many important services so cheaply, we should not expect it to do no harm or avoid all ethically thorny situations.

Google is no better and no worse—and no less complicated and conflicted—than the rest of our institutions. "Don't be evil" is sometimes no more than a motto—a pose for public-relations purposes—but it is often something more. Those who work for Google support a wide range of interpretations and applications of the motto. When I asked them about it, a few of them cynically rolled their eyes, acknowledging that Google is subject to the same pressures and temptations as any other media or advertising company in a rickety global economy. Others took the creed seriously, citing it as one of the chief motivations for devoting so many hours of their lives to the projects and experiments that the company encourages. Many of Google's workers correctly see that the company's size and influence are the result of a million good, modest decisions by engineers who preceded them, by the founders of Google, and by the millions of people who use Google every day. Most of Google's management has explained away the phrase as a useful standard, a measure that they may invoke as a test of a business decision, but not an answer to any particular dilemma. They argue that the phrase was meant to be a reminder that a firm founded by and for idealistic engineers should not become just another company—or worse, another Microsoft.

Despite its embrace of benevolence, in other words, Google may sin, just as any of us may sin. However, its sins are our sins, too. One of the main reasons we have faith in Google is because we think that we can do anything we want if we have the right tools. That is the sin of pride. We have a blind faith in technology: techno-fundamentalism.

SUPERBIA

In an Oxford-style debate in New York City in October 2008, to be broadcast on the National Public Radio program *Intelligence Squared,* I joined an
illustrious team that included Randall Picker of the University of Chicago
Law School faculty and Harry Lewis, a professor of computer science
at Harvard.[57] We argued to support the motion "Resolved: Google vio-
lates its 'Don't be evil' motto." The opposition was just as formidable. It
included the author and blogger Jeff Jarvis, the libertarian legal advocate
Jim Harper, and one of the smartest people involved in the promotion
and governance of the Internet, Esther Dyson.

I opened my statement by noting that we had failed to define "evil." I
told the crowd that I would invoke an authority, something of an expert
on evil and sin: Dante Alighieri, who provides in *The Divine Comedy* a
list of the seven deadly sins. They are *luxuria* (extravagance or lust); *gula*
(gluttony); *avaritia* (greed); *acedia* (sloth); *ira* (wrath); *invidia* (envy); and
superbia (pride or hubris). I claimed I could demonstrate that Google had
committed every one of them.

I was joking about all the other sins, but I was serious about *superbia*.
The particular kind of hubris that energizes Google is the notion that you
can always invent something to solve the problem that the last invention created. That's techno-fundamentalism. It's an extreme form of the
pragmatic orientation that, as we've seen, lies behind the acceptance of
Google as the world's primary search engine. Techno-fundamentalism
assumes not only the means and will to triumph over adversity through
gadgets and schemes but also the sense that invention is the best of all
possible methods of confronting problems.

At the beginning of the twenty-first century, we pay a heavy price
for techno-fundamentalism. We build new and wider highways under
the mistaken belief that they will ease congestion. We rush to ingest
pharmaceuticals that are no more effective than a placebo at alleviat-
ing our ills.[58] We make investment and policy decisions based on principles such as the so-called Moore's law, which predicts that computer
processing power will double every eighteen months, as if such
progress had its own momentum, independent of specific decisions

by firms and engineers.[59] Perhaps most dangerously, we neglect real problems with the structures and devices we depend on to preserve our lives, as we did for decades with the levees that failed to protect the poorest residents of New Orleans after Hurricane Katrina.[60] And now it seems techno-fundamentalism stands as the operative ideology in defense and security policy. We need not depend on messy diplomacy or credible military threats to curb the activities of hostile states. We have Star Wars.[61]

The faith that technology can redeem all of our sins and fix all of our problems is the ultimate hubris. There are many examples in human history in which techno-fundamentalism has led to great suffering. For Dante, pride is actually the gravest of the seven deadly sins, because it was the sin that Lucifer committed. Lucifer, we should remember, was originally a good guy. He fell because he thought he could be equal to God, and instead he became Satan. The "Don't be evil" motto is itself evil, because it embodies pride, the belief that the company is capable of avoiding ordinary failings.

The theologian Reinhold Niebuhr wrote about the claims of benevolence in world affairs by American political leaders that "the pretensions of virtue are as offensive to God as the pretensions of power." Niebuhr was concerned that such pretensions blind leaders "to the ambiguity of all human virtues and competencies."[62]

THE BLINDNESS OF HUBRIS

Pretensions to virtue create other forms of blindness as well. Blind faith in the information to which Google provides access, for example, often allows us merely to confirm our prejudices and illusions. The actor and model Jenny McCarthy has spent the past several years trying to convince new parents that they should avoid vaccinating their babies against life-threatening diseases. She embarked on her campaign after her child was diagnosed with autism. Despite the absence of any evidence tying vaccines to the development of autism in children, McCarthy decided that the medical and public-health experts were wrong about the conclusions they reached using real data and the scientific method.[63] She believed she could find out "the truth" about the imagined vaccination-autism connection by enrolling in what she described as "the University of Google."[64]

The University of Google lacks accreditation, to be sure. It's too simple to say it's only as good as its sources. Google is designed to favor sites with the most "votes" from others who use the Web, rather than those endorsed by knowledgeable experts. This is usually not a problem. In fact, no one has come up with a better way to navigate the mess of tangled documents and claims that make up the Web. However, it's sometimes harmful when people, even those who should know better, trust a simple Google search as the first step toward the truth.[65]

Poor searches by faithful Google users are only part of the problem with the Googlization of knowledge. The ways that Google structures, judges, and delivers knowledge to us exacerbate our worst tendencies to jump to erroneous conclusions and act on them in ways that cause harm. On September 8, 2008, a reporter for an obscure news company called Income Securities Advisors typed "bankruptcy 2008" into a search box on Google.com. Google News instantly pointed the reporter to an article from a newspaper called the *South Florida Sun-Sentinel* announcing that UAL, the parent company of United Airlines, had filed for bankruptcy protection. The reporter, who worked for a company that feeds stories to the powerful Bloomberg news service, posted a simple alert with no story or background attached: "United Airlines files for Ch. 11 to cut costs." This alert, apparently informing readers that the airline was seeking legal protection from its debtors, went out to thousands of influential readers of Bloomberg's financial news network.[66]

The problem was that the *Sun-Sentinel* archive did not display a publication date for the story, thus allowing Google News to list it among recent or current stories. Google's computers then placed a new date on the link to the article: September 6, 2008—the day Google's Web-crawling software found and indexed the article. But the UAL bankruptcy filing it referred to occurred in 2002. The company emerged successfully from protection and reorganization in 2006. Sadly, the reporter, apparently unfamiliar with the earlier travails of UAL and incautious about what might get tossed up from the sea of Web content, did not attempt to verify the report.

When the NASDAQ market opened on the morning of September 8, 2008, UAL stock was trading at $12.17 per share. Once the alert zoomed around Bloomberg at approximately 11:00 A.M. Eastern Standard Time, panicked sellers unloaded 15 million shares of UAL and drove the price per share down to $3.00.

By 11:16 A.M., Bloomberg had issued an alert denying that UAL had filed for bankruptcy. As word spread that the bankruptcy alert was false, the stock recovered. But it still finished the day at $10.92 per share, down $1.38 from its opening price. This simple glitch cost UAL shareholders— including most of its employees—11.2 percent of the company's market value. In addition, the panic drove down shares of two other airlines, Continental Airlines and AMR (the parent of American Airlines) as well. The airlines had done nothing wrong. They had released no bad news. Yet they were all worth less at the end of the day than at the beginning because Google's Web crawlers found a mislabeled story in an open newspaper archive.[67]

This anecdote offers valuable lessons about our dependence on cheap, shallow, instant information and the chief delivery system for such information—Google. Certainly, had those responsible for posting the *Sun-Sentinel* article used proper metadata—the elements in a file that tell us its context, such as a date of origin—Google's computers would not have placed the story in front of the Income Securities Advisors reporter. And had the reporter been better informed and a more critical and less credulous reader, no one would ever have heard about the mistake. If anyone in this story understood that aggregators of information like Google News are only as good as their sources, no one would have overreacted. If either Bloomberg or Google News had been set up to enhance understanding, rather than simply to pass on what, under its brand, instantly becomes credible as trustworthy information, someone could have put the brakes on the error. And finally, if traders and investors around the world read more than headlines and tickers before making huge decisions that could cost innocent people money and jobs, the errors that preceded the sell-off might not have mattered at all.[68]

But that is not the world in which we live. We are flooded with data, much of it poorly labeled and promiscuously copied. We seek maximum speed and dexterity rather than deliberation and wisdom. Many of our systems, not least electronic journalism, are biased toward the new and the now. The habits and values of markets infect all areas of our lives at all times of day. And even after living intimately with networked computers for almost two decades, we lack understanding of what such complex information systems can and cannot do, or even how they work. We trust them with far too much that is dear to us and fail to confront or even to acknowledge their limits and problems.

Despite all the loud accusations of fault that flew between Google and those responsible for the journalistic errors, it's clear that Google itself did nothing wrong.[69] It's hard to expect that Google's programmers would consider the possibility of the basic metadata error that the *Sun-Sentinel* made. Nor should we expect them to have predicted the collective stupidity of the rest of the humans involved in the chain reaction.[70]

So the chief lesson here is not that Google is the cause of the problem: the lesson is that we are flawed. One of our flaws—which we recognize—is that we often lack the knowledge that we need to live our lives both happily and responsibly. We believe that Google offers a powerful way to overcome that flaw. But our faith in Google leaves us vulnerable to other flaws: the tendency to believe what we want to believe, like Jenny McCarthy, and belief itself, the credulity that makes us functioning social beings and that sometimes can betray us, as in the case of the false UAL bankruptcy report. When we choose to rely blindly on a pervasive, powerful gatekeeper that we do not understand, we are destined to make monumental mistakes.

THE TEMPTATION

Faith in Google is dangerous not because of anything specific that Google does. It's dangerous because of how we allow it to affect our expectations and information about the world. Using Google habitually raises our expectations about matters both deep and shallow. In the space between expectations and reality lie happiness and anxiety. When expectations about significant issues—justice, peace, health, and knowledge—exceed reality by significant margins, the difference can motivate us to achieve marvelous things both collectively and individually. But when that tension is constant and loud about trivial things—the speed of information delivery, access to services, and acquisition of the latest and coolest goods—we indulge in decisions and actions that merely satiate us rather than enrich us.[71]

THREE THE GOOGLIZATION OF US

UNIVERSAL SURVEILLANCE AND INFRASTRUCTURAL IMPERIALISM

In 2006, *Time* declared its Person of the Year to be you, me, and everyone who contributes content to new-media aggregators such as MySpace, Amazon, Facebook, YouTube, eBay, Flickr, blogs, and Google. The flagship publication of one of the most powerful media conglomerates in the world declared that flagship publications and powerful media conglomerates no longer choose where to hoist flags or exercise power. "It's about the many wresting power from the few and helping one another for nothing and how that will not only change the world, but also change the ways the world changes," Lev Grossman breathlessly wrote in *Time*. "And for seizing the reins of the global media, for founding and framing the new digital democracy, for working for nothing and beating the pros at their own game, Time's Person of the Year for 2006 is you."[1]

Almost every major marketing campaign these days is likewise framed as being about "you." "You" have freedom of choice. "You" can let yourself be profiled so that "you" receive solicitations only from companies that interest "you." "You" could customize "your" mobile phone with a ringtone. "You" go to the Nike Store to design your own shoes.

This emphasis on "you," however, is only a smokescreen for what is actually happening online. As I have stressed throughout this book, the Googlization of everything entails the harvesting, copying, aggregating, and ranking of information about and contributions made by each of us. This process exploits our profound need to connect and share, and our remarkable ability to create together—each person contributing a little bit to a poem, a song, a quilt, or a conversation. It is not about "you" at all. It should be about "us"—the Googlization of us.

Google, for instance, makes money because it harvests, copies, aggregates, and ranks billions of Web contributions by millions of authors who tacitly grant Google the right to capitalize, or "free ride," on their work. So in this process of aggregation, who are you? Who are you to Google? Who are you to Amazon? Are you the sum of your consumer preferences and MySpace personas? What is your contribution worth? Do "you" really deserve an award for allowing yourself to be rendered so flatly and cravenly? Do you deserve an award because Rupert Murdoch can make money capturing your creativity with his expensive toy, MySpace?

Because Google makes its money by using our profiles to present us with advertisements keyed to the words we search, precision is its goal. Google wants advertisers to trust that the people who see their paid placements are likely customers for the advertised products or services. These advertisers have little interest in broadcasting. That's a waste of money. The more Google knows about us, the more effective its advertising services can be. Understanding the nature of this profiling and targeting is the first step to understanding the Googlization of us.

How much does Google know about us? How much data does it keep, and how much does it discard? How long does it keep that information? And why?[2] Our blind faith in Google has allowed the company to claim that it gives users substantial control over how their actions and preferences are collected and used. Google pulls this off by telling the truth: at any time, we may opt out of the system that Google uses to perfect its search engine and its revenue generation. But as long as control over our personal information and profiles is granted at the pleasure of Google and similar companies, such choices mean very little. There is simply no consistency, reciprocity, or accountability in the system. We must constantly monitor fast-changing "privacy policies." We must be willing to walk away from a valuable service if its practices cause us concern. The amount of work we must to do protect our dignity online is daunting. And in the end, policies matter less than design choices. With Google, the design of the system rigs it in favor of the interests of the company and against the interests of users.

Google complicates the ways we manage information about ourselves in three major ways. It collects information from us when we use its services; it copies and makes available trivial or harmful information about us that lies in disparate corners of the Internet; and it actively captures images of public spaces around the world, opening potentially embarrassing or private scenes to scrutiny by strangers—or, sometimes worse, by loved ones. In theory, Google always gives the victim of exposure the opportunity to remove troubling information from Google's collection. But the system is designed to favor maximum collection, maximum exposure, and the permanent availability of everything. One can only manage one's global electronic profile through Google if one understands how the system works—and that there is a system at all.[3] Google is a system of almost universal surveillance, yet it operates so quietly that at times it's hard to discern.

Google's privacy policy is not much help in this regard. In fact, it's pretty much a lack-of-privacy policy. For instance, the policy outlines what Google will collect from users—a reasonable, yet significant amount: IP (Internet Protocol) addresses (numbers assigned to a computer when it logs into an Internet service provider, which indicate the provider and the user's general location), search queries (which constitute a record of everything we care about, wonder about, or fantasize about), and information about Web browsers and preference settings (fairly trivial, but necessary to make Google work well). Google promises not to distribute this data—with two major exceptions. First, "We provide such information to our subsidiaries, affiliated companies or other trusted businesses or persons for the purpose of processing personal information on our behalf." Second, "We have a good faith belief that access, use, preservation or disclosure of such information is reasonably necessary to (a) satisfy any applicable law, regulation, legal process or enforceable governmental request, (b) enforce applicable Terms of Service, including investigation of potential violations thereof, (c) detect, prevent, or otherwise address fraud, security or technical issues, or (d) protect against imminent harm to the rights, property or safety of Google, its users or the public as required or permitted by law."[4]

Google's privacy policy is a pledge from the company to us. It is binding in that if the company violated its policy, a user could sue Google in the United States for deceptive trade practices (though proving deception is always a difficult burden). However, Google changes its policy often and without warning. So today's policy—for all its strengths and weaknesses—might not be the policy tomorrow or next year. You might have engaged with Google and donated your data trail to it under the provisions of an early version of the policy, only to discover that Google changed the policy while you were not looking. The policy does pledge that "we will not reduce your rights under this Privacy Policy without your explicit consent, and we expect most such changes will be minor." But that is cold comfort, because the policy already gives Google substantial power over the data.

If you read the privacy policy carefully, it's clear that Google retains the right to make significant decisions about our data without regard for our interests. Google will not share information with other companies without user consent, but it asserts the right to provide such information to law enforcement or government agencies as it sees fit.

If another company were to acquire Google, the policy states, the company would inform users of the transfer of the data. But there is no promise that users would have a chance to purge their data from Google's system in time to avoid a less scrupulous company's acquisition of it. Although Google's commitments to fairness and transparency are sincere and important, they are only as durable as the company. If

Google's revenues slip or its management changes significantly, all the trust we place in the company today might be eroded.

To complicate matters more, each Google service has its own privacy policy. The index page for these policies contains a series of videos that outline the terms by which Google collects and retains data. One of the videos echoes the statement that Google retains personally identifiable information for only eighteen months after acquiring it. After eighteen months, information such as IP addresses is "anonymized" so that it's difficult to trace a search query to a particular user. However, that pledge is not made in the policy itself. Anonymization simply involves the removal of the last few digits of a user's IP address, and many cases of anonymization by information brokers have been exposed as ineffective at untethering people's identities from their habits.[5] The "cookies" left by many websites on users' computers contain information that could still be employed to identify a user.[6]

Although Google's public pronouncements about privacy and its general privacy statement fail to explain this point, Google actually has two classes of users, and consequently two distinct levels of data accumulation and processing. The larger, general Google user population simply uses the classic blank page with the search box in the center. Such general users leave limited data trails for Google to read and build services around. The second class might be called power users: those who have registered for Google services such as Gmail, Blogger, or iGoogle. Google has much richer and more detailed dossiers on these users. In exchange for access to this information, Google rightly claims that it serves these power users better than it serves general users. They get more subtle, personalized search results and a host of valuable services.

Google does empower users to control the information the company holds about them, but not in subtle or specific ways. Google's settings page offers a series of on-off switches that can prevent Google from placing cookies in a browser or from retaining a list of websites a user has visited. Power users can delete specific items from the list of website visits.

The default settings for all Google interfaces grant Google maximum access to information. Users must already be aware of and concerned about the amount and nature of Google's data collection to seek out the page that offers all these choices.

Google's data-retention policies have come under significant scrutiny, especially in Europe. Most of the changes in its privacy policies in recent years have resulted from pressure by European policy officials. The United States government has offered consumers and citizens no help in these matters. In fact, it has acted to erode privacy. In 2006, the U.S. Department of Justice issued subpoenas to collect general information from the major search-engine companies in an effort to support its unsurprising contention that Internet users often search for pornography. The department wanted to use such data—which would not have been linked to any particular user, but instead would have offered generalized, statistical information about what users like to do online—in its legal defense of a law called the Child Online Protection Act. Of the major search companies, only Google resisted the subpoena, and then not to protect its users' privacy but to protect its trade secrets. Google's ability to analyze search queries for patterns is its greatest strength in the market. To give up such data could reduce the company's chief competitive advantage.[7] Google prevailed, and the government abandoned its efforts to collect such information.

Understandably, Google officials have practiced responses to questions about data retention and privacy. For instance, Google vice president Marissa Mayer explained to U.S. television host Charlie Rose in early 2009: "In all cases it's a trade-off, right, where you will give up some of your privacy in order to gain some functionality, and so we really need to make those trade-offs really clear to people, what information are we using and what's the benefit to them, and then ultimately leave it to user choice."[8] Mayer, who is very disciplined in her answers to questions about privacy, always offers statements very close to this. But Mayer and Google in general both misunderstand privacy. *Privacy* is not something that can be counted, divided, or "traded." It is not a substance or collection of data points. It's just a word that we clumsily use to stand in for a wide array of values and practices that influence how we manage our reputations in various contexts. There is no formula for assessing it: I can't give Google three of my privacy points in exchange for 10 percent better service. More seriously, Mayer and Google fail to acknowledge the power of default settings in a regime ostensibly based on choice.

THE IRRELEVANCE OF CHOICE

In their 2007 book *Nudge: Improving Decisions about Health, Wealth, and Happiness,* the economist Richard Thaler and law professor Cass Sunstein describe a concept they call "choice architecture." Plainly put, the structure and order of the choices offered to us profoundly influence the decisions we make. So, for instance, the arrangement of foods in a school cafeteria can influence children to eat better. The positions of restrooms and break rooms can influence the creativity and communality of office staff. And, in the best-known example of how defaults can influence an ostensibly free choice, studies have demonstrated that when employer-based retirement plans in the United States required employees to opt in to them, more than 40 percent of employees either failed to enroll or contributed too little to get matching contributions from their employers. When the default was set to enroll employees automatically, while giving them an opportunity to opt out, enrollment reached 98 percent within six months. The default setting of automatic enrollment, Thaler and Sunstein explain, helped employees overcome the "inertia" caused by business, distraction, and forgetfulness.[9]

That choice architecture could have such an important effect on so many human behaviors without overt coercion or even elaborate incentives convinced Thaler and Sunstein that taking advantage of it can accomplish many important public-policy goals without significant cost to either the state or private firms. They call this approach "libertarian paternalism." If a system is designed to privilege a particular choice, they observe, people will tend to choose that option more than the alternatives, even though they have an entirely free choice. "There is no such thing as a 'neutral' design."[10]

It's clear that Google understands the power of choice architecture. It's in the company's interest to set all user-preference defaults to collect the greatest quantity of usable data in the most contexts. By default, Google places a cookie in your Web browser to help the service remember who you are and what you have searched. By default, Google tracks your searches and clicks; it retains that data for a specified period and uses it to target advertisements and refine search results. Google gives us the power to switch off all these features. It even provides videos explaining how to do this.[11] But unless you act to change them, the company's default settings constitute your choices.

When Mayer and others at Google speak about the practices and policies governing their private-data collection and processing (otherwise known as privacy policies), they never discuss the power of defaults. They emphasize only the freedom and power that users have over their data. Celebrating freedom and user autonomy is one of the great rhetorical ploys of the global information economy. We are conditioned to believe that having more choices—empty though they may be—is the very essence of human freedom. But meaningful freedom implies real control over the conditions of one's life. Merely setting up a menu with switches does not serve the interests of any but the most adept, engaged, and well-informed.

Setting the defaults to maximize the benefits for the firm and hiding the switches beneath a series of pages are irresponsible, but we should not expect any firm to behave differently. If we want a different choice architecture in complex ecosystems such as the Web, we are going to have to rely on firms' acceding collectively to pressure from consumer groups or ask the state to regulate such defaults.

Google officials also don't acknowledge that completely opting out of Google's data-collection practices significantly degrades the user's experience. For those few Google users who click through the three pages it takes to find and adjust their privacy options, the cost of opting out becomes plain. If you do not allow Google to track your moves, you get less precise results to queries that would lead you to local restaurants and shops or sites catering to your interests. Google has to guess whether a search for "jaguar" is intended to generate information about the car or the cat. But if Google understands your interests, it can save you time when you shop. It can seem like it's almost reading your mind.

In addition, full citizenship in the Googleverse includes use of functions like Gmail and posting videos on YouTube, which require registration and allow Google to amass a much richer collection of data about your interests. Moreover, exploring such options can give you a pretty clear idea of the nature of the transaction between Google and its users; but for the vast majority of users, the fate of their personal data remains a mystery.

Opting out of any Google service puts the Web user at a disadvantage in relation to other users. The more Google integrates its services, and the more interesting and essential the services that Google offers, the more important Google use is for effective commerce, self-promotion, and cultural citizenship. So the broader Google's reach becomes—the more it Googlizes us—the more likely it is that even informed and critical Internet users will stay in the Google universe and allow Google to use their personal information. For Google, quantity yields quality. For us, resigning ourselves to the Google defaults enhances convenience, utility, and status. But at what cost?

THE PROBLEM WITH PRIVACY

Google is far from the most egregious offender in the world of personal data acquisition. Google promises (for now) not to sell your data to third parties, and it promises not to give it to agents of the state unless the agents of the state ask for it in a legal capacity. (The criteria for such requests are lax, however, and getting more lax around the world.) But Google is the master at using information in the service of revenue generation, and many of its actions and policies are illustrative of a much larger and deeper set of social and cultural problems.

In November 2007, Facebook, the social networking site most popular among university students and faculty, snuck in a surprise for its then-almost 60 million users (by 2010 it had 150 million users). With minimal warning, Facebook instituted what it called its Beacon program, which posted notes about users' Web purchases in the personal news feeds on Facebook profiles. So if a user had purchased a gift for a friend on one of the Web commerce sites that were partners in the program, the purchase would be broadcast to all of that person's Facebook associates—most likely including the intended recipient of the gift. Facebook ruined a few surprises, but it had a bigger surprise in store for itself: a user rebellion. Within days, more than fifty thousand Facebook users signed up for a special Facebook group protesting the Beacon service and Facebook's decision to deny users the chance to opt out of it. The furor spread beyond Facebook. Major news media covered the story and quoted users who until then had been quite happy with Facebook but were now deeply alarmed at the inability to control Beacon or their Facebook profiles.[12]

This reaction caught Facebook executives by surprise. In 2006, when they had released the news feed itself as a way of letting people find out what their Facebook friends were up to, there had been a small protest. But within a few weeks, users got used to it and quieted down. Over time, users did not find news feeds too intrusive or troublesome, and they could turn off the service if they wished.

Facebook executives assumed that their users were not the sort who cared very much about personal privacy. After all, they readily posted photos from wild parties, lists of their favorite bands and books, and frank comments on others' profiles. All the while, Facebook executives were led to believe that young people today were some sort of new species who were used to online exposure of themselves and others, immersed in the details of celebrity lives via sites like PerezHilton.com and Gawker.com, obsessed with the eccentricities of reality television show contestants, and more than happy to post videos of themselves dancing goofily on YouTube.[13]

Then came the great Facebook revolt of 2010. By May of that year, users had alerted each other to the various ways that Facebook had abused their trust. Where once the service had allowed easy and trustworthy management of personal information (it was simple to choose who could and could not view particular elements of one's profile), it had slyly eliminated many of those controls. It had rendered much personal information openly available by default and made privacy settings absurdly complicated to navigate and change. In addition, Facebook suffered some serious security lapses in early 2010. Soon a movement was born to urge friends to quit Facebook in protest. There is no way to tell how many people actually did quit, largely because Facebook would never release that number; moreover, completely deleting an account is very difficult. Facebook membership continued to grow worldwide throughout 2010, as did disgruntlement. Fundamentally, Facebook had become too valuable to people's lives to allow them to quit. The value, however, is in its membership, not in its platform. Facebook was only slightly chastened by the public anger.[14]

The cultural journalist Emily Nussbaum, writing in *New York* magazine in February 2007, stitched together some anecdotes about young people who have no qualms about baring their body parts and secrets on LiveJournal or YouTube. "Younger people, one could point out, are the only ones for whom it seems to have sunk in that the idea of a truly private life is already an illusion," Nussbaum wrote. "Every street in New York has a surveillance camera. Each time you swipe your debit card at Duane Reade or use your MetroCard, that transaction is tracked. Your employer owns your e-mails. The NSA owns your phone calls. Your life is being lived in public whether you choose to acknowledge it or not. So it may be time to consider the possibility that young people who behave as if privacy doesn't exist are actually the sane people, not the insane ones."[15]

Yet if young people don't care about privacy, why do they react angrily when Facebook broadcasts their purchases to hundreds of acquaintances? In fact, a study conducted by Eszter Hargittai of Northwestern University and danah boyd of Microsoft research demonstrated that young people in America have higher levels of awareness and concern about online privacy than older Americans do.[16] But still, isn't privacy a quaint notion in this era in which Google and Amazon—not to mention MI5, the U.S. National Security Agency, and the FBI—have substantial and detailed dossiers on all of us? Despite frequent warnings from nervous watchdogs and almost weekly stories about massive data leaks from Visa or AOL, we keep searching on Google, buying from Amazon, clicking through user agreements and "privacy" policies (that rarely if ever actually protect privacy), and voting for leaders who gladly empower the government to spy on us.

Broad assumptions about the apparent indifference to privacy share a basic misunderstanding of the issue. Too often we assume that a concern with privacy merely represents a desire to withhold information about personal conduct, such as sexual activity or drug use. But privacy is not just about personal choices, or some group of traits or behaviors we call "private" things. Nor are privacy concerns the same for every context in which we live and move. *Privacy* is an unfortunate term, because it carries no sense of its own customizability and contingency. When we complain about infringements of privacy, what we really demand is some measure of control over our reputations. Who should have the power to collect, cross-reference, publicize, or share information about us? If I choose to declare my romantic status or sexual orientation on Facebook, I may still consider that I am preserving my privacy because I assume I am managing the release of that information in a context I think I understand. *Privacy* refers to the terms of control over information, not the nature of the information we share.[16]

Through a combination of weak policies, poor public discussions, and some remarkable inventions, we cede more and more control over our reputations every day. And it's clear that people are being harmed by the actions that follow from widespread behavioral profiling, whether it's done by the Transportation Security Agency through its "no-fly list" or Capital One Bank through its no-escape, high-fee credit cards for those with poor credit ratings.

Jay Gatsby could not exist today. The digital ghost of Jay Gatz would follow him everywhere. There are no second acts, or second chances, in the digital age. Rehabilitation demands substantial autonomy and control over one's record. As long as our past indiscretions can be easily Googled by potential employers or U.S. security agents, our social, intellectual, and actual mobility is limited.[17]

We learn early on that there are public matters and private matters, and that we manage information differently inside our homes and outside them. Yet that distinction fails to capture the true complexity of the privacy tangle. Because it's so hard to define and describe what we mean by privacy and because it so often seems futile to resist mass surveillance, we need better terms, models, metaphors, and strategies for controlling our personal information. Here's one way to begin to think more effectively about the issue.

We each have at least five major "privacy interfaces," or domains, through which we negotiate what is known about us.[18] Each of these interfaces offers varying levels of control and surveillance.

The first privacy interface is what I call "person to peer." Early on, we develop the skills necessary to manage what our friends and families know of our predilections, preferences, and histories. A boy growing up gay in a homophobic family learns to exert control over others' knowledge of his sexual orientation. A teenager smoking marijuana in her bedroom learns to hide the evidence. If we cheat on our partners, we practice lying. These are all privacy strategies for the most personal spheres.

The second interface is one I call "person to power." There is always some information we wish to keep from our teachers, parents, employers, or prison guards because it could be used to manipulate us or expose us to harsh punishment. The common teenage call "Stay out of my room!" exemplifies the frustration of learning to manage this essential interface. Later in life, an employee may find it prudent to conceal a serious medical condition from her employer to prevent being dismissed to protect the company's insurance costs.

The third privacy interface is "person to firm." In this interface, we decide whether we wish to answer the checkout person at Babies "R" Us when she asks us (almost always at a moment when we are feeling weak and frustrated) for a home phone number. We gladly accept what we think are free services, such as discount cards at supermarkets and bookstores, that actually operate as record-keeping account tokens. The clerk at the store almost never explains this other side of the bargain.

The fourth interface is the most important because the consequences of error and abuse are so high: "person to state." Through the census, tax forms, drivers' license records, and myriad other bureaucratic functions, the state records traces of our movements and activities. The mysterious and problem-riddled "no-fly list" that bars people from boarding commercial flights in the United States for unaccountable reasons is the best example. Because the state has a monopoly on legitimate violence, imprisonment, and deportation, the cost of being falsely caught in a dragnet warrants concern, no matter how unlikely it seems.

The fifth privacy interface is poorly understood and has only recently gained notice, although Nathaniel Hawthorne explained it well in *The Scarlet Letter*. It's what I call "person to public." At this interface, which is now located largely online, people have found their lives exposed, their names and faces ridiculed, and their well-being harmed immeasurably by the rapid proliferation of images, the asocial nature of much ostensibly "social" Web behavior, and the permanence of the digital record. Whereas in our real social lives we have learned to manage our reputations, the online environments in which we work and play have broken down the barriers that separate the different social contexts in which we move. On Facebook, MySpace, or YouTube, a coworker may be an online friend, fan, or critic. A supervisor could be a stalker. A parent could be a lurker. A prospective lover could use the same online dating service as a former lover. In real life, we may be able to keep relationships separate, to switch masks and manage what people know (or think they know) about us. But most online environments are intentionally engineered to serve our professional, educational, and personal desires simultaneously. These contexts or interfaces blend, and legal distinctions between public and private no longer hold up.[19] We are just beginning to figure out how to manage our reputations online, but as long as the companies that host these environments benefit directly from the confusion, the task will not be easy.

In *The Future of Reputation*, the law professor Daniel Solove relates the sad story of the "Star Wars Kid." In November 2002, a Canadian teenager used a school camera to record himself acting like a character from *Star Wars*, wielding a golf-ball retriever as a light saber. Some months later, other students at his school discovered the recording and posted it on a file-sharing network. Within days, the image of a geeky teen playing at *Star Wars* became the hit of the Internet. Thousands—perhaps millions—downloaded the video. Soon, many downloaders used their computers to enhance the video, adding costumes, special effects, and even opponents for the young man to slay. Hundreds of versions still haunt the Web. Many Web sites hosted nasty comments about the boy's weight and appearance. Soon his name and high school became public knowledge. By the time YouTube debuted in 2005, the "Star Wars Kid" was a miserable and unwilling star of user-generated culture. He had to quit school. The real-world harassment drove his family to move to a new town. The very nature of digital images, the Internet, and Google made it impossible for the young man to erase the record of one afternoon of harmless fantasy. But it was not the technology that was at fault, Solove reminds us. It was our willingness to ridicule others publicly and our ease at appealing to free-speech principles to justify the spreading of everything everywhere, exposing and hurting the innocent along the way.[20]

No one made any money from this or the other events that Solove describes, and the state is neutral toward such incidents, so we can't blame market forces or security overreactions. But our appetite for public humiliation of others (undeserved or otherwise) should trouble us deeply. Like Hester Prynne in *The Scarlet Letter,* any one of us may be unable to escape the traces of our mistakes. We are no longer in control of our public personas, because so many of our fellow citizens carry with them instruments of surveillance and exposure such as cameras and video recorders. An advocate of Internet creativity and its potential to contribute to democratic culture, Solove treads lightly around any idea that might stifle creative experimentation. But even those of us who celebrate this cultural "mashup" moment would be delinquent if we ignored the real harms that Solove exposes.

The sociologist James Rule, in *Privacy in Peril,* emphasizes one point that is either muted in or absent from most other discussions about privacy and surveillance: data collected by one institution is easily transferred, mined, used, and abused by others. Companies such as Choice-Point buy our supermarket and bookstore shopping records and sell them to direct-mail marketers, political parties, and even the federal government. These data-mining companies also collect state records such as voter registration forms, deeds, car titles, and liens in order to sell consumer profiles to direct-marketing firms. As a result of this cross-referencing of so many data points, ChoicePoint knows me better than my parents do—which explains why the catalogs that arrive at my home better reflect my tastes than the ties my father gives me each birthday. Each data point, each consumer choice, says something about you. If you purchase several prepaid cell phones and a whole lot of hummus, you might be profiled as a potential jihadist. If you use your American Express Platinum card to buy a latte from Starbucks the same day that you purchase a new biography of Alexander Hamilton from Barnes and Noble in an affluent Atlanta ZIP code, you might be identified as a potential donor to a Republican election campaign.[21]

The privacy laws of the 1970s, for which Rule can claim some credit after his 1974 book *Private Lives and Public Surveillance*, sought to guarantee some measure of transparency in state data retention. Individuals should be entitled to know what the federal government knew about them and thus be able to correct errors. And there were to be strong limits on how government agencies shared such data.[22] As Rule explains in *Privacy in Peril*, such commonsense guidelines were eroded almost as soon as they became law. And in recent years, following pressure from the great enemy of public transparency and accountability, former vice president Dick Cheney, they have been pushed off the public agenda altogether. It's as if Watergate, the Church Committee report (which in 1975 exposed massive government surveillance of U.S. citizens and other illegal abuses of power by the CIA), and the revelations of FBI infiltration of antiwar protest groups never happened.[23]

Mass surveillance has been a fact of life since the eighteenth century. There is nothing new about the bureaucratic imperative to record and manipulate data on citizens and consumers. Digital tools just make it easier to collect, merge, and sell databases. Every incentive in a market economy pushes firms to collect more and better data on us. Every incentive in a state bureaucracy encourages massive surveillance. Small changes, such as the adoption of better privacy policies by companies like Google and Amazon, are not going to make much difference in the long run. So the only remedy is widespread political action in the public interest, much as we had in the 1970s. Passivity in the face of these threats to dignity and personal security will only invite the deployment of more unaccountable technologies of surveillance. The challenge is too large and the risks too great.

"STREET VIEW" AND THE UNIVERSALIZATION OF SURVEILLANCE

Although there is indeed nothing new about the incentives for the state and businesses to keep tabs on private individuals, Google, with its Street View service in Google Maps, now enables individuals to undertake forms of surveillance of each other that have never been possible before. Our first reactions to seeing other people's streets and neighborhoods on our screens are hyperbolic. Once the service has been in place for a while, however, it generates broad interest and some utility. It also causes much anxiety without causing demonstrable harm. Only in a handful of places has Google been urged or forced to alter Street View significantly.

Google Street View allows users of Google Maps to take a 360-degree view, at ground level, of streets and intersections in many cities in (as of 2009) the Netherlands, France, Italy, Spain, Australia, New Zealand, and Japan, in addition to the United States and the United Kingdom. Google captures these images by sending automobiles known as Googlemobiles (Vauxhall Astras in the United Kingdom; Chevrolet Cobalts in the United States; Toyota Priuses in Japan), with special cameras mounted on their roofs, to drive along every street in a city.[24] Launched first in May 2007 in New York, San Francisco, and a handful of other large U.S. cities, Google Street View now covers thousands of small towns across the United States—even Charlottesville, Virginia (population 50,000). At first, American users flocked to the service to check for a record of their own lives, and perhaps to discover embarrassing or revealing aspects that Google might disclose. Many commentators declared the service to be too invasive for comfort.[25]

Generally, Google introduces a service in a standard way in all locations. If it generates attention or complaints, Google might tailor some policies for a specific locality. But the defaults Google sets for itself are consistent, if not constant. Responding to the initial criticisms of Street

View, Google defended the service by saying—as it always does—that if anyone reported an image to be troubling, embarrassing, or revealing of personal information such as faces or vehicle license plates, Google would be happy to remove or smudge the image. But, as usual, the defaults were set for maximum exposure.

Critical suspicion of Google Street View faded after a few weeks. Over time, as no horror stories emerged, American Google users became accustomed to the new function and started coming up with creative ways to employ it. Google accurately gauged the sensibilities toward privacy and publicity of users in the United States, where practicality has a way of sweeping away any number of nebulous concerns.

As I studied the reaction in the spring of 2009, I wondered to what interesting uses my fellow Americans had put Google Street View in the two years since its launch. I solicited some input via Twitter, Facebook, and my blog. Overwhelmingly, my respondents (mostly technologically adept and highly educated) reported using Street View to scout out potential homes. Some used it to assess the prospects for parking in a busy area. Others wrote that they often remembered where a restaurant was, but could not remember its name or precise address, so they used Street View to locate it and recommend it to friends.[26]

A few of my responders had particularly interesting applications for Street View. David de la Peña, an architect based in Davis, California, uses Street View daily in his work:

> [Google Street View] is a very useful tool that I use regularly on community design and streetscape projects. It saves me from the drudgery of taking hundreds of photographs of a site, and the user interface is more intuitive than flipping through, say, 100 photographs of a street. For community design projects, it allows designers to see a neighborhood scene more or less from eye-level perspective. When we see a neighborhood from this experiential level, rather than from an aerial photograph, we have a better shot at creating more livable environments. The eye-level views also allow us to verify elements of a streetscape that just aren't apparent from a plan or an aerial photo, such as architectural character, yard and porch layouts, and tree types. For streetscape projects, the eye-level views give a very realistic view of a street's character, which are comprised of building facades; types and

varieties of street trees; locations of street lights and power poles; and arrangements of drive lanes, bicycle lanes, parking and sidewalks.

I started using it as soon as it was available. I immediately saw it as a useful tool to be added to my toolbox. Before [Google Street View], we relied primarily upon aerial photographs, MS Live 3D aerials, and photos we would take ourselves. Of course, none of these replaces on-the-ground research. I have been using [Google Street View], for example, on a project near Sacramento that is located 30 minutes from my office. We are trying to locate a new community center and park within a low-income neighborhood on foreclosed fourplexes that the city owns. GSV gave me a better sense than any other visual tool about the feel of each of the potential sites. Today I visited the sites to confirm our intuitions and to take more photographs. While walking the neighborhood, I was approached by eight different neighbors asking what I was doing. People naturally get suspicious when you're taking pictures of their homes, but if you're open to talking with them, other doors will open. I met a few single mothers who had great suggestions for locating a tot lot, and an on-site building manager who had suggestions for how the city deals with code compliance. These chance encounters gave me more information than any visual tool could, and more important, they helped me to establish as sense of trust.[27]

Cory Doctorow, an author, blogger, and activist, told me that he had used Google Street View to describe in detail a scene in San Francisco when he was writing his successful young-adult novel *Little Brother*. Here is the scene from his novel: "I picked up the WiFi signal with my phone's wifinder about three blocks up O'Farrell, just before Hyde Street, in front of a dodgy 'Asian Massage Parlor' with a red blinking CLOSED sign in the window. The network's name was HarajukuFM, so we knew we had the right spot."[28]

Doctorow wrote to me that he had written much of the novel while living in Los Angeles, but had done a lot of globe-trotting during that time, as well. "I think I was writing from Heathrow that day, or possibly Croatia. I know O'Farrell [Street] pretty well, but it had been a few years. I zoomed up and down the street with [Google Street View] for a few seconds until I had refreshed my memory, then wrote."[29]

One objection to Street View in the United States came from Aaron and Christine Boring, a couple living in Pittsburgh, Pennsylvania.

Concerned that Street View included clear images of their driveway and house, which was sited far back from the street, the couple sued Google in April 2008 seeking $25,000 in damages and alleging Google had in effect trespassed on their property through the power of its lenses. The judge in the case dismissed their claims in February 2009 because the couple had not taken the simple step of requesting that Google remove the offending images. In other words, as far as the court was concerned, as soon as the Borings had discovered the images of their property, they could have acted in a low-cost way to alleviate the conflict. However, that decision did not take account of how long the images had been public or how many people might have seen them.[30]

Today Google Street View, perhaps the most pervasive example of the Googlization of us, barely causes a gasp in the United States. That was not the case in Canada, parts of Europe, or in Japan.

In late spring 2009, Google was planning to extend Street View to Canadian cities. Canada has much stronger data-privacy laws than the United States does, and its people are far less likely to acquiesce in the aims of rich American companies. Along with much of Western Europe, Canada upholds a general prohibition on the photography of people without their permission, with special exceptions for journalism and art. As early as 2007, Google announced that it would tailor Street View to conform to Canadian law by blurring faces and license plates—as if that were a special concession for Canada.[31] In fact, faces and license plates were blurred in street views of the United States and the rest of the world as well. By April 2009, just before the Canadian launch of Street View, Google still claimed that its imperfect, machine-driven blurring technology would comply with Canadian law.[32]

The problem with the blurring process, in addition to a small rate of complete failure, is that a face is not the only feature that defines one's identity. For example, I used to live near the corner of Bleecker Street and LaGuardia Place in New York City. Every day I walked a white dog with brown spots. I drove a black car. And I am more than two meters tall, bald, and heavy. Any shot of me on Google Street View in that neighborhood would be instantly recognizable to hundreds of people who know me even casually. If one of those images seemed to implicate me in, for example, the activities of one of the many illegal gambling establishments within ten blocks of my apartment, my personal and professional reputation could be harmed severely. Canadian privacy advocates articulated the same concerns about the blurring technology in the weeks leading up to the launch of Google Street View, but their arguments did not sway either the company or the Canadian government.

In May 2009, a data-privacy official in the city of Hamburg, Germany, threatened to fine Google over Street View unless the city received a written guarantee that the service would conform with German privacy laws—specifically, the prohibition against the publication of images of people or their property without their explicit consent. Other German cities also protested Street View. Residents of the city of Kiel had put stickers on their front doors demanding that Google not photograph their homes—a nonelectronic way of opting out of Street View.[33] The city of Molfsee forbade Google vehicles from trawling the streets in 2008.[34] And in May 2010 German privacy officials criticized Google for collecting the addresses of unsecured wireless routers throughout Germany with the same cars that the company uses to create Street View. Law-enforcement officials around the world, including the United States, started investigations of Google's data-surveillance practices.[35]

In May 2009 Greece banned Street View on the grounds that Google did not have an adequate plan for notifying residents of town and cities that Google cars would be coming through. Greek authorities also wanted details about the data-storage and protection measures Google would use for the images. In reaction to the Greek decisions, a Google spokesperson uttered the standard mantra to the *Times* of London: "Google takes privacy very seriously, and that's why we have put in place a number of features, including the blurring of faces and license plates, to ensure that Street View will respect local norms when it launches in Greece."[36]

The tension over local norms revealed itself through the reaction in Japan when Street View was launched in 2008. A group of lawyers and professors called the Campaign against a Surveillance Society staged a protest against the service, but these initial objections did not deter the company or generate government reaction.[37] Once Japanese Web users found the standard array of embarrassing images on the service, however, concern about it started to build.[38]

One search-engine professional, Osamu Higuchi, posted an open letter to Google staff in Japan on his blog in August 2008. The letter urged Google staff to explain to their partners in the United States that Street View demonstrates a lack of understanding of some important aspects of daily life in Japan. Osamu urged Google to remove largely residential roads from Street View. "The residential roads of Japan's urban areas are part of people's living space, and it is impolite to photograph other people's living spaces," wrote Osamu. He pointed out that in the United States, the boundary between private space and public space is the property line that abuts a public road. "For people living in Japan, though, the situation is quite the opposite," wrote Osamu. "The residential street in front of a house, the so-called 'alleyway,' feels more like a part of one's own living space, like part of the yard." Osamu explained that private citizens care for, personalize, and decorate these narrow public streets as if they were part of their own land. "When we walk along an alleyway like that, we don't stare at and scrutinize the houses along the way," Osamu wrote. The population density of urban Japan demands a strong sense of mutual discretion, he argued. One does not peep into people's limited and exposed living spaces.

The main problem with Street View, Osamu explained, is the asymmetry of the gaze. A person walking down the street peering into residents' yards would be watched right back by offended residents, who would consider calling the police to report such dangerous and antisocial behavior. But with Google Street View, the residents can't see or know who is peeping.[39] Osamu's pleas and concerns were shared by enough others in Japan that, by May 2009, Google announced it would reshoot its Street View images of Japanese cities with the cameras mounted lower, to avoid peering over hedges and fences.[40]

Certainly, the physical and social geography of Japan and its accompanying notions of privacy are aspects of its culture that Google's engineers and corporate leaders might understandably have failed to grasp. But Osamu's analysis of the asymmetry of the gaze explains much of the more general, global aversion to Street View. Only in a handful of places do Google's defaults run afoul of local laws; in most of the world, the utility of Street View has so far trumped poorly articulated concerns about asymmetry or lack of reciprocity. But everywhere in the world, at least some people find Street View a little bit creepy; some, as in Japan, are deeply offended by it.

The reaction in Britain in 2009 echoed the American reaction from 2007—but with a few significant amplifications and ironies. On the day it unveiled Street View, Google had its busiest day ever in the United Kingdom, with a 41 percent increase in traffic.[41] Google already controlled more than 90 percent of the Web search traffic in the United Kingdom.[42]

Many of the problems that first day were fairly predictable: a few embarrassing scenes were caught on camera; a few sensitive images had to be deleted on request. And the *Independent* newspaper misquoted a Google engineer as saying that Google's technology catches and blurs "99.9" percent of faces and license plates automatically. That turned out to be "a figure of speech," as a Google spokesperson told the *Independent* later. "The technique is not totally perfect. The idea is not to blur every single face, only those that can be clearly identified."[43]

In fact, enough identifying details were preserved in British Street View images to cause a public backlash. Thousands of people requested that Google remove specific images of their homes and businesses, including the former prime minister Tony Blair. A former criminal wrote a column in the *Sun* claiming that Street View would be a gift to criminals. Bloggers quickly found and copied embarrassing images, including a man vomiting outside a pub and another leaving an adult video store. The ensuing fury exceeded all reactions in the United States two years before. And although Google acted quickly to remove these troubling images, they were preserved in other parts of the Web—and easily discoverable via Google Image Search.[44]

The most dramatic reaction to Google Street View came from residents of an affluent village in Cambridgeshire called Broughton. When one of the village residents spotted the Googlemobile, with a camera perched on its roof, slowly cruising his neighborhood, he raced into the street to block it, called the police, and started calling for neighbors to join him. Dozens formed a human chain to prevent the Google car from continuing. The residents of Broughton claimed that the presence of their homes on Google Street View would invite the attention of burglars (though they offered no evidence that a burglar has actually ever used Google Street View to plan a crime or that such information would be more useful to burglars than simply walking the neighborhood themselves). The move to block the Google car from the streets of Broughton generated significant worldwide attention, but it also provoked a blowback. Soon, Google Street View defenders started a campaign to drive the streets of Broughton, taking photographs and posting them on the social photography site Flickr.[45]

Ultimately, neither Broughton nor Google suffered substantial or long-term damage from these high-profile incidents. If anything, the news coverage and peer-to-peer buzz about Street View enhanced Google's presence in Britain. In other words, the very panic that journalists, politicians, activists, or angry citizens generate at the imposition of something as strange and unnerving as Street View creates a tremendous amount of interest in the service, as well as voyeuristic curiosity about what it shows. Google officials can then boast of the increase in usage as evidence of public acceptance, rather than evidence of wariness and concern about the service.

Wherever Street View has been launched, a company spokesperson has repeated that "privacy is very important to Google" without ever defining exactly what the company means by privacy or addressing what a culture considers private or sacrosanct. The company always reiterates that individuals may opt out and request that an image be removed; it does not, however, explain that such a request takes at least three steps of effort and that several hours, or even days, may elapse before the offending images disappear from Google Street View.

In March 2009, just days after the launch of Google Street View in the United Kingdom, Google had to remove an image of a naked toddler who was playing in a garden square in North London.[46] Although Google's policy operated as the company promised, the public exposure could still have subjected this child or his parents to ridicule and shame. Street View had been up for at least forty-eight hours by the time the image of the child was discovered and Google alerted. There is no way to tell how many people saw or made copies of the image in that period. It's likely that friends and neighbors of that child could identify him from such an image, even if it his face were blurred, simply from the setting or from the images of adults in the area.

Moreover, not everyone featured in an embarrassing image is likely to find it within forty-eight hours of its appearance on the Internet. Not everyone uses Google Maps or Street View. Not every neighborhood is filled with computer users. To defeat Google's default settings, you have to be looking out for yourself, your property, your family, and your neighborhood. As always, the technologically proficient and aware suffer little harm and gain greatly from the convenience of Google Street View. Those who are not proficient, perhaps by choice but perhaps because of age, disability, or lack of means, are much more vulnerable under such a system. Because of this and other high-profile incidents, by April 2010 the United Kingdom's information commissioner, Christopher Graham, had called for Google to flip its defaults and grant privacy protection first, rather than placing the burden on the individual to opt out. "It is unacceptable," Graham wrote to Eric Schmidt, "to roll out a product that unilaterally renders personal information public, with the intention of repairing problems later as they arise."[47]

A few days after the Broughton incident, I had a long conversation with Peter Barron, head of communication and public affairs for Google in the United Kingdom, Ireland, Belgium, the Netherlands, and Luxembourg. "This was actually a fantastically successful launch" in the United Kingdom, Barron told me over a Skype connection.

> We had record numbers of people visiting Google Maps. Many, many millions of people used and enjoyed and found the product extremely useful. We had a very small number of complaints—complaints in the hundreds—about the fact that people's houses were up or maybe their faces weren't blurred. We explained to people that these images could be removed if you wanted that and this was carried out very, very quickly, usually within an hour or two. . . . The truth is, we expected

a degree of controversy. In many countries where Street View has launched, there is a degree of controversy within the first few weeks. There is an element of the shock of the new. People aren't used to Street View and perhaps feel a bit uncomfortable with it in the beginning. But after a couple of weeks it tends to die down.[48]

INFRASTRUCTURAL IMPERIALISM

Barron was correct about the ebb of panic and concern about Google Street View after a few weeks. British newspapers moved on to other issues. The public began to use Google Maps and Street View to find its way around London. Barron emphasized that there was a substantial difference between the ways urban and rural areas of the United Kingdom reacted to Google Street View. "People in the cities are very used to having themselves publicly photographed, and in the countryside less so," Barron told me. That's certainly true in the United Kingdom, with the heaviest surveillance of any liberal and industrialized state in the world. Video cameras are posted on almost every street corner in the major cities of the United Kingdom.[49] The BBC estimates that there are as many as 4.2 million surveillance cameras—both public and private—operating in Britain. That's about one for every fourteen people.[50] After decades of terrorism at the hands of Irish Republican Army members, and more recently Islamic radicals, the people of the United Kingdom have grown to accept high levels of surveillance in their cities, even though such a lattice of lenses has not contributed to any measurable decrease in crime or increase in security.[51] There has certainly been a cost, however. Privacy International ranks the United Kingdom as the worst democracy at protecting individual privacy. (Again, the group is fuzzy on its definition of privacy.) The United Kingdom ranks with Malaysia and China in terms of the levels and reach of state surveillance.[52]

It's puzzling why people in the United Kingdom, who are so used to assuming their image is being captured on camera, reacted so viscerally to the idea of an American corporation taking static photographs in which most people are difficult to identify, and making those photographs available to anyone with a computer. The negative reactions in

Germany and Japan are more readily understandable. After the invasive and destructive state surveillance that Germans experienced during the Nazi era and in Soviet-dominated East Germany, one can understand the wariness with which German citizens consider Google's initiatives. And the density of Japanese cities explains the Japanese aversion to Street View. The people of the United Kingdom, by contrast, have consistently elected leaders who support expanding technologies of surveillance rather than limiting them. And Britain after Margaret Thatcher, John Major, Tony Blair, and Gordon Brown is hardly an anticorporate or anti-American culture. So it's possible that the reaction to Google Street View was a reflection of the sensationalism endemic to British journalism rather than a deeper cultural issue. Or perhaps some people in the United Kingdom have had enough of living under constant state and commercial scrutiny.[53] Maybe a few of them chose to make a stand against an obvious and less powerful offender than their own state and corporate bureaucracy.

After examining this array of reactions to Street View and Google's unvarying approach to its introduction in diverse cultural, political, and historical contexts, I wondered whether Google operated with a universalizing ideology. Did the company consider local differences and concerns? I didn't see any evidence of it in the Street View saga.

Google's CEO, Eric Schmidt, has commented that he sees few, if any important cultural differences among Google users around the world. In a conversation at Princeton University with the computer scientist Ed Felten in May 2009, Schmidt said, "The most common question I get about Google is 'How is it different everywhere else?' and I am sorry to tell you that it's not. People still care about Britney Spears in these other countries. It's really very disturbing." Schmidt said his experience analyzing Google users' habits around the world had convinced him that "people are the same everywhere." Schmidt went on to give the standard Google line that the company respects local laws (as, of course, it must). But his universalist statements are consistent with much of the company's behavior.[54]

The tension between universalism and particularism in the age of rapid globalization is well documented. It's clear after decades of argument that ideologies such as market fundamentalism, liberalism (with its imperative for free speech), techno-fundamentalism, and free trade are no longer simply "Western"—if they ever were.[55] It's too simple (and ahistorical) to tag such ideologies as merely imperialistic. But it is true that they are universalizing. They carry strong assumptions that people everywhere have the same needs, values, and desires—even if they don't yet know it themselves.

Cultural imperialism has become a useless cliché. The academic cultural-imperialism thesis is in severe need of revision. Once dominant among leftist critics in the 1970s and 1980s, it has been supplanted and modified by the rise of cultural studies.[56] Yet it still resonates in public discourse about the global North and the global South and in some anxious corners of academia.[57] While those who complain about cultural imperialism cite the ubiquity of KFC in Cairo and McDonald's in Manila, anxious cultural protectionists in the United States quiver at the sound of Spanish spoken in public or mosques opening in Ohio. Some American nationalists argue that cultural imperialism would be good for the world, because Americans have so much figured out.[58] Others dodge its complications by celebrating "creolization" at all costs, while ignoring real and serious imbalances in the political economy of culture.[59]

Although the evidence for cultural imperialism is powerful only when selectively examined, the evidence for the recent emergence of what we might call "infrastructural imperialism" is much stronger. There are imbalances of power in global flows of culture, but they are not what traditional cultural-imperialism theorists claim them to be.

If there is a dominant form of cultural imperialism, it concerns the pipelines and protocols of culture, not its products—the formats of distribution of information and the terms of access and use.[60] It is not exactly content-neutral, but it is less necessarily content-specific than theorists of cultural imperialism assume. The texts, signs, and messages that flow through global communications networks do not carry a clear and unambiguous celebration of ideas and ideologies we might lazily label Western, such as consumerism, individualism, and secularism.[61] These commercial pipelines may instead carry texts that overtly criticize and threaten the tenets of global capitalism, such as albums by the leftist rock band Rage against the Machine, films by Michael Moore, and books by Naomi Klein. Time Warner does not care if the data inscribed on the compact discs it sells simulates the voice of Madonna or of Ali Farka Touré. What flows from North to South does not matter as much as how it flows, how much revenue the flows generate, and who uses and reuses them. In this way, the Googlization of us has profound consequences. It's not so much the ubiquity of Google's brand that is troubling, danger-ous, or even interesting: it's that Google's defaults and ways of doing spread and structure ways of seeking, finding, exploring, buying, and presenting that influence (though they do not control) habits of thought and action. These default settings, these nudges, are expressions of an ideology.[62]

Because Barron had watched closely as Google introduced a number of high-profile services to several European countries, I asked him how Google navigates cultural differences and whether he was concerned that Google's universalist tendencies would cause trouble in places that do not embrace either the technocratic imperative or a cultural commit-ment to free expression.

"Google starts from a position that we seek to make information avail-able to the widest number of people," Barron explained to me. "Google is built on free expression. In the United States, that has been embraced enthusiastically. Elsewhere, there are different cultural norms, different laws, and different customs. We are committed to abiding by the laws of the countries that we operate in, but also taking into account local norms and local customs."[63]

This was the standard line. So I asked Barron for an example of how Google had tailored its practices to conform to a local concern. He had a good one at hand. "Over the last year, we had some prob-lems with gang-related videos, with boys brandishing weapons and making general threats on these videos." Under YouTube's estab-lished guidelines, these videos would not have been considered viola-tions, Barron said. But "because of the nature of the concern in the UK, YouTube decided to alter their guidelines for the UK to cover gang-related videos."

In this case, and that of the decision to reshoot the entire nation of Japan for Google Street View, Google altered its operations in response to reactions in particular environments. This is good practice, even if, as in Japan, it took a year for the company to concede the point. Google has found this approach to globalization workable in almost every context in which it operates. The vast majority of those who use Google find services such as Street View more beneficial to them than harmful. The few who might be offended by the standard and universal policies of Google are of little importance to the company. After all, we are not Google's customers: we are its products. Google can afford to alienate a few thousand of us, because for most of those who are connected to the cosmopolitan global culture of the Internet, living without Google is not tenable. For every person who complains about Street View, millions more find it useful.

THE GOOGLIZED SUBJECT

This universalization of surveillance via infrastructural imperialism, and its general acceptance, merits critical attention. However, most work surveying the troubling implications of mass surveillance has fundamentally misrepresented its nature. It assumes that surveillance of the kind that Google makes possible is analogous to the theory of social control described by Michel Foucault as the Panopticon. But this trope has exhausted its utility. The original Panopticon, conceived by Jeremy Bentham, was a design for a circular prison with a central watchtower, in which all the inmates would behave because they would assume that they were being observed at all times. Foucault argued that state programs to monitor and record our comings and goings create imaginary prisons that lead citizens to limit what they do out of fear of being observed by those in power. The gaze, the theory goes, works as well as iron bars to control the behavior of most people.[64] Those who write about privacy and surveillance usually can't help invoking the Panopticon to argue that the great harm of mass surveillance is social control.[65]

However, the Panopticon model does not suffice to describe our current predicaments. First, mass surveillance does not inhibit behavior: people may act weird regardless of the number of cameras pointed at them. The thousands of surveillance cameras in London and New York City do not deter the eccentric and avant-garde. Long before closed-circuit cameras, cities were places to be seen, not to disappear. Today, reality television suggests that there may be a positive relationship between the number of cameras and observers pointed at subjects and their willingness to act strangely and relinquish all pretensions of dignity. There is no empirical reason to believe that awareness of surveillance limits the imagination or cows creativity in a market economy under a nontotalitarian state.

Certainly the Stasi in East Germany exploited the controlling power generated by widespread awareness of surveillance and the potential for brutal punishment for thought crimes.[66] But that is not the environment in which most of us now live. And unless the Panopticon is as visible and ubiquitous as agencies like the Stasi, it cannot influence behavior as Bentham and Foucault assumed it would.

But more important, the forces at work in Europe, North America, and much of the rest of the world are the opposite of a Panopticon: they involve not the subjection of the individual to the gaze of a single, centralized authority, but the surveillance of the individual, potentially by all, always by many. We have a "cryptopticon" (for lack of a better word). Unlike Bentham's prisoners, we don't know all the ways in which we are being watched or profiled—we simply know that we are. And we don't regulate our behavior under the gaze of surveillance: instead, we don't seem to care.

In fact, that's just how those doing most of today's surveillance want it. ChoicePoint, Facebook, Google, and Amazon want us to relax and be ourselves. They have an interest in exploiting niche markets that our consumer choices have generated. These companies are devoted to tracking our eccentricities because they understand that the ways we set ourselves apart from the mass are the things about which we are most passionate. Our passions, predilections, fancies, and fetishes are what we are likely to spend our surplus cash on and thus make us easy targets for precise marketing. For example, almost everybody kind of likes Fleetwood Mac's 1977 album *Rumours*, so the fact that I bought it long ago says nothing special about me. But I am one of the few people who really digs their earlier, bluesy *Then Play On*. That says something about me that might be useful to marketers. As Joseph Turow explained in *Niche Envy*, and *Wired* editor Chris Anderson describes in *The Long Tail*, market segmentation is vital to today's commerce. In order for marketers and vendors to target messages and products to us, they must know our eccentricities—what makes us distinctive, or, at least, to which small interest groups we belong. Forging a mass audience or market is a waste of time and money unless you are selling soap.[67]

Even the modern liberal state, like those of North America and Western Europe, wants us to be ourselves. It wants subversive and potentially dangerous people to reveal themselves through their habits and social connections, not to slink away and hide in the dark.[68] Repressing dissent and subversion does not eliminate them: the Stasi lost its efforts to control the East German people despite the enormous scale of its operations and the long-lasting damage it inflicted on both the observers and the observed. In the twenty-first-century liberal state, domination does not demand social or cultural conformity. The state, like every private firm that employs a sophisticated method of marketing, wants us to express ourselves—to choose—because mere expression of difference is usually both harmless and remarkably useful to the powerful.

Living so long under the dominance of market fundamentalism and techno-fundamentalism, we have come to accept the concept of choice and the exhortation of both the Isley Brothers and Madonna, "Express yourself," as essential to living a good life. So comforted are we by offers of "options" and "settings" made by commercial systems such as Facebook and Google that we neglect the larger issues. We weave these services so firmly and quickly into the fabrics of our daily social and intellectual lives that we neglect to consider what dependence might cost us. And many of us who are technically sophisticated can tread confidently through the hazards of these systems, forgetting that the vast majority of people using them are not aware of their pitfalls or the techniques by which users can master them. Settings only help you if you know enough to care about them. Defaults matter all the time. Google's great trick is to make everyone feel satisfied with the possibility of choice, without actually exercising it to change the system's default settings. But as I show in the next chapter, for people living in illiberal political contexts, different vulnerabilities exist.

FOUR

THE GOOGLIZATION OF THE WORLD

PROSPECTS FOR A GLOBAL PUBLIC SPHERE

In early 2009, the leaders of Eu, a small town in the north of France, decided to change its official name. It seems that Google searches for "Eu" generated too many results for Europe in general, largely because the European Union is colloquially known as "EU" and because there is a general European Web domain name ".eu." Even some results pointing to the chemical element Europium outranked those for the little town. Voters in the town were asked to choose among longer strings of text such as "Eu-en-Normandie" or "la Ville d'Eu." And municipal leaders considered purchasing ads on Google and hiring a firm that specializes in optimizing search-engine ranks to raise the profile of the town.[1] It seems that if a town—or anyone or anything—can't be found with Google, it might as well not exist.

As Google steadily expands and globalizes its services, localities and nations deal with it in very different ways. Instead of pandering to the

biases of Google searches, as the town of Eu did, other European entities have taken a more hostile stance. In February 2010 Google's top
lawyer, David Drummond, and three other top Google executives were
convicted in Italy on privacy-violation charges for failing to prevent the
posting to YouTube of a video of an autistic child being bullied. The
video remained on the Italian version of YouTube for two months in
2006. Under widely agreed practice and most European law, Google
and its executives should have been free from risk of suit or prosecu-
tion. In this case, Google did what it always does, and what every Web
service provider does: it removed the illegal content as soon as authorities notified the company. But for some reason Italian prosecutors were
not satisfied with that move. Instead, they pursued the Google executives for more than a year, convicting three of the four. Google immediately appealed the ruling and proclaimed—with justification—that if
Web service companies were to be held responsible for the content their
users upload, then none would host such content. The risks would be
too high. If more countries were to prosecute such cases, the Web would
not be as free, open, or interesting as it could be.[2]

In a very different situation, the government of Iran in February
2010 blocked access to Google's e-mail system, Gmail, and instituted
a national e-mail system to take its place. This occurred just before the
celebration of the thirtieth anniversary of the Iranian revolution of 1979
and a few months after massive protests against the government over
a stolen election that resulted in thousands of cases of imprisonment,
torture, rape, and murder of government critics. The Iranian government had already infiltrated social networking systems such as Facebook
and Twitter to monitor protest plans. When activists turned to using
Gmail, largely because it can be encrypted, the government took action
against the service.[3] Not coincidentally, just three weeks earlier Google
had activated Gmail encryption by default in reaction to the news that
hackers from China had breached the security of several Gmail users
who were considered troublesome dissidents by the Chinese government. Google had immediately threatened to dismantle aspects of its
carefully designed operation in China and said it would consider pulling
out of providing services to China entirely.[4]

Such cases demonstrate the extent to which the world has been Googl-ized. Even cities, towns, and universities obsess about their visibility, rankings, and reputations on Google and bend to the biases of this pow-erful search service. At the same time, more and more people around the world have been resisting the universalizing tendencies of Google. They are demanding exceptions and reconsiderations. Thus Google is strug-gling to maintain its vision and principles while itself bending slightly to the wills of states, institutions, and communities in a diverse world. And increasingly, the company devoted to liberating information and connecting the world has to deal with life-and-death consequences of its investments and activities.

In 2009, Google faced a conflict that put it between two countries with nuclear powers and the world's most important growing econ-omies, China and India. For more than fifty years, the two countries have been contesting their shared border between Tibet and the Indian state of Arunachal Pradesh, occasionally to the point of combat. Google Maps originally depicted the territory as Indian. As of late 2009, Google Maps users in China saw the area marked as part of Tibet; those in India still saw it designated as part of India. Google Maps applied the same treatment to disputed areas of the Indian states of Jammu and Kashmir, which have majority Muslim populations and have been claimed by Pakistan since the two nations were divided in 1947.[5] As its influence and operations expand around the world, Google is finding it difficult to keep everyone happy and stay true to its mission.

THE CHINA SYNDROME

Of all the issues that have tangled and troubled Google, none is as serious and complex as the company's relationship with the People's Republic of China. The story of Google in China started around 2004 and seemed to end with a whimper in 2010. In the summer of 2009, the Chinese government had deployed all its technologies of Internet censorship to block its residents' access to social networking services such as Twitter and Facebook, and it has also blocked access to many Google services, such as Blogger and YouTube.

All of this tension was put into sharp relief in January 2010 in an incident that revealed to the world the level of insecurity in global online systems and the extent to which the Chinese government was willing to go in order to hunt down its critics. Just a week before U.S. secretary of state Hillary Clinton was scheduled to make a major speech emphasizing her country's commitment to freedom of communication in digital networks, Google announced that servers located far from China had been breached by someone operating within the People's Republic. Many assumed that the hackers were working at the behest of the Chinese security services, as several of the Gmail accounts that had been compromised belonged to dissidents and critics of the government. But that assumption was impossible to prove, and the Chinese government denied it. In the days that followed, Google made it clear that at least thirty U.S. companies had also had their servers breached by the same attackers from China. Realizing that its security was inadequate, Google immediately bolstered some features. It also announced that China had made it impossible to continue to operate as it had been doing. Google would no longer cooperate with the government in its efforts to censor search results, the company pledged. Instead of facing a major scandal and stories of the dangerous lack of security among major Internet companies, Google managed to turn the story into a defense of human rights and free speech.

Google risked quite a bit by taking a stand against the breaches of security by someone in China. For its action, the company received much applause and an affirmation of support from the U.S. government. Clinton specifically mentioned Google and China in her speech on Internet freedom, thus embarrassing China and heightening tensions. Google also received praise from the same human rights groups that had been criticizing Google's longtime arrangement with China, despite the fact that Google merely expressed a desire to stop censoring Web searches and did nothing to ensure that people in China were able to fight or evade censorship. Then, after more than two months of stasis, Google announced in March 2010 that it would no longer offer Google

.cn, the Mandarin-language search service operated within China under the critical eye of Chinese censors.[6]

The Google move was mischaracterized as a "pullout" and celebrated as a victory for human rights by activists in the United States. But it was neither. Google merely redirected users in China to its Hong Kong–based search service, which was not actively censored by Google. However, the Chinese government itself censors and often blocks access to the Hong Kong–based Chinese-language version of Google. So no one in China ever sees an uncensored version of Google search results. In addition, Google retained its partnerships with Chinese firms to produce mobile phones. It also maintained its research activities and offices in China. There was no "pullout," merely a redirection of data and a misdirection of public understanding.

In closing down Google.cn, Google made the decision to abandon many millions of users—and thus potential advertising revenue. For decades, American companies have been weighing the risks and benefits of engaging with China for manufacturing and marketing. Despite risking worldwide shame for colluding with a brutal regime, companies have realized that China has the potential to generate many important ideas, technologies, and scientific breakthroughs. More immediately, the importance of a population of 1.3 billion people as a source of labor and a market for products and services is undeniable.[7]

Ultimately, Google's concessions gave the government of the People's Republic of China exactly what it wanted—to be rid of a troublesome company that was never comfortable operating under Chinese law. In its efforts to enlist the Obama administration and Secretary of State Hillary Clinton to its cause, Google managed to get itself tarred by nationalists in China and the Chinese government as a puppet of the U.S. government, thus undermining at least some of the goodwill it had built up as a cosmopolitan, apolitical technology company. Web users in China now must use one of the homegrown, completely controlled search engines or the censored, Hong Kong–based version of Google. The company lost out in this move, and the people of China gained nothing. And the Chinese government can rest easier now that

Google will not be the source of troublesome influences leaking into the country.

Human rights and free-speech advocates had argued for years that in its relations with the Chinese government, Google was rendering itself a part of that government's structures of oppression. They argued that it abrogated the duties and obligations of corporate responsibility. As the Harvard computer science professor Harry Lewis put it in the debate on National Public Radio in November 2008 (see chapter 2), Google violated its "Don't be evil" motto by creating Google.cn along the very lines that the Chinese government demanded: Google merely "chose the more profitable of the two evils," passively allowing censorship rather than actively engaging in it. The results for the Chinese people are, of course, the same.[8]

From the point of view of both promarket neoliberals and techno-fundamentalists, however, Google's presence in China improved transparency and offered aid to those who struggle for basic human rights; it thus worked to reform a corrupt system by allowing a little bit of light into an otherwise dark environment. Esther Dyson, one of the visionaries of the information age, responded to Lewis by arguing for the transformative, perhaps revolutionary power of information technology. "The great virtue of the Internet is that it erodes power, it sucks power out of the center, and takes it to the periphery, it erodes the power of institutions over people while giving to individuals the power to run their own lives," she said. "Google by its very presence and its operation, even if it's incomplete, creates increasing expectations for transparency, it starts people answering questions. It gets them to expect to be able to find out stuff."[9]

In fact, Google played no role in actively oppressing the Chinese people—and almost no role in their potential liberation either. These two diametric positions—that Google is part of the problem in China and that it is part of the solution—emerge from a lack of understanding of both the Internet in general and Google's policies and services in China. If the People's Republic of China ever opens itself up to the turmoil of free speech and democratic accountability, it will not be merely because the Internet was free and open or because Google did not help the government limit access to certain sites. Nothing is that simple.

TECHNOLOGY AND REVOLUTION

When I started to research this book, I expected to berate Google for its lack of corporate accountability in taking an acquiescent stance toward the Chinese government. The prodemocracy events of 1989, in China and elsewhere, forged my political consciousness. As the journalism scholar Jay Rosen has said, "There are 1945 democrats. There are 1968 democrats. I am a 1989 democrat." I too am a 1989 democrat. On June 4, the day the Chinese military slaughtered hundreds of peaceful demonstrators in Beijing, the freshly legalized Polish labor union, Solidarity, unseated the Communist government in a fair election, thus sparking a series of democratic revolutions throughout the world. By October 1989, the East German dictator Erik Honecker had resigned, and Hungary had become a parliamentary republic. By November, the pro-apartheid National Party in South Africa had begun dismantling the racist system and inviting full political participation by the oppressed black majority. Also in November 1989, the "Velvet Revolution" began in Czechoslovakia, and the country's Communist Party announced it would hold free elections in December. The Czech poet Václav Havel later was elected president. Brazil also held its first free elections that December, after twenty-nine years of military rule. The year ended with the Romanian dictator Nicolae Ceauşescu being overthrown and executed in Romania. These and other events contributed to the dissolution of the Soviet empire and eventually the Soviet Union itself by late 1991.

In 1989, as a young man of twenty-three, I could not have been more optimistic about the prospects for justice and democracy in my country and the rest of the world. As accounts of these revolutions emerged, stories circulated of how new communication technologies had played a part in the successful resistance to oppression. The proliferation of fax machines in Eastern Europe and the Soviet Union, for instance, reportedly facilitated activism and awareness among networks of dissidents.[10]

One business writer voiced this common belief by boldly stating, "The fall of Communism in Eastern Europe is the direct result of new information technologies."[11] To a naive young American like me, fascinated by new technology and devoted to the belief that free speech can be deeply and positively transformative, this simple connection between a new technology and stunning historical events was irresistible. Such a techno-optimistic story accorded well with other views I held at that time: that the Reformation and Enlightenment were driven, or made necessary, by the emergence of the printing press in fifteenth-century Europe, and that mass-market pamphlets such as Thomas Paine's *Common Sense* were essential factors in the birth of the American republic.[12] Of course, this view was far too simple an explanation for the sudden (and, in many places, temporary) spread of democracy and free speech. Historians of both politics and technology knew the story was more complex.[13]

New communicative methods and technologies certainly play a role in rapid social and political change. But like many others, I put too much emphasis on them and discounted the remarkable human struggle, raw courage, and ideological effort that were more instrumental in the overthrow of oppressive regimes—especially in places like South Africa and Brazil. In *Postwar: A History of Europe since 1945*, the historian Tony Judt credits different factors for the success of liberation movements in each country of Eastern Europe. In Hungary, Judt explains, a youthful reform movement within the Hungarian Communist Party pushed the government at its weakest points. In East Germany, the decision to alter a solidly analog technology—the Berlin Wall—and allow Berliners to travel back and forth had by late 1989 created a political tide the Communist Party could not withstand. All of this change in the satellite nations was reinforced by the progressive weakening of the Soviet state, caused in part by its futile war in Afghanistan.

In addition, change was rapid within Soviet society itself. The Soviet leader Mikhail Gorbachev invited the growth of a nascent public sphere, Judt writes, by engaging in glasnost, or a policy of openness, thus allowing dissent to be expressed through clubs, meetings, and publications. Glasnost even liberalized what appeared on Soviet television—a far more powerful and universal medium than the fax machine. Gorbachev himself decided to break the Communist Party's monopoly on news and information. Once Moscow was weakened, dozens of other factors—including the efforts of labor unions, religious leaders, poets, and criminals—could chip away at the foundation of Communist oppression across the Soviet Union and its satellites.[14]

Judt acknowledges that the most surprising thing about the revolutions of 1989 (in Europe, anyway) is that they all happened within such a short period, despite the distinct causes and conditions in each nation. He concludes that communication technology did play an important role in the speed and spread of the revolutionary spirit, but it was not the fax machine that motivated people to rise up: it was television. When viewers in Czechoslovakia and Germany could see local uprisings on television in their own living rooms, they encountered what Judt calls "instant political education, drumming home a double message: 'they are powerless,' and 'we did it.'" Just as important, Eastern Europeans, along with the rest of the world, watched the events in Tiananmen Square. They were struck, as I was, by the bravery of the protesters and the brutality of the state. They were no doubt inspired by the peaceful revolts that seemed to spring forth almost simultaneously all over the world. Global television, which relayed these events instantly, gave them both inspiration and a set of models to emulate. For the first time, they knew they were not alone.[15]

By focusing on the novelty of communicative technologies and assuming that their arrival in a place causes—rather than coincides with or aids—rapid change, we tend to downgrade the importance of factors as obvious and powerful as changing a government policy, opening a gate, or waging a disastrous and debilitating war in Central Asia. The introduction of a powerful and efficient mode of communication such as the fax machine or the Internet can amplify or accelerate a movement, provided that the movement already has form, support, substance, and momentum. Technologies are far from neutral, but neither do they inherently support either freedom or oppression. The same technologies, as we have already seen, can be used both to monitor and oppress a group of people and to connect them in powerful ways.[16] The way a society or a state uses a technology is as important as the design and capacities of that technology.

Communicative technologies certainly matter to the struggle for freedom, but how and how much? In any oppressed society, dissenting ideas and criticisms exist and flow, even when impeded by technology and law. They seep through the cracks in the system, and every system has cracks. As Robert Darnton writes about systems of censorship and their flaws before the French Revolution, "It was not simply a story that pitted liberty against oppression but rather one of complicity and collaboration."[17] Recent events in China demonstrate how the complex relations of technology with oppressive regimes and liberation movements play out, and the ways in which technological innovations, such as those offered by Google, function in collaboration and complicity with both the forces of repression and the forces of liberation.

THE MYTH OF THE "GREAT FIREWALL"

Despite common perceptions, China is hardly sealed off from the rest of the world. It never has been, even during the brutal Cultural Revolution of the late 1960s and early 1970s. The outside world was shocked to discover, after the fact, that millions of Chinese had starved during the economic "reforms" of the Great Leap Forward in the late 1950s and that Chinese society had been fractured right down to the level of the family during the Cultural Revolution. But there had been hints and indications all along that life in China during these periods was intolerable for many. Only the scale was hidden.

The standard views of China vacillate between a rising and dynamic economic giant and a brutal totalitarian society that forces its citizens to curb their associations and imaginations. Neither of these models is accurate. China has a thriving market economy whose macroeconomic and large-scale investment policies are significantly guided by the central state. It has a state apparatus that is just as corrupt and incompetent as it is vicious—although it displays its brutal effectiveness without hesitation when it needs to, as events in Tibet in 2008 demonstrated.[18]

China is still authoritarian, tolerating little overt dissent over certain policies, such as treatment of dissident religious groups, pornography, its efforts to destroy Tibetan culture, or the protests in Tiananmen Square on June 4, 1989.[19] Yet despite these repressive and restrictive measures, China has plugged itself into to the world's social, economic, and technological flows. It has more Internet users than any other country, despite the fact that only 16 percent of the population was online regularly as of 2009.[20]

The style of state censorship in China thus is complex. There is no "Great Firewall," as many of those reporting on China have asserted.[21] China's Internet filtering and blocking policy is not sturdy and impenetrable: it's fluid and situational, more like the dystopian model described in Aldous Huxley's *Brave New World* than that of George Orwell's *Nineteen Eighty-Four*. Distraction and consumerism crowd out meaningful dissent and troublesome expression.[22] China has ways of blocking, however imperfectly, most of the sites and messages to which it objects, but for most people in China, site censorship affects daily life very little.

China cranks up the tools of censorship during times of potential social unrest, such as the 2008 Olympics, the twentieth anniversary of the June 4 massacre, and protests in Tibet. When they do block access to a site or a service, Chinese censors mask the nature of the disruption by indicating that a connection has failed or been reset, rather than blocked or forbidden. This subtle tactic serves to frustrate the general user in China without generating clear and targeted resentment against the state.

Forbidden material is not completely unavailable to Chinese Internet users. It's just a challenge to get it, and searching for it puts users at risk of state reprisal if their usage is being monitored. Those adept at technology may find their way through the cracks in the system by using encrypted messages or proxy servers to hide or fool the government's censoring and surveillance technologies. The Chinese Internet censorship project does not pretend to seal China off completely from certain sources or ideas. It just hopes to marginalize and track potential dissidents. The Chinese government has a strong interest in deterring those who would use the Internet to coordinate trouble or unrest and in generating fear among them, but it has just as strong an interest in ensuring that commerce flowers in China. Global commerce depends on a reliable and malleable communication infrastructure such as the Internet. Commerce also requires tools such as strong encryption and virtual private networks (VPNs) to protect sensitive data and trade secrets. So China will not outlaw use of the Internet or enforce restrictions on methods of protecting information.

As a result, China has built a fascinating and flexible system that simultaneously allows it to grant private firms the ability to exploit the Internet with almost as much freedom as American and European companies have, to distract the greater population with the prospects of consumption and entertainment, and yet to hamper political and religious dissidents enough to limit their influence on daily life. That's not to say that China's Internet is "open" or "free"—far from it.[23] Elites, as always, can wangle more freedom than the rest of Chinese society. As the journalist James Fallows has explained, the most effective aspect of Chinese Internet policy is its unpredictability. China has harnessed the power of inconvenience as its most effective weapon in stifling political dissent and even awareness.[24]

The result of this unpredictability is that global technology companies operating in China simultaneously enable new forms of dissent and the repression of it. It's in this more subtle way that Internet technology companies are simultaneously complicit with repressive regimes and subversive of them.

China's Internet is penetrable by technologically adept dissidents and others who seek to communicate the truth about the regime; it is also a means of conducting surveillance of them. Amnesty International reminds us that China has imprisoned more journalists and bloggers than any other state.[25] Chinese officials can use Internet surveillance techniques to crack down on anyone who crosses an invisible and unpredictably shifting line. China's Internet is more centralized than most of the world's networks. All traffic flows through three fiber-optic cable nodes and then to the rest of the world. This architecture allows the government to block access to certain sources of data.[26] China also employs several thousand officials who share the duty of policing Internet use, mostly in cafes. The government sponsors several important Internet firms, such as the search-engine company Baidu. And China extracts important provisions and promises from foreign companies that offer Internet services in China.[27]

China offers foreign companies, including Internet technology companies, vast opportunities for growth in market share, revenue, and human capital. The lure is irresistible. But as Yahoo discovered, the technology a company provides in China can serve contradictory ends. When an activist named Wang Xiaoning used his Yahoo e-mail account to distribute some anonymous writings criticizing the Chinese government's handling of the events of May and June 1989, he was arrested; he began serving a ten-year sentence in 2003. During his trial, prosecutors introduced evidence obtained from Yahoo's China branch identifying Wang as the distributor of the incriminating messages.[28] Then, in 2003, Chinese authorities arrested a dissident named Li Zhi and sentenced him to eight years for "inciting subversion." Again, Yahoo supplied the information needed to track Li's messages.[29] Another, more famous case involved a poet and journalist named Shi Tao, who had sent an e-mail revealing a Communist Party directive concerning Tiananmen Square dissidents to someone in the United States. Shi was well known to Chinese authorities for his criticisms of human rights abuses. So when Yahoo revealed his e-mail account information to Chinese authorities, they were able to track Shi as the source of the offending e-mail. Shi was sentenced to ten years in prison in April 2005.[30]

Once word reached the United States that Yahoo was complicit in the persecution of political dissidents, a furor ensued. Yahoo has faced a lawsuit filed by human rights organizations, widespread criticism among bloggers and activists, shareholder objections, and a grilling by a U.S. congressional committee examining the roles of American companies such as Yahoo, Cisco (which supplies the servers that facilitate much of the surveillance and site blocking in China), and Google. Yahoo, of course, defended its actions by saying that it cannot violate the laws of a country in which it does business, and it cannot be held responsible if its users violate laws. It also claimed that its American affiliate owned only 40 percent of Yahoo China. The majority owner was another Chinese search-engine and service provider, Alibaba.com. Since 2005, Alibaba.com has assumed complete control over Yahoo in China.

In every discussion about the role and responsibilities of Internet companies in China, the plight of dissidents has played a central role. These cases have generated calls for American companies to forge a set of best practices or a code of conduct that would limit the extent to which their resources could be used by the Chinese government to violate basic human rights. In the 1980s, many American and European companies signed the Sullivan Principles, which established a code of just conduct, when the South African government practiced brutal oppression against its black majority. So far, foreign companies have failed to outline such provisions for China.

The Yahoo saga has cast a shadow over Google as well, even though Google has operated in a very different way in China. The application of Internet technology in China shows an inevitable interplay between complicity with repression and the potential for liberation. Contrary to the assertions of techno-fundamentalists, such technology does not inherently further either liberal democratic or neoliberal economic and political ends. There is no "Great Firewall" in China, but neither has Internet technology led to the ends that its proponents predicted. China certainly embraces Internet technology, but it uses it in its own way.

CHINA AND RESISTANCE TO INFRASTRUCTURAL IMPERIALISM

Google never put itself in a position to turn over information about Chinese dissidents' e-mail accounts to the government, because the company decided years ago not to host e-mail or any other service that might require such revelations within China. But because of the nature of its relations with China, Google could not escape complicity with the repressive policies of the Chinese regime. Google.cn offered only a filtered version of Google's search engine to Chinese users. To do business there, it had to compromise its avowed commitment to providing access to everything by everybody. Rather than impose its own values, it had to accede to the way the Chinese regime does things.

Before 2006, Google did not have servers or services located in the People's Republic of China. Chinese users could reach Google by connecting to Google.com and its servers in the United States. Of course, this meant that the Chinese censors could block all Google services if they decided that something offended or troubled them. This happened often between 2002 and 2006. Moreover, having Google's data pass through China's three central nodes and filters meant that Google was significantly slower than search engines with servers based inside China. Google was facing the prospect of becoming irrelevant to Chinese users, excluded from gathering advertising revenue from one of the fastest-growing consumer economies in history, and facing irregular and arbitrary blackouts of its service for which the company would most likely be blamed.

Consequently, by late 2002, it became clear that Google was not going to be able to gain purchase in the Chinese market if it retained its public commitment to universal access to free thought and expression. "We faced a choice at that point," Google vice president Elliot Schrage told a congressional subcommittee in 2006. "Hold fast to our commitment to free speech and risk a long-term cut-off from our Chinese users, or compromise our principles by entering the Chinese market directly and subjecting ourselves to Chinese laws and regulations." For a while, at least, Google actually stayed out of China. Then, in 2005 the company began a series of discussions with government and human rights leaders in an effort to construct a model that would allow Google to offer dependable service in China without putting itself or its users in danger.[31]

The company launched a new service, Google.cn, in 2006. Because it was based in China, it worked quickly and was tailored to local needs and search habits. In addition, it included a feature that revealed to users whether certain sites had been blocked or removed by the state. Most important, Google has refused to operate any services that could put users in jeopardy. Chinese users of Gmail and Blogger must sign in through the U.S.-based Chinese-language sites of Google.com. And search results generated by Google.com remain unfiltered and uncensored by Google, though not by China itself. As a result, of course, the Chinese government still frequently blocks access to YouTube and Blogger with mysterious messages that "the connection has timed out."[32]

China's ability to resist the values of infrastructural imperialism, as espoused by Google in its formats of distribution and terms of access and use, stems in part from Google's status as an international corporation. Google would be foolish to abandon the Chinese market. In fact, it would commit something close to commercial malpractice to avoid or vacate China. Google is not a free-speech engine: it is an advertising company. It is also a publicly traded corporation with a duty to provide returns to its shareholders, and access to the Chinese market is potentially very profitable. And although both the company and its critics in the human rights community profess a shared commitment to free speech, Google can't possibly rise to the level of its own rhetoric on such matters.[33]

In many areas of speech and in many places in the world, Google similarly compromises its principles, usually to conform to local laws. In Germany and France, Google limits access to sites that promote anti-Semitism. In most of the world, Google limits access to images that display significant amounts of human skin. In the United States, Google quickly removes videos from YouTube if a just few people flag them as inappropriate. And because United States copyright law makes it easy for a company to remove a digital file from any Web server if it potentially infringes on copyright, such claims can be an effective tool of censorship as well.

It's hardly fair to compare the practice of conforming to standards of decency and copyright laws in relatively liberal nations with the participation in widespread practices of political censorship in places like China. But the company invites such a comparison by consistently asserting—no matter the context or issue—that it conforms to local laws and standards in matters of censorship. If you have a problem, the company is saying, take it up with local officials.[34]

Even so, Google officials continue to insist that the company is committed to the principles of free speech and that instances of censorship by the company are exceptions, rather than standards.[35] This contradiction creates a point of friction between Google's public philosophy—that is, what it says and believes about itself—and how it negotiates its positions and practices around the world. Certainly, Google is bound to conform to the laws of the countries in which it operates; so if Chinese officials demand that Google remove access to certain sites or subjects, the company claims it must obey. Human rights groups counter that Google is obliged to obey *all* of Chinese law and point out that the constitution of the People's Republic of China guarantees free speech. So Google, they say, is choosing to conform to Chinese law only in a way that causes it the least trouble and inconvenience.

China's ability to resist the values of infrastructural imperialism stems in part from its sheer size and geopolitical power. The contradiction between Google's principles and practices and the public outcry over the Yahoo decision to expose activists to persecution have generated a firm call for a shared code of conduct for global Internet corporations that deal with China. However, it's not clear whether pressure by liberal groups in North America and Western Europe is sufficient to counter the potential revenue that companies stand to gain from operating in China with the government's approval. Holding fast to principle might be easier in a smaller, poorer, and more oppressive country, such as Burma or Saudi Arabia.[36]

In recent decades, as global corporations have grown in influence, lawyers and theorists have been working to expand the reach of human rights law to cover corporate actors as well as states. The roles of the diamond industry in the slaughters and civil wars of Central Africa, of petroleum companies such as Shell in the support of the totalitarian junta in Burma, and of mining companies in the degradation of places such as Irian Jaya in Indonesia have sparked strong reactions. The connection between the interests of these companies and the brutality that exists in these places is impossible to deny. So far, however, this effort has not yielded tangible results. There is scant legal foundation for sanctioning companies for cooperating with states in the oppression of their own people. In addition, states sign human rights treaties; companies do not. Because current law does not hold companies liable for complicity in human rights violations, legal reformers are pushing for changes to international law that would treat such complicity as a crime.[37]

In fact, Google's role in China never precipitated a serious human rights showdown, because the company lacked leverage to either open up China or make it more oppressive. In 2009, Google controlled less than 21 percent of the China search market (as defined by the share of total searches; its share of search-based advertising revenue was higher, at 29.8 percent). That figure was more than two points lower than in the last quarter of 2008, so Google's market share was actually falling slightly in China in 2008–9. Because the number of searches within China rose 41.2 percent between the first quarter of 2008 and the first quarter of 2009, even a 21 percent share of the searches represented a lot of business to be done and money to be made. Nonetheless, Google was hardly the cultural and political factor in China that it is in North America and Europe.[38]

The Chinese search site Baidu.com controls more than 74 percent of the search market.[39] There are many reasons for its dominance. First and foremost, its early lead in market share gave Baidu more data with which to customize search results and services. Second, as of mid-2009, Google.cn offered fewer search services and features than Baidu did: while Google holds back from China many of its most attractive services to avoid human rights dilemmas, Baidu offers a wide array of locally based (and thus fast) services (online chat, children's material searches, legal searches, and access to government websites). Baidu also appeals to the growing nationalistic spirit in China, because many young people are wary of the influence of multinational corporations and proud that a Chinese firm can best one of the most powerful and popular in the world. Baidu also has the advantage of building its code from the ground up to serve searches in simplified Mandarin, whereas Google has had to translate many of its tools and services into Mandarin. Perhaps most important, for several years Baidu has taken advantage of China's notoriously lax copyright enforcement to allow its users to find unauthorized audio and video files easily. In early 2009 Google announced a deal with major global music companies to offer free, authorized music downloads to users in China to compete with Baidu.[40]

Google has been most popular among the cosmopolitan elite and international businesspeople in China, rather than the young and poor people who make up both the vast majority of the Chinese population in general and—more important—most of the potential market for Internet services. Given Baidu's much greater overall popularity, there is no reason to believe that Google's market share would have grown significantly over the next few years. But by commanding a valuable slice of the market—those who buy and travel more—Google had the potential to continue increasing its revenues and share of total revenues, even if its total market share continued to shrink.[41]

If we consider the wide array of tools that the Chinese government uses for security, surveillance, and censorship on the Internet and also consider how small are Google's market share and thus its influence in China, we can't help but conclude that Google has never mattered much in issues of commerce, politics, or justice in China. If that is the case, Esther Dyson was wrong to believe that Google's compromise with Chinese laws and standards could generate any measurable benefit to Chinese dissidents or promoters of religious freedom and democracy. The elites in China, those most likely to find value in Google, are also most likely to be aware of the global criticism of the Chinese stance on human rights, the technologies of censorship and surveillance, and the fate of the leaders of the uprisings in 1989. The vast majority of people in China, however, are satisfied with the commercial and entertainment services that Baidu offers. Even if Google.cn had offered access to somewhat more of the complicating and troublesome political information available in the world, there might not have been a demand for it. Web search is inherently conservative: the key to providing effective and attractive search services is to limit the number of surprises users will encounter. Largely because of Google's expertise, such services now deliver to users almost exactly what they think they want. If they don't want to look for trouble, they don't find it. Powerful and effective Web search thus inhibits rather than promotes social and political change.

Political change in China and elsewhere can only arrive when Chinese public culture demands it and presses the state at its points of greatest weakness.[42] We make a grave mistake by relying on technologies to change societies. Technologies are embedded in societies and cultures. They are not distinct and independent drivers.[43]

GOOGLE AND THE PROSPECTS FOR A GLOBAL CIVIL SOCIETY

Resistance to infrastructural imperialism and the spread of the values espoused by techno-fundamentalists is scarcely limited to oppressive regimes. China is hardly the sole example of a state that effectively censors Internet traffic and thwarts political dissent. As the Internet scholar Rebecca MacKinnon wrote during the June 2009 crackdown on Google and other Internet services in China, "The Internet censorship club is expanding and now includes a growing number of democracies. Legislators are under growing pressure from family groups to 'do something' in the face of all the threats sloshing around the Internet, and the risk of overstepping is high." Germany was considering a national censorship system through which Internet service providers would be required to block a secret list of sites. Australia and the United Kingdom have for a number of years maintained a similar national censorship list.[44] While none of these states censor as pervasively, disruptively, or effectively as China does, it's clear that China has strong partners in efforts to restrict the use of the Internet.

In each of these countries, Google follows orders from the state and thus actively (albeit tangentially and grudgingly) participates in the censorship of the Internet. Even in the United States, digital copyright laws have forced Google to aid the Church of Scientology in its efforts to squelch Web critics. In addition, the United States has for a decade been requiring libraries and schools to install Web filter software similar to the software that the Chinese government attempted to mandate for all Chinese computers for the same overt reason: to restrict access to sites suspected of supplying pornography. Such software, of course, also restricts material of political significance. As I have stated above, measuring by scale or effect, it's improper to compare the Chinese efforts to restrict the flow of information with those of the United States and other democracies. But it's a mistake to single out China as the only significant place where Web censorship is a matter of policy.[45]

The liberal values espoused by techno-fundamentalists and corporations such as Google encounter resistance when they meet the realities of corporate and nation-state behavior. The struggle to speak freely on the global network of networks illustrates the daunting challenges of forging a "global civil society" or a media environment in which citizens around the world can organize, communicate, and participate openly and equally. What, then, are the potentials for actually realizing those ideals?

In part, the answer lies in the development of entities that lie outside state sovereignty and outside the economic imperatives and constraints of the corporation. As communication and transportation technologies have connected people in more efficient ways over the past three decades, we have seen the rise in importance of organizations and social networks that operate across borders and outside state control. Paradigmatic civil-society organizations include Amnesty International, Oxfam, Falun Gong, the Catholic Church, the International Olympic Committee, FIFA, and the International Red Cross. But this category also includes smaller and more diverse collections of people who come together temporarily to support protesters against the government of Iran, Swedish Internet hackers who enable massive file sharing, and advocates of a violent, bigoted brand of Hinduism.

"Civil society" is a messy and not always benevolent construct.[46] The political theorist John Keane defines global civil society as "a vast, interconnected and multi-layered non-governmental space that comprises many hundreds of thousands of self-directing institutions and ways of life."[47] Certainly, global civil society already exists. Elements of it are divergently global, civil, and societal, and most of these institutions antedate the Web. An ideal global civil society, different from the actual civil society we have now, would foster a cosmopolitan sense of identity and a commitment to the common good of the whole planet. So we must ask to what extent and in what ways Google can help create and support such a society, to what extent and in what ways it hinders it, and what we can do to promote the common good on a global scale.[48]

A "public sphere," according to the German philosopher Jürgen Habermas, is "a realm of our social life in which something approaching public opinion can be formed. Access is guaranteed to all citizens. A portion of the public sphere comes into being in every conversation in which private individuals assemble to form a public body."[49]

According to Habermas, early examples of public spheres emerged in Europe soon after the rise of nation-states and a commercial middle class in the eighteenth century. The tragedy of the public sphere, Habermas argues, is that its core institutions, such as newspapers and broadcasting, became so rampantly commercialized in the nineteenth and twentieth centuries that they failed to support the goals of keeping a republic informed and engaged. When it comes to the Web and the influence of Google on the Web, we can see a case study in which Habermas's narrative of the collapse of the public sphere has unfolded in a very short time.[50]

The global network of networks that we call the Internet represents the first major revolution in communications to occur since Habermas's influential historical work, *The Structural Transformation of the Public Sphere*, was first published in 1962.[51] Habermas described a moment in the social and political history of Europe in which a rising bourgeoisie was able to gather in salons and cafes to discuss matters of public concern. The public sphere represented a set of sites and conventions in the eighteenth century in which (almost exclusively male) members of the bourgeoisie could forge a third space between the domestic sphere and the sphere of formal state power. It was a social phenomenon assisted by a communicative development: the spread of literacy and the rise of cheap printing in Europe.

Habermas asserts that such a space had not existed in Europe in a strong form before the eighteenth century and that by the end of the nineteenth century it had undergone some profound changes. On the one hand, the democratic revolutions in the United States and France, parliamentary reform efforts in England, and the unsteady lurches toward republics in Germany and other parts of Europe eventually codified many of the democratic aspirations of the public sphere: openness, inclusiveness, and fairness. On the other, by the dawn of the twentieth century, the corporatization of communicative functions across nation-states had drained the bourgeois public sphere of its deliberative potential and much of its purpose.

Habermas leaves those of us who worry about the health of democratic practice with a nostalgic model of rational discourse with liberatory potential. It's been a powerful and useful model. Habermas's book has influenced media-reform efforts and—to a much lesser extent—media policy. Exhausted by trying to rebuild the classical Greek agora, we have set about trying to build a better coffeehouse.[52]

It's no surprise, then, that as soon as the Internet entered public consciousness in the 1990s, cultural and communication theorists started asking whether it would enable the generation of a "global public sphere," or, in the words of Yochai Benkler, a "networked public sphere."[53] Influenced perhaps too much by Marshall McLuhan's model of a global village, scholars, journalists, and activists drove Habermasian terms into mainstream discussions of Internet policy and its political potential.[54]

Alas, the public sphere is not the best model to idealize when we think globally and dream democratically. Habermas's public sphere is as temporally and geographically specific as Benedict Anderson's notion of "imagined communities" and has been similarly misapplied to disparate experiences that don't correspond to the specific historical situation examined by the original work. In Habermas's story of the emergence and deflation of the public sphere, both nationalism (with the rise of the nation-state) and capitalism play a major role. Concern for the fate of the nation or local affairs, he argues, drove people to assemble and deliberate. A global public sphere, however, is necessarily cosmopolitan in temperament. Therefore, members of a global public sphere must culturally cohere in some way. Either they must share a language, or they must share a value system and a common notion of truth and validity. We are far from having such a system, and it's not clear that it's in everyone's interest to create one.[55]

In addition, any consideration of the potential for a global public sphere enabled by the Internet must confront the discrepancies of access and skills across the world. Often discussions of the effects of Internet and other communicative technologies take on the shallowest analysis of access. Either they assume something close to universal access to the network of networks or they assume that people everywhere experience electronic networks the same way that most Americans do: as fast, cheap, and out of control. In fact, fewer than one in five people in the world have domestic access to the Internet at speeds that allow the viewing of the simplest YouTube video. As late as 2009, only ten countries had high-speed Internet access that reached at least 80 percent of their populations; and those ten countries account for less than 2 percent of the world's population. In countries where high-speed Internet is available in public cafes and libraries, many users have to deal with significant filtering, censorship, and surveillance. So they already have a suboptimal Internet experience.[56]

But the most significant gap separating potential citizens of the world is not necessarily access to Internet technologies and networks. It is the skills needed to participate in the emerging global conversation. Being able to use a search engine, click on a link, and even post to Facebook does not require much skill or investment, but producing video, running an influential blog, participating in the Wikipedia community, hosting a proxy server, and even navigating between links and information sources on the Internet demand much more money and knowledge than most people in the world have. To acquire such skills, people need at least minimal free time and significant means, and many with disabilities are excluded regardless of education or means. The barriers to entry for such productions are lower than ever in human history, but they are far from free, open, and universal.[57]

To consider the prospects for a cosmopolitan global civil society or its cousin, a global public sphere, and the role that Google might play in it, we should consider the role of powerful and flexible communicative technologies in places as dynamic and diverse as China, Russia, and India. Doing so will also allow us to assess the degree to which Google is now inseparable from the Web in general.

Despite its global and universalizing ambitions and cosmopolitan outlook, Google's search functions are not effective in connecting and unifying a diverse world of Web users. Instead, its carefully customized services and search results reinforce the fragmentary state of knowledge that has marked global consciousness for centuries. Over time, as users in a diverse array of countries train Google's algorithms to respond to specialized queries with localized results, each place in the world will have a different list of what is important, true, or "relevant" in response to any query. Already, a search done using the Indian version of Google,

Google.in, while seated at a computer in Charlottesville, Virginia, generates a different set of search results from the same search run in New Delhi, India. Google knows the general location of the searcher and structures the results to reflect the habits expressed by others in that location.

As Google continues to localize, personalize, and particularize its services and results, it fractures a sense of common knowledge or common priorities rather than enhances it. Google might indeed be "organizing the world's information and making it universally accessible," but it is not making universal knowledge universally accessible. Everything might eventually be available to everyone (although we are far from that state of affairs, and Google is not necessarily contributing to that mission equally across the world), but essential information could be highly ranked on Google searches in Sydney and buried on the ninth page of results in São Paulo. There might be significant differences in results (and thus effective access to knowledge) between Kiev and St. Petersburg, or Tel Aviv and Hebron.

Just as important, the Internet itself does not simply or automatically universalize experience, knowledge, or communication. Although it connects along certain axes, it severs along others. In Bangalore, India, a growing and technologically sophisticated upper middle class has been turning this once sleepy southern university city into a hub of investment, research, and technological expertise. The standard story of Bangalore's transformation describes the city's shiny new buildings, dependable electricity, and burgeoning taste for consumer goods.[58] As the city has grown over the past two decades, it has served the infrastructural and lifestyle desires of global corporations and the workers and investors who support them. However, it has not necessarily served the needs of the vast majority of those who live in and around Bangalore—the very poor. The Bangalore lawyer and media researcher Lawrence Liang describes this and other major cities in India, such as Hyderabad and New Delhi: "This urbanism in India has become a significant theatre of elite engagement with claims of globalization. . . . Imprints of the media industry like multiplexes, malls, and lifestyle suburbia go hand-in-hand with the cries of urban decay and pollution, and managing populations that are increasingly restless in the new arrangements."[59] And as the media scholar Ravi Sundaram has said, "Cities are being actively remapped" in India. "You have sections of the city that are meant only for the elite, with their own power supply, air conditioning, and private security."[60] So although a small, but growing segment of Indian society is firmly embedded in the cosmopolitan flows of culture, knowledge, and power as a result of the remarkable investments of the past twenty years in India, the poor pay a disproportionate price and receive an inadequate return.

If there is a cosmopolitan civil society in India, it is composed of the few and the elite. Indian elites both contribute to and benefit from being members of global civil society and contributors to its commercial wings. And in many ways, the members of the global, cosmopolitan, technological Indian elites have more in common (and thus feel stronger communal ties) with American and European society and similar elites in Bahrain or Brazil. "This space is generating an elite hybrid culture that is emancipated from any dialogue with issues such as public space and is securely anchored on the West," Sundaram has said.[61] However, as members of India's technological elites converse and connect with expatriate Indians in the United States, Canada, and Europe, they rarely work to forge a sense of cosmopolitan justice. They are cosmopolitan in style, but not in politics.

At the same time, the Internet has provided ample space and occasion for the development of affinity groups, which may be simultaneously parochial and international. Radical Hindu fundamentalism, which has contributed to the rapes and deaths of thousands of Muslim Indians in the past two decades, has been aided greatly by the rise of global Internet communities devoted to developing a "pure" and portable sense of Hindu identity and thus eroding the eclectic and tolerant traditions of India. The Internet has thus fomented political and religious hatred and violence. Millions of poor people have been able to access Internet services in recent years, thanks to the proliferation of cafes and hot spots in urban India, and they have generated what Liang calls significant "illegal information cities" by using pirated software, discarded or hacked hardware, and stolen electricity. But the marginal improvements to their lives have been trivial compared with the environmental and civic costs they have incurred and the outlandish benefits rendered to the elites. The major effects of the Internet on India thus far have been incivility and inequality, not the makings of a global civil society.[62]

Linguistic differences are, or course, another barrier to the creation of a genuinely global civil society. Here, too, although the Internet connects along certain axes, it divides along others. One exceptional aspect of Google's global role is its automatic translation tool, which enables people to read very rough translations of documents written in other languages. It works very well for simple documents, such as most Web pages. However, complex and long documents remain beyond its expertise. My recent attempt to read the Italian-language book *Luci e ombre di Google: Futuro e passato dell'industria dei metadati*, composed by an Italian collective, was frustrated by the poor quality of Google's translation.[63] But as Google imports more text into its linguistic-analysis computers and obtains feedback from users, it is certain to improve. In the meantime, Google is striving to add new languages to its translator software as events demand. When the protests over the disputed June 2009 elections in Iran broke out, Google rolled out a Farsi translation tool within a week.[64]

Even so, because language skills differ markedly throughout the world, Google has different effects and influence in different regions. The current trends in Web search and Web use point toward the evolution of at least two Webs with very little interaction: one using the Latin alphabet (with English dominating that realm) and another in simple Mandarin (but with as global a reach as the Chinese diaspora itself). The utility and universality of English on the Web in general, according to some scholars, have been reinforcing its position as the dominant language of commerce in the world. But two factors have complicated this trajectory: the rise of Mandarin as the fastest-growing language area of the Web, and the ability of Google to customize, search, and translate elements of the Web into dozens of languages. So the next ten years of the Web might see the domination of two languages on the Internet, or of none.[65]

Google is most dominant in Latvia, Lithuania, Hungary, Poland, Romania, Belgium, and the Netherlands, where it controls more than 95 percent of the Web search market. Venezuela, Switzerland, Spain, Portugal, Italy, Germany, France, Finland, Denmark, Colombia, Chile, Brazil, Argentina, and the United Kingdom are close behind, with Google controlling between 90 and 95 percent of their Web search traffic, according to various search industry reports in 2009.[66] In examining the linguistic characteristics of countries where Google leads the pack, it's hard to find a common denominator. Most of them use the Latin alphabet, but several, including Latvia, Lithuania, Hungary, and Finland, use a script heavily marked with diacritics and thus differ significantly from the Latinate languages of Western Europe.

Because Google does not handle diacritics well, it's surprising that some new local search engine has not challenged Google in Eastern Europe and the Baltic states.[67] Most countries that use Asian syllabic scripts and non-Latin alphabets find locally developed search engines better suited for their needs. Google is far behind the local competition in China, Hong Kong, Japan, Taiwan, South Korea, and Russia. Each of these nation-states grants Google less than 40 percent of the search market. And each of these countries has major languages that use scripts that are very different from Latin.

Linguistic diversity does not explain everything, of course. As of 2009, most of the major Web search services worked better in English and the languages of Western Europe than they did in other languages. In addition, regardless of the local language of the search engine, the legacy strength of English-language websites (the greater traffic they receive as a result of having been up longer) biases most search engines in favor of English sites.[68] The world, and thus the set of markets that promise greatest growth, is hardly biased toward English and is highly diverse. Web-search and portal companies certainly understand this. So it's clear that linguistic diversification is central to the long-term success of any Web company.[69]

There are also important differences between countries using non-Latin languages. Google actually does worse in Taiwan, with just 18 percent of market share, than in mainland China, with 21 percent. So technologies of censorship might not be the most important factor to searchers. In South Korea (which now has a rich commitment to democracy and high-speed Internet services accessible to 70 percent of the population), Google has only 3 percent of the search market.[70] Naver, the search leader in South Korea, exploits local knowledge generated by generous Web users to tailor search results, resulting in a sort of blend of Wikipedia and Google. And the fact that few Google users use Korean text means that Google's computers have not been able to master the data in Korea the way they have in other parts of the world. Naver got in early on this market, so Google has had nothing but trouble and frustration in South Korea.[71] Moreover, the Korean government has been pressuring Google to adopt a system by which users must identify themselves truthfully when posting videos or comments on YouTube, a policy that Google does not want to enforce. Google has been limiting access to some services for South Korean users rather than abandon the protection of user anonymity.[72]

Google has offered its service in Arabic since 2005, but I have not been able to find any information on its market shares in Arab countries. Google does have offices in Amman, Jordan, and Cairo, Egypt. It offers Gmail to users in Egypt, despite the fact that the Egyptian government is just as aggressive as China in tracking down, jailing, and torturing political dissidents and critics. Google has not been as forthcoming about its concerns for the fate of its users in Egypt as it has in China, and no one in the U.S. Congress or major human rights groups seems to have raised the issue of Google's policies in other oppressive regimes.

As Russia has lurched from fragile democracy to nationalist, authoritarian, one-party rule under the direction of Vladimir Putin, Google has been able to operate freely within the country. Although Putin's regime has stifled journalism deemed critical of the government (to put it mildly), it has kept the Web relatively open. We often assume that greater Internet use and freedom correspond with greater political liberty, but in Russia over the past ten years, a steady rise of Internet use and freedom has been accompanied by a harsh crackdown on dissent. It's as if the Russian regime believes that the Web is for shopping, and that whatever political organization might occur over it is a mere nuisance.[73]

Despite the structural openness of the Russian Internet, Google has not been able to establish a significant or influential share of the search market in the birthplace of its cofounder, Sergey Brin. Yandex, a Russian company with close connections to the state, had 44 percent of the search market in 2008; Google had only 34 percent. At the time, only about 25 percent of Russians were regular users of the Internet, so the potential for growth and change in that market was significant. Yandex also controls many wi-fi access locations and a popular photo-sharing site. Yandex and Rambler, the second most popular Russian search engine, have the advantage of being programmed natively in Russian, using the Cyrillic alphabet. Yandex specializes in offering Cyrillic-text sites in other related languages, such as Ukrainian and Belarusian.

Russian grammar is complex and very different from that of most European languages. Because search techniques now demand complex linguistic analysis, Google's lead in these areas of research for Western European languages is no help in the Russian market. What growth Google has experienced since its debut in Russia in 2006 can therefore be attributed to its influential ancillary services, such as YouTube and Google Maps. And in Russian markets, political connections and the support of the state can matter just as much as or more than the quality of the service. Because of this complex ecosystem, it's hard to imagine Google prevailing or even growing significantly if Russia becomes even more nationalistic than it already has. If, on the other hand, Russian society and government open up and liberalize, one could imagine Google playing an important role in that process. Once again, social and cultural conditions would drive the change in the media environment, rather than the other way around.[74]

Perhaps Google does better in countries with more internal linguistic diversity. The United States, which is largely monolingual (although Spanish is America's second language), gives Google only about 72 percent of its Web-search business—although this number has been climbing steadily since 2005. Google does slightly better in bilingual Canada, with 78 percent of the market. India, the most multilingual of major economic powers (with twenty-one major languages in use), is a much better market for Google, with more than 81 percent of the search market.[75]

Many of the searches in India are done in English, which is the standard language of commerce across the country of more than a billion people—more than 17 percent of the world's population. Unlike Korea, where mastery of one script and one language has been the key to success for Naver.com, India offers Google an ideal environment to demonstrate its flexibility, adaptability, and computational power. Google has invested much in automatic translation within and among Indian languages. As of mid-2009, Google offered its service in nine of India's languages: Hindi, Bengali, Telegu, Marathi, Tamil, Gujurati, Kannada, Malayalam, and Punjabi. Although India is a major high-technology incubator, its software engineers have yet to produce an effective local search engine that does anything more than mimic Google's look and feel.[76]

LOCAL CULTURE AND THE RESISTANCE TO COSMOPOLITANISM

Although the Internet may have great potential to unite the world, it has done so unevenly over the past twenty years. Rather than act as a membrane that connects everyone with everyone and everyone with every piece of knowledge equally, the Internet allows for punctuated connections. It succeeds best at uniting diasporic communities and at forging political alliances both within and across borders. Google's role in these phenomena has been anything but simple. In its search functions, Google has increased the "tribalization" of the Web, letting Dutch football fans and people of Maori descent find each other and reinforce their shared opinions. It fractures the world in new ways even as it unites it in other new ways. One aspect of global civil society, what we might call "local-culture movements," has benefited greatly from this simultaneous aggregation and disaggregation of people and places. It demonstrates how global civil society and the potential global public sphere conflict rather than cohere.

Local-culture movements have little use for the global public sphere. In fact, they see it as a problem. These movements represent the interests of long-marginalized culture groups, particularly those that have struggled to assert and maintain identities under intense pressure from illiberal, authoritarian, or totalitarian nation-states intent on eliding difference for the sake of a forged and coerced nationalism. Under these conditions, many of these culture groups were unable to transmit their traditions openly or teach their languages to their young members. For example, both Spain and France have sought to suppress the culture and language of the Basque country, which straddles their border. The Internet has allowed Basque nationalism to reassert itself, making connections between members of the Basque diaspora worldwide; disseminating Euskara, the ancient Basque language; and extending the concept of Basque identity to those who would embrace it via the Web, regardless of their actual ancestry.[77] Similar local-culture movements have flourished in places such as Wales and Cornwall.

However, because globalization has allowed the resurgence of such movements in many places (including generally liberal states such as Australia and Canada), these culture groups face a new threat: the corporate exploitation of their signs, stories, and cultural practices. In this view, a public sphere is merely an opportunity for others to cheapen their experiences, traditions, and beliefs by rapid repetition and distribution in new and often insulting contexts.[78] The local-culture movement thus opposes the torrent of proprietary media images and texts that pour out of multinational corporations via closed networks of satellite, cable, broadcast, and retail outlets.[79]

The tension between the very liberal Web movements and more communitarian local-culture movements exposes the frustrations and limitations of efforts to generate a global public sphere that can wrestle with cultural, trade, health, or environmental questions. The public sphere in Habermas's model mediates between the private and the state. However, although local and even individual interests clearly can find expression on the Web, rarely does any supranational body have effective sovereignty over any global issue. Sometimes the World Trade Organization seems able to enforce its agenda, but its actions might just be a mask for the interests of a particular nation-state. At other times, UNESCO and the World Intellectual Property Organization (WIPO) may seem to have authority in their respective areas of concern. But again, such organizations might just be acting as instruments of a nation-state seeking multilateral cover. Moreover, public spheres imply and perhaps require real, physical spaces for deliberation and debate.

The very marginality of a local-culture movement—its reason for being—renders it peripheral to global discussions of cultural policy. Only when represented by a friendly and supportive nation-state (again, such as Canada or Australia) do members of local-culture movements find their claims considered by policymaking officials. But this is action driven by the state, not by a global public sphere.[80]

The Internet does not in itself provide the social space or norms that Habermas describes and prescribes for a healthy public sphere. It is not designed to be a force for civility. Paradoxically, the Internet does a better job of stimulating (or simulating) rational spaces and norms in illiberal contexts, as when it is employed by democratic dissident movements.[81] Much Internet-mediated global political action is markedly uncivil. On the margins, "hactivism" (using disruptive communicative technology toward political ends) and cybervandalism have become important tools for the disaffected (including members of local-culture movements).[82] The Internet is not enough. Perhaps some technology applied to the Internet—a filter such as Google, for instance—could "civilize" the networks.

For a time, Google appeared to offer uniformity and consistency of experience in the use of the Web, lending weight to the notion that technology could unite and connect people everywhere. By basing its search results on consensus choices, it promised to filter out the marginal and to contribute to the stability and universality of knowledge on the Web. But, as we have seen, recent moves to localize and customize search results have undermined that potential. And we now understand that the very nature of Google's search algorithms privilege highly organized, technologically savvy groups over others. Google in fact disrupts the prospects of building a global public sphere.

To understand why such disruptive behavior remains important in global politics, we must consider the peculiar role of culture in the postmodern global market economy. Culture is contentious. Seyla Benhabib argues that "culture" has traditionally been considered central to the maintenance of worldviews of dominant political structures, not a distinct field or locus of symbolic generation and differentiation. The distinction of "culture" from the regimentation and reification of science, politics, economics, or militarism is a distinctly modern phenomenon, the result of a process that Max Weber called *Wertausdifferenzierung*, or "value differentiation." Weber claimed that culture under the modern state and capitalist economy tends to foster oppositional poses as much as legitimizing ones. Under the political canopy of the twentieth-century industrial and welfare state, cultural politics was merely an adjunct to questions of resource distribution, but calling for resource distribution in a neoliberal context seems futile and is dismissed as counterproductive. Consequently, in recent years, Benhabib explains, cultural groups have been employing political strategies to assert recognition, rather than redistribution, although there can be redistributive consequences of cultural recognition.[83] In a desperate, divided, Darwinian world economy, cultural recognition can seem as important as life itself.[84] Attempts at forging a global public sphere discount the importance of cultural recognition in favor of procedural equality. Not that there is anything wrong with that; but failing to consider the visceral power of specific cultural claims is likely to exclude and alienate much of the postcolonial world.

With its powerful trends toward localization in search results and thus the customization of knowledge, Google's search functions actually reinforce the interests of the local-culture movements and thus inhibit rather than further the expansion of a genuine global civil society. However, several major aspects of Google's business have influenced the expansion of global civil society in its present form and have offered a glimpse of what a global public sphere might look like: YouTube, Blogger, and Google News. These are some of the main factors in the Googlization of the world. If the development of a global public sphere is a good thing and a goal to be pursued—and despite the obstacles to such a development that I've been analyzing, there are people and forces that would assert that it is—we need to ponder ways in which we can influence the Googlization of the world to achieve that end. One way to do that is to analyze further another major aspect of the Googlization of everything: the Googlization of knowledge.

FIVE

THE GOOGLIZATION OF KNOWLEDGE

THE FUTURE OF BOOKS

Those of us who take liberalism and Enlightenment values seriously often quote Sir Francis Bacon's aphorism that "knowledge is power." But, as the historian Stephen Gaukroger argues, this is not a claim about knowledge: it is a claim about power. "Knowledge plays a hitherto unrecognized role in power," Gaukroger writes. "The model is not Plato but Machiavelli."[1] Knowledge, in other words, is an instrument of the powerful. Access to knowledge gives access to that instrument of power, but merely having knowledge or using it does not automatically confer power. The powerful always have the ways and means to use knowledge toward their own ends.

However, expanding access to knowledge brings more people with more and different ends into the space where those ends can be made known, be advocated, and take their place on the agendas of nations and transnational movements alike. Indeed, advocates for increased access to knowledge have put that issue itself on the international agenda regarding questions ranging from access to patent medicines to access to proprietary software. The issue of access to knowledge is thus central to the prospects for expanding the public sphere and thereby contesting the claims of the powerful to all the instruments of power.

Much of human knowledge exists in the form of long arrays of text, what we still call books. We are dazzled and distracted by the new methods of transmitting and using this knowledge, but most of the best expressions of deep human thinking still rest on paper, bound with glue, nestled and protected by cloth covers, on the shelves of libraries around the world. How can we simultaneously preserve and extend that knowledge? How can we vet and judge its utility and truth? How can we connect the most people with the best knowledge? Google, of course, offers some answers to those questions. It's up to us to decide whether Google's answers are good enough.

SHUFFLING THE PAGES

In May 2006, the *Wired* magazine contributor Kevin Kelly published in the *New York Times Magazine* his predictive account of flux and change in the book-publishing world. That article outlined what he claimed "will" (not "might" or "could") happen to the book business and the practices of writing and reading under a new regime fostered by Google's plan to scan millions of books from university and public libraries and offer searchable texts to Internet users. "So what happens when all the books in the world become a single liquid fabric of interconnected words and ideas?" Kelly wrote. "First, works on the margins of popularity will find a small audience larger than the near-zero audience they usually have now. . . . Second, the universal library will deepen our grasp of history, as every original document in the course of civilization is scanned and cross-linked. Third, the universal library of all books will cultivate a new sense of authority."[2]

Kelly suggested that the linkages of text to text, book to book, page to page, and passage to passage will fill the knowledge gaps that have made certain people winners and others losers. "If you can truly incorporate all texts—past and present, multilingual—on a particular subject," he wrote, "then you can have a clearer sense of what we as a civilization, a species, do know and don't know. The white spaces of our collective ignorance are highlighted, while the golden peaks of our knowledge are drawn with completeness. This degree of authority is only rarely achieved in scholarship today, but it will become routine."[3]

Such heady predictions of technological revolution have become so common, so accepted in our techno-fundamentalist culture, that even when John Updike criticized Kelly's vision in an essay published a month later in the *New York Times Book Review,* he did not doubt that it would someday come to pass. Updike just lamented the change, musing about how wonderful his old bookstore haunts were for him and everyone else who strolled the streets of New York, Oxford, and Boston in the 1950s.[4] His elitist comments served only to bolster the democratic credentials of Kelly and others who have been asserting that Google's plan to scan millions of books would spread knowledge to those not as lucky as Updike.

As it turns out, universal access to book knowledge is proving not so easy to accomplish. Kelly's predictions depend, of course, on the cooperation of one part of the system that he slights in his article: the copyright system. He mentions copyright as a mere nuisance: to acknowledge that a system built by lawyers might defeat one built by engineers would have run counter to his vision. In fact, when he wrote his article, it seemed entirely possible that the current American copyright system would crush Google's plan to scan the entire collections of dozens of university libraries.

THE GOOGLIZATION OF BOOKS

For several years, Kelly's vision for a universal digital library seemed to be approaching realization through a project known at different times as Google Print, Google Book Search, and Google Books. The project foundered and then apparently recovered, thanks to the legal settlement that Google reached in October 2008 with the Association of American Publishers and the Authors' Guild. That settlement came after four years of argument over what copyright would look like in a digital age. It dodged the legal and philosophical questions at the heart of the dispute, and it proposed a bold new system for book research and distribution that, instead of promoting access to knowledge, raised even more questions: the lack of competition, increased monopolization, and the increasing privatization of the information ecosystem.[5]

In 2004, Google began scanning and indexing millions of books from more than twenty-five university libraries. This service has been the subject of much hyperbolic speculation. On first learning of Google's plans, legal scholars such as Lawrence Lessig claimed that they would radically democratize information for the public, not just for academics. Authors such as Cory Doctorow initially applauded Google Books for offering ways to connect interested readers to particular texts and thus prevent small books from getting lost in the mass market. And techno-libertarians such as Kelly celebrated the transformative nature of electronic texts, arguing that Google Books would allow users to connect disparate pieces of information as they saw fit, thus evading the tyranny of the book cover and library catalog. These were expressions by true believers in the potential of digital culture—when properly supported by a benevolent force such as Google—to transform, extend, and democratize knowledge. Publishers and authors, meanwhile, took a less rosy view, and two high-profile lawsuits were initiated against the program for copyright infringement.

Google Book service has failed to live up to any of the exaggerated claims that its early proponents made for it. Not only has it failed to deliver on its promises, but along the way it has disrupted the copyright system and the economy of publishing. Google had hoped to take the modes and standards of Web copyright practice and apply them to books in the real world, where they do not fit. Once people discovered the contours and details of the settlement proposal engineered by publishers' lawyers and Google in the fall of 2008, they saw some big problems. Copyright and cyberlaw professors who had cheered Google's bold embrace of the principle of fair use of copyrighted material realized that Google had actually designed a system that would give it important competitive advantages, making it too powerful within the economy and culture of books.[6] When it was first announced, the Harvard law professor and copyright reform advocate Lawrence Lessig called the settlement "a good deal that could be the basis for something really fantastic."[7] But after considering all the debates and issues surrounding the settlement and Google's plans, Lessig soon concluded that the settlement would not only fail to loosen up American copyright law but might even restrict and commercialize the flow of digital knowledge, and he withdrew his support for the project.[8]

More significantly, the head of one of the original Google library partners, Harvard University Libraries, publicly declared that he opposed the project. The historian Robert Darnton had been a professor at Princeton University when Harvard entered its partnership with Google. Once he became head of the libraries at Harvard, he began to question whether it was in the best interest of the university to contribute to the privatization of knowledge through Google. In February 2009, Darnton published an influential article in the *New York Review of Books* in which he declared Google's efforts to control so much of our historical heritage a danger to the future of learning.[9]

In addition, the governments of France and Germany issued opinions that Google Books would give Google an unfair advantage in the market for out-of-print texts. Authors in China sued Google for infringing their copyrights by scanning their books without permission, prompting a rare apology from the company.[10] In September 2009 the U.S. Department of Justice issued an opinion that the Google Books settlement would violate U.S. antitrust laws unless it were significantly redrawn. Google and the publishers withdrew the settlement to revise it and resubmit it for a hearing before a judge, which occurred in February 2010. Even the revised version failed to allay the Justice Department's concerns that because the settlement would facilitate the sale of digital copies of these books through Google, the proposed system would effectively make Google the sole vendor of most of the books published in the twentieth century.[11]

As I finished updating this chapter for the paperback edition in October 2011, Google was back to negotiating with the Authors' Guild and publishers that had sued the company after federal judge Denny Chin rejected the class-action settlement of the case in March 2011. If Judge Chin had approved the complex settlement, Google would have been in a position to offer for sale millions of digital files of out-of-print books published in the twentieth century. In addition, Google would have offered access to many millions of books that were never protected by copyright or whose copyright has expired. The settlement would have facilitated a remarkable change in the relationship among books, readers, publishers, authors, libraries, and Google. Access to so many great works would be greater than anyone imagined just ten years ago. But American libraries would be commercialized, essentially hosting Google vending machines on their premises. Publishers and authors might make a little more money than they did before. Occasionally, a long-lost work might emerge to be a surprise best seller. But Google would have asserted itself as the mediator of the accessibility and affordability for this vast collection. No other firm could realistically hope to mount a competing service. Readers would seamlessly shift between the safe, anonymous, republican space of the public library and the commercialized environment of Google without a warning that their reading and browsing habits would be tracked. And, perhaps most costly, we might never be willing to design and fund high-quality, durable, publicly run, noncommercial services with the mission of spreading knowledge rather than selling books or placing advertisements.

We are fortunate, then, that Judge Chin rejected the settlement and put the copyright lawsuits between authors and Google and publishers and Google back into court. Still, now the stakes are higher. Google, after trying to settle, should not convincingly and in good faith be able to mount a credible defense against the accusations of copyright infringement. And publishers have little incentive to renegotiate and settle on lesser terms than Google offered in the first place. Any future settlement would certainly be modest in scope and would limit Google's outsized ambitions. But a trial over massive copying of books still covered by

THE GOOGLIZATION OF KNOWLEDGE   155

American copyright law could jeopardize Google, the essential concept of fair use, and even Web search itself.

The most troubling aspect of the settlement went beyond any of the legalities and specifics, and it has nothing to do with how we will find and experience books and knowledge in the next few decades. The scanning project that has been bringing the collected works of dozens of libraries into easy-to-use forms and the changes in policy and practice that would flow from the settlement are monumental in scope. The Google Books project is one of the most revolutionary information policy changes in a century or more. If the settlement had been approved, it would have altered how we think about copyright, culture, books, history, access, and libraries. Yet the public has had no say in how it will be constructed and run. No public policymaking body oversaw its creation. No legislature considered the notion of creating what amounts to a compulsory-license system (through which the copyright holder is never asked beforehand if she agrees to the copying; instead the copier may assume the right to copy) to allow a company to scan copyrighted books by the millions. It would have generated substantial change in both information policy and our entire information ecosystem foisted upon us by private actors with no public deliberation or input.

The Google Books plan is a perfect example of public failure. The great national, public, and university libraries of the world never garnered the funds or the political will and vision needed to create a universal, digital delivery service like Google envisions. The public institutions failed to see and thus satisfy a desire—perhaps a need—for such a service. Google stepped in and declared that it could offer something close to universal access for no cost to the public. The catch, of course, was that it would have to be done on Google's terms, with no attention paid to long-term preservation needs or quality standards. Essentially, the Google Books settlement is a radical change in information policy executed by a class-action settlement. If it had gone into effect, private law will determine public policy.

How did such a seemingly benign project balloon into the most controversial and risky effort Google ever initiated? Google's leaders may not have realized it at the time, but many people were growing wary of its increasing power over the global information ecosystem, and the details of its proposal to digitize millions of copyrighted books touched on some very controversial issues: copyright, competition, privacy, the privatization of public libraries, and the future of books themselves. Hanging over the promise of access to knowledge offered by Google Books is the specter of its opposite—restrictions on open access to books, their contents, and the power that such access might help provide.

BOOKS, COPYRIGHT, AND THE FREE RIDE

In an op-ed piece in the *New York Times* in October 2009, Google's cofounder Sergey Brin defended the Books program and declared that Google was interested in digitizing books because such a project fit the idealistic mission of the firm. "Because books are such an important part of the world's collective knowledge and cultural heritage, Larry Page, the cofounder of Google, first proposed that we digitize all books a decade ago, when we were a fledgling startup," Brin wrote. "At the time, it was viewed as so ambitious and challenging a project that we were unable to attract anyone to work on it. But five years later, in 2004, Google Books (then called Google Print) was born, allowing users to search hundreds of thousands of books. Today, they number over 10 million and counting."[12]

Brin lamented that the project had attracted lawsuits from publishers and a few wealthy authors, but he wrote that the settlement was in the best interest of everyone—including the public. "While we [Google and the publishers that sued Google] have had disagreements, we have a common goal—to unlock the wisdom held in the enormous number of out-of-print books, while fairly compensating the rights holders," Brin wrote. "As a result, we were able to work together to devise a settlement that accomplishes our shared vision. While this settlement is a win-win for authors, publishers and Google, the real winners are the readers who will now have access to a greatly expanded world of books." Brin also presented the project as a way to preserve the knowledge of centuries from the perils of physical harm, such as fire and flood.[13]

Oddly, Brin wrote this piece without conceding that the quality of Google's document scans was too poor to serve the aims of preservation. In many cases, human hands obscure the text in Google Books images, and pages are missing or blurry. The quality of Google's scanned images is far below that of library-run digital preservation efforts. More interesting, though, is Brin's failure to mention the fact that Google Books is a revenue-generating project for the company. It is not a public service. And Google is not a library.

Google may have been the biggest and most controversial player in the effort to digitize books, but it was hardly the first. The saga of digital books offered on the Web is tortured and long. Back in the early 1990s, several groups of tech-savvy bibliophiles began posting plain-text versions of classic works that have entered the public domain. Among the best-known of these services are Project Gutenberg and Eldritch Press. As public participation in the Web grew through the 1990s and more people expressed a desire to read substantial texts on mobile devices and laptops, these services grew in importance, but they suffered from several limitations. First, public-domain works were simply not in high demand in electronic form; second, the plain-text format made files portable and searchable but were often unattractive to read. Firms such as Random House had experimented with electronic versions of their popular books as early as 1994, but the early reading devices on which these works were offered either did not work well or were too expensive—or both. Meanwhile, as Amazon.com established itself as the leading retail outlet for printed books on the Web, it began offering a "Look Inside" feature, presenting electronic glimpses of tables of contents and samples of text to assist customers. But searching, researching, and acquiring access to the full texts of electronic works on Amazon remained impossible. Amazon was offering digital images of text purely as a sales technique, not as a public good.

Before embarking publicly on the massive scanning of library collections without permission, Google launched what it called its "partner program." Inspired by Amazon's success in book sales online, beginning in early 2003 Google began negotiating with commercial and academic publishers to secure digital rights for what was initially called Google Print. The terms of access to the millions of book-page images Google collected depended on the particular wishes of the publishers.

Some titles offered nearly full-text access. Others offered only excerpts. In general, users could view only a few pages of a book at a time, and they could not copy, print, or download the images. The margins of the pages Google offered contained links to sources where a user could purchase the books, as well as bibliographic information and links to the publishers' sites.

Then, in December 2004, Google shocked publishers and the public by announcing its plans to digitize millions of bound books from five major English-language libraries.[14] The libraries' initial contributions in 2004 were as follows.

- Harvard University libraries: 40,000 public-domain books during the pilot phase of the project, with the possibility of extension. The library has more than 15 million volumes.
- Stanford University libraries: hundreds of thousands of public-domain books, with the possibility of extending the program to cover the entire collection of 7.6 million books.
- University of Michigan at Ann Arbor: all 7.8 million books in the collection, even those under copyright.
- Oxford University: all books published before 1900. The library holds a total of 6.5 million books.
- The New York Public Library: between ten thousand and one hundred thousand public-domain volumes as part of the pilot project. The library holds 20 million volumes.[15]

Over the next several months, dozens of other university libraries joined the project. These included the University of Wisconsin, the University of Virginia, and, most significant, the University of California system, which planned to scan more than 2.5 million books at a rate of three thousand volumes per day. In total, Google planned to add more than 17 million library volumes to its electronic index at an estimated cost of $10 per book. Most of the more recent library partners offered Google their special collections, as well as access to select volumes not included in the Michigan collection. In return for access to the books, Google promised to provide the libraries with electronic copies of the works they contributed to the project.[16] However, in some of the more recent partnership agreements, Google held back from scanning certain works while they determined the status of lawsuits and the utility of the files for the Google project.

Under the original, unauthorized library-scanning project—which is distinct from the "partner" project authorized by publishers—search results and the user experience depended on the copyright status of the book. The company announced that for works published before 1923 (and thus mostly in the public domain in the United States), users would have access to the entire text. For works published since 1923 (and thus potentially still under copyright protection), the user would see the bibliographic information, as well as a few text excerpts ("snippets") containing the term that the user had typed into the search box. Google claims that viewing the displayed results of copyrighted works is comparable to the "experience of flipping through a book in a bookstore."[17] As with the authorized "partner" content, Google provided links to allow users to buy books from numerous vendors, as well as targeted advertisements that depended on the nature of the book and possibly also the inferred interests of the searcher.

When major commercial publishers learned of this clandestine library-scanning project, their initial reactions were panicked, alarmist, and largely unwarranted. They expressed concerns that the Google project would threaten book sales and risk hacking and the widespread pirating of texts. Gradually it became clear that Google's library project posed no threat to publishers' core markets and projects. If anything, the project could have been a marketing boon: if the searches yielded books that met users' needs, they would be likely to purchase at least some of those works.[18] Since then, it has become clear that publishers were most offended by the prospect of a wealthy corporation free riding on their content to offer a commercial and potentially lucrative service without any regard to compensation or quality control. The publishers wanted a piece of the revenue—and some control over the manner of display and search results.

Copyright, which has traditionally protected the rights of authors and publishers to control the copying and distribution of their works, has rarely been used to govern ancillary markets for goods that enhance the value or utility of the copyrighted works.[19] As the author and activist Cory Doctorow has pointed out, booksellers have never tried to extract licensing revenues from bookcase makers, bookmark makers, or eyeglass producers. By analogy, a searchable, online, full-text index, similar to what Google had originally planned to offer, is a supplement to a book (and to book culture), not a substitute for it. However, creating such an index requires that Google make digital copies of the complete physical books, thus violating the fundamental provisions of the copyright act.[20] So although the publishers' complaints were hyperbolic, they might indeed have had the law on their side.

The conflict over Google's bold initial library project raised questions that get to the heart of copyright. Now that the settlement has been rejected and the possibility remains that Google and its plaintiffs could fight out the issues in court, we might witness some fascinating public discussions about the role, scope, purpose, and design of the copyright system. But we might also experience significant—perhaps radical—changes to it. If the publishers prevail, Google's core mission and the openness of the Web could be threatened—as would all the revenue that Google has accumulated from advertisements and capital markets. If Google prevails, we could see a serious shift of power in information markets, from analog-era firms devoted to creating and taxing scarcity by pricing and selling books to digital firms (like Google) designed to manage the abundance of information by collecting information about its users and selling advertising access to them. More directly, the peculiarly American notion of fair use of copyrighted material—and perhaps even the copying of entire works for clearly commercial purposes—would be expanded and solidified after a Google win. It would be a shift far beyond what Congress had ever imagined when it codified fair use in 1976, when the advent of the photocopier supposedly threatened commercial publishing with extinction. Fair use, in short, is a defense one may use in U.S. courts when accused of copyright infringement. One may argue that the use of the original material is small enough that it does not threaten the market for the original, or that the use is clearly in the service of journalism, criticism, research, or education. Nothing about fair use is clear and simple. Courts are supposed to consider fair-use arguments on a case-by-case basis. And there are very few certainties about how well such a defense would work. Fair use was developed to allow individuals to avoid going through the time and expense of securing permission to use copyrighted material when the public clearly benefits from the unauthorized use of it. Still, Google will have to make a huge, wholesale argument about the general permissibility of its massive copying. If Google pursues that argument and prevails, fair use would become a significantly stronger users' right than it had been designed to be. If Google loses in court, fair use might be severely curtailed.

The rejected settlement of October 2008 avoided any such revolutionary change to the law, yet it generated a new, hybrid set of rules to govern our information ecosystem and set the terms of access to our cultural heritage. Here are some of the major elements of the settlement:

- The members of the Authors Guild and the Association of American Publishers agreed to cease pursuing damages for copyright infringement.

- Google offered to pay $125 million to publishers to settle the case.

- Google undertook plans to establish and run a not-for-profit rights registry to allow rights holders to claim or establish control over out-of-print works. This registry was intended to serve as a database through which scholars and publishers could find rights holders in order to clear rights. Because no such registry existed previously, this provision had the potential to be a boon to research and publishing. In addition, it could help rights holders accrue royalties (meager though they might be) by exploiting a market that has never worked efficiently or effectively: that for reprints or selections from out-of-print works. Google was undertaking to do what the U.S. Copyright Office should have done years ago.

- Google agreed to offer (with strict controls on the ability to print and share) full-text copies of certain out-of-print books for sale as downloads.

- Google undertook to offer much better access to many out-of-print works still under copyright. Before the settlement, Google offered largely useless excerpts of these texts. The settlement provided for much richer and broader access.

- Google agreed to provide designated computer terminals in U.S. libraries that would offer free full-text, online viewing of millions

of out-of-print books. Google would forbid printing from these
terminals, but users would be able purchase electronic copies of the
books from these terminals.

Compared with the severe limitations on user access to most twentieth-century works under the original model for Google Books, this new
model promised to improve the service substantially. In addition, the
settlement aimed to avoid the threat of the great copyright meltdown
outlined above. Clearly both sides saw real risks in forcing a courtroom showdown. However, back when Google introduced the library-
scanning project as part of the Books program, many copyright critics
celebrated the fact that a big, rich, powerful company was taking a
stand to strengthen fair use. That never happened. Fair use in the digital
world is just as murky and unpredictable as it was the day before the
settlement. But what of the other problems and pitfalls inherent in the
settlement? Critics of Google Books expressed serious concerns about a
wide range of issues. Immediately after the announcement of the settlement, I asked Google's legal department the following questions:

"Isn't this a tremendous antitrust problem?" I asked. Google had
essentially proposed a huge compulsory licensing system without the
legislation that usually makes such systems work. In addition, this proposed system excludes many publishers, such as university presses, and
authors who are not members of the Authors' Guild. More important,
this system would have excluded the other major search engines and the
one competitor Google has in the digital book race, the Open Content
Alliance. Wouldn't these parties have had a very strong claim for an
antitrust action?[21]

The Google legal team did not believe that this agreement was structured in such a way as to exclude others from developing a competing
service. The agreements with and about publishers, libraries, and the
registry were all nonexclusive, as is typical of Google's approach to competition in the Web business. The registry would be started with Google
funds, but it would be an independent nonprofit entity able to deal with
the Open Content Alliance and other services without restriction from
Google. Generally, Google's lawyers did not see this service as presenting a typical antitrust problem. There are so many segments to the book

market in the world, including real bookstores, online stores such as Amazon.com, and used-book outlets, they claimed, that no single entity or sector can set prices for books (even out-of-print books) effectively. There are always competing sources, including libraries themselves.[22]

"But isn't this a potential privacy nightmare for libraries?" I asked. Would Google compile personally identifiable information from users of its free terminals (for example, by requiring them to log in to Google Docs or some other service)? Would Google collect search and usage data from these library terminals to "improve" searches? Would such data be open for study by publishers or media scholars? How long would Google retain such data if it were compiled?

The response from Google's lawyers, in November 2008, exhibited a willingness to examine this potential problem. They indicated that much about the design of the program was yet to be determined. Google had not agreed to share personal information with publishers, but the company might share aggregate data collected through the service. And although Google had not yet designed the system, the legal department predicted that users would not have to log in to Google to use the public terminals. The legal department assured me that the company would "build in privacy protections" with the guidance and assistance of the library partners.

SELLING OUT LIBRARIES AND CORPORATE WELFARE

The strongest criticism of the Google Book program had always concerned the actions of the university libraries that have participated in this program, rather than Google itself or the effects of the program on libraries in general. The advantages to libraries of the settlement are twofold. First, they might face much less legal risk by permitting Google to scan books in their collections that are still protected by copyright (although future lawsuits by authors and publishers who live outside the United States, Canada, Australia, and the United Kingdom—the only countries covered by the settlement—remain a risk). Second, because Google has pledged to place designated terminals in public and university libraries across the United States, many libraries that never had the funds or space to build large collections of works would be able to offer their users greatly expanded access to electronic texts.

But the negative effects of these changes could be significant as well. Libraries might choose to remove physical books from their collections if they considered electronic access via Google to be sufficient. Of greater concern is the fact that every library in the United States might soon have what is in effect an electronic book-vending machine, run by and for Google, operating in an otherwise noncommercial space. Every library would soon be a bookstore. The commercialization of libraries and academia is not a new story, but it remains a troubling one. Inviting Google into the republican space of the library directly challenges its core purpose: to act as an information commons for the community in which it operates.

Companies such as Google should always do what is best for them. But libraries, and especially university libraries, have a different, more altruistic mission and clear ethical obligations. From the beginning, Google Books has seemed to be a major example of corporate welfare. Libraries at public universities all over this country (including the one that employs me) have spent many billions of dollars collecting these books. Now libraries are offering these books to one company that is cornering the market on online access. They accepted Google's specifications for the service uncritically, without concern for user confidentiality, image preservation, image quality, search prowess, metadata standards, or long-term sustainability. They chose the expedient way, rather than the best way, to extend their collections. They have been complicit in centralizing and commercializing access to knowledge under a single corporate umbrella.

Under the rejected settlement, elements of library collections would have been offered for sale through a private contractor. Perhaps this change is only a matter of degree, but perhaps it is instead a major mission shift. Ultimately, we have to ask, is this really the best possible system for extending access to knowledge?

The privatization of some library functions is not necessarily a bad thing. We should not pretend that libraries operate independently of market forces or without outsourcing many of their functions to private firms; but many of the thorniest problems facing libraries today are a direct result of rapid privatization and onerous contract terms. There are too many devils in too many details.

Even by offering apparently benign services like free library access to electronic texts, Google serves its own masters: its stockholders and its partners. It does not serve the people of the state of Michigan or the students and faculty of Harvard University. The main risk of privatization is simple: libraries and universities last, but companies wither and fail. Should we entrust our heritage and collective knowledge to a company that has been around for less than fifteen years? What will happen if stockholders decide that Google Books is a money loser or too much of a liability? What if they decide that the infrastructure costs of keeping all those files on all those servers are not justifiable?

The early celebration of Google's library project revealed an unfounded and unfortunate assumption: that the role of the librarian in the global digital information ecosystem is superfluous. It also ignored serious quality-control issues. Google has never publicly discussed the principles on which the book search engine will operate. In contrast, librarians and libraries operate with open and public standards for metadata and organization. Metadata—data about data—is particularly important.[23] Without metadata—such as subject headings, keywords, and quality indicators—embedded in the files, a search for books about the Holocaust is just as likely to yield books denying the event as examining it. Good metadata standards generate better search results. Poor metadata standards can yield ridiculous or dangerously misleading results.[24] So far, we have no reason to believe that the transfer of this indexing function from a public university library to a private entity will involve good or open metadata standards.

COPYRIGHT AND THE PRIVATIZATION OF KNOWLEDGE

Now that Judge Chin has rejected the settlement agreement between the publishers and Google, we are back where we were in 2008, when Google was mounting a fair-use defense against the publishers. This time, however, Google will have a harder time convincing the public and courts that it has the right under fair use to continue to scan the contents of libraries for its own use. By settling the lawsuit with publishers (and thereby surrendering its claims that the wholesale scanning of books is fair and legal), Google has managed to lock in a tremendous advantage for itself. No other institution could reasonably have pursued a massive scanning project in the knowledge that publishers would sue right away; and no other entity would be able to compel the plaintiffs to settle on terms anywhere close to those Google has negotiated. So, regardless of the disposition of the settlement, unless we reform copyright to allow more innovative uses of material that is now sitting on shelves, underused, we are stuck with the Googlization of books and nothing more. If Google shuts down the project out of fear of losing a monumental judgment in court, then we will be stuck with much less access than we have today.

The music-downloading controversy of the early 2000s provides an introduction to the parameters of these issues. Peer-to-peer music downloading was described by music copyright holders as the greatest threat to the historically successful copyright system and all the industries that depend on it.[25] The 2004 case *MGM v. Grokster* was expected to be the showdown over the issue.[26] In an amicus curiae brief I wrote on behalf of media studies professors, I argued that there is no functional distinction between the peer-to-peer interface Grokster and the popular search engine Google.[27] Both are search engines that facilitate the discovery, access, and unauthorized use of others' copyrighted works. Both "free ride" on others' copyrighted works. Both provide a service to the public for no direct remuneration from their users, yet both are commercial entities that benefit from increased traffic and the data gathered from their users. So if you hold Grokster liable for inducing infringement, Google's Web Search service is liable, as well.[28]

Of course, there is one big difference. Grokster itself did not actually do any copying: it just facilitated copying by others. Google, by contrast, makes copies of all kinds of copyrighted material. For years, it has been making cache copies of the Web pages it indexes, because its search function cannot operate without a cache index. In two cases, courts ruled that this practice does not infringe copyrights.[29]

Copyright on the Web, however, works in peculiar ways. A series of important court cases in the United States gave search engines and other Web enterprises confidence to innovate.[30] We could not navigate the Web effectively if Google and other search engines could not freely copy and cache others' copyrighted material. Every time you post an entry on a blog or create a new Web page, you are granting search engines a presumed license to copy it. If you wish to opt out of the Web search system, you must act. The burden is on the copyright holder. Courts have ruled that if the burden were on the search-engine companies to ask permission and negotiate terms with every one of the millions of people who generate copyrighted content on the Web every day, they would simply quit, because the costs of doing business would be too high. And thus we would have no search engines, and the Web would be unnavigable.

By copying and caching actual physical books, Google is reaching beyond the Internet and the copying and caching of Web pages. In the real world, off the Web, a copyright holder must grant explicit permission to allow someone to copy an entire work for a commercial purpose. That's how copyright has worked for three centuries: the burden of securing permission is on the party that wants to copy the work. The default is that everything in the real world is protected. The default on the Web is that everything can be copied.

Through its scanning program, Google had hoped to impose the copyright norms of the digital world onto the analog world. Publishers, accustomed to the norms of the real world and skittish about those of the Web world, panicked and sued.[31] By provoking a lawsuit over Google Books, Google not only gambled the value of the company: in the words of the University of Pittsburgh law professor Michael Madison, it "bet the Internet" on this case. If the case goes to court and Google loses, an appeals court or the U.S. Supreme Court might write a decision that would undermine the rights of search engines in general to make cache copies of Web documents without permission. In that event, the very concept of a navigable World Wide Web would collapse. No company, not even one as wealthy and successful as Google, could afford the time, labor, and funds it would take to secure permission to copy the billions of text pages, images, and videos that Google now scours for its indexes.[32]

That is far from the outcome that copyright laws are intended to produce, yet it was the threat that their imposition posed in the instance of Google Books.

Copyright in recent years has become too strong for its own good. It protects more content and outlaws more acts than ever before. When abused, it can stifle individual creativity and hamper the discovery and sharing of culture and knowledge.[33] But the Google scanning project threatened the very foundation of copyright law. Google had hoped to exploit the instability of the copyright system in a digital age by resting a huge, ambitious, and potentially revolutionary project on the most rickety, least understood, most provincial, and most contested perch among the few remaining public-interest provisions of American copyright law: fair use.

When it settled the publishers' lawsuit, Google managed to avoid the fundamental issues of copyright by conceding that the company had no clear fair-use right to scan millions of copyrighted works just to display them on a restricted, yet commercial platform. But this was more than a dodge. Google vaulted over the copyright conundrum and exploited its own dominance as the chief search platform in the world to corner the market on electronic library searches and delivery. It was a bold move that raised as many hard issues as it settled.

By settling, Google engineered a better position for its commercial services than it would have had it won the lawsuit. To some observers, the slim prospect of Google prevailing with its fair-use defense was clear as early as 2004. Soon after the Google Books library-scanning project was made public, Paul Ganley, a London solicitor, wrote an analysis of the Google library case under both U.S. and U.K. law. He concluded that although Google had a slight chance to prevail under the flexible fair-use provisions of U.S. law, it had absolutely no chance of surviving a challenge in British courts. Ganley presents the case as a "teaching moment" because it generates two wonderful potential exam questions: Can Google do this under existing copyright law? Should Google be able to do this under copyright law?[34]

I added a third question to public debate about the project, one that spoke directly to the first two: Is Google the right agent to do this? If it is, then copyright law certainly should allow ambitious and potentially beneficial uses of copyrighted material that on balance do not threaten existing markets for works. However, it is possible that copyright law already allows other institutions better suited for these efforts to undertake them.[35]

Within weeks of the announcement of Google's plan to scan library collections, I concluded that legally, politically, and practically, Google was not the right agent for the job. Instead, I argued, libraries should pool their efforts and resources to accomplish such massive digitization and access projects themselves. Because Google is such an inappropriate choice, its legal argument is inherently weakened: thus the answer to Ganley's first question is no. However, by avoiding a courtroom showdown over the scanning project, Google's actions injected uncertainty into the projects that other organizations might pursue. If public and university libraries were to team up to generate a similar service, would they be bold enough to create cached copies of millions of scanned books still under copyright? Would the existence of a new market for out-of-print books available from Google Books prejudice a court against a fair-use defense mounted by libraries? Answers to these questions depend on the answer to a more general formulation of Ganley's second question: Under copyright law, *should* any entity be able to create cached copies of millions of scanned books still under copyright?

Back when it looked as though Google would mount a bold case to expand fair use, distinguished scholars and litigators such as Jonathan Band, William Patry, Fred von Lohmann, Cory Doctorow, and Lawrence Lessig all voiced enthusiasm for the Google project and launched defenses of the firm's copyright strategy.[36] Each of these writers relied on the traditional (and statutory) "four-factor" analysis of Google's use of the works: the character of the intended use, the nature of the work to be used, how much of the work would be used, and the harm to potential markets.[37] Each of them minimized the fourth factor, declaring that the Google project would not harm the sale of books and might enhance it. In addition, they concurred, several important cases in recent years have shown that commercially viable uses are not beyond the scope of fair use.[38] All their arguments treated the snippet of text that Google users would encounter when clicking on a link to a copyrighted work as the operative use of the work and minimized the importance of the original scanning of the book—the very copying that the publishers wanted the court to consider as operational and significant. They argued that the snippet-based interface is "transformative," thus invoking the magic word that Justice David Souter employed in his ruling for the hip-hop group 2 Live Crew in the case of *Campbell v. Acuff Rose.*[39] In this view, by "transforming" the original song—Roy Orbison's classic hit "Oh, Pretty Woman"—the defendant, Luther Campbell, created something entirely new—in this case, a parody of the original song.

Tranformative stands now as a concept distinct from *derivative*. If a work is derivative of a copyrighted work, it falls under the control of the copyright holder; if the work is considered transformative, it can be considered fair use.[40] Much is at stake in this distinction. But as Michael Madison points out, courts are wildly inconsistent in their determinations of whether a use is transformative.[41]

In addition, the defenders of Google's copyright strategy all relied on the claim that a snippet displayed as a search result would obviously be a small portion of a book and thus of a work. Thus they aided Google in the consideration of the third factor: the amount and substantiality of the taking. The problem with this assertion is that often books are composed of small, distinct works—an anthology of poetry, for instance. A standard "four-factor" fair-use analysis of the excerption of Leo Tolstoy's *War and Peace* differs substantially from an analysis concerning a collection of haiku or limericks. For these and other reasons, the pedestrian exercise and almost arbitrary nature of the four-factor test has driven some scholars and judges to question its utility.[42]

Lessig's defense of Google back in 2005 depended on the courts' agreeing with his assertion that the Google library-scanning project "could be the most important contribution to the spread of knowledge since Jefferson dreamed of national libraries. It is an astonishing opportunity to revive our cultural past, and make it accessible."[43] Such hyperbole was essential to Google's argument. If the Google library-scanning project did not promise to deliver a valuable service, then the fair-use argument would be too weak to stand. The problem with Lessig's argument was that Google's search algorithms, while effective (yet imperfect) for something as dynamic and ephemeral as the Web, are wholly inappropriate for stable texts such as books. Any simple search of terms such as "It was the best of times" or "copyright" yields very bad results. Google would have had a hard time convincing a court that we are actually better off with this service than without it. Although Google's PageRank algorithm is good enough for the Web, the rudimentary search engine that Google has applied to Books has none of the subtlety and brilliance of PageRank or the constant feedback mechanisms that have refined Web search so effectively. It generates too many irrelevant results for simple searches. And Google offers no simple information-seeking training to its customers.

Privileging internal text searching over more established forms of book indexing is troublesome. Relying on Google's engineers to do the work that librarians do is an even bigger mistake. Searching inside the text of books is rarely a better way to search than searching among books. Books are discrete documents that operate with internal cohesion more than external linkages. They are not, in David Weinberger's phrase, "small pieces loosely joined," nor should they be.[44] Their value is in their comprehensiveness. Printed and bound books are examples of a portable, reliable technology that has worked extremely well for more than five hundred years. No one has yet shown that searches for "key words in context" have much value to readers, researchers, or writers.

The same reasons that libraries and librarians are best able to provide access to knowledge in the form of access to books, including copyrighted material, apply to noncommercial publishers, as well—especially university presses. In the early days of the conflict over Google Books, representatives of American university presses complained that there was already an emerging and mutually beneficial market for electronic access to and indexes for books that academic presses would provide to libraries. For more than a decade, many university presses have been creating electronic files of back-catalog and out-of-print works. Some of these were intended to generate a "print-on-demand" capability for books for which demand was too limited to justify even the minimum feasible standard print run of several hundred copies. With the support of foundations, university presses were forming a consortium that would standardize the format and index of such files and offer electronic books to libraries for a subscription fee. Microsoft and Yahoo had been helping a not-for-profit venture, the Open Content Alliance, scan books from a small number of academic libraries (although Microsoft withdrew its support in 2008).[45]

Once Google came into the race in 2004, with a financial commitment exceeded only by its ambition, it became hard, if not impossible, to argue for funding a diverse array of participants in this market. Google was just too big and fast, and it crowded out lesser initiatives. After the settlement, in which Google effectively set the price for royalty distribution to copyright holders for books downloaded from its system, Google stood alone, and since the announcement of the Google library project, many academic publishers and libraries have suspended such projects.[46]

University press directors were not particularly troubled by the open Web-search capabilities that Google offered. Instead, they worried about the propriety and legality of the transfer of the electronic copy from Google back to the university libraries. We should be troubled as well. I have asked many scholars and activists who support Google's position on this project what possible justification, under fair use or any other provision or exemption under copyright, exists for Google's distribution of an entire copyrighted work as payment for a commercial transaction. I have yet to receive an answer. Hence my answer to the third question I proposed to add to Ganley's law school exam: Google is not the not right agent to create cached copies of millions of scanned books still under copyright. If we want large-scale projects that allow digital access to copyrighted books, we should generate the necessary political will to change copyright law instead of resting our hopes on a narrow exception like fair use and hoping that the courts take a liking to the idea.

THE LEGACY

The legal saga of Google Book service has had two significant effects. First, it has threatened to put Google in sole possession of the means of search and distribution for most of the books published in the United States in the twentieth century. With this power, Google has staked a claim on the ability to fix prices for royalties. Through its size and willingness to throw away money, Google has crowded out any reasonable alternative service. No competitor will ever have the leverage to negotiate a similar deal with authors and publishers. But perhaps more important, Google is positioned to be the chief way we discover new books as well as old. As newspapers and magazines contract and reduce their reviews and discussion of books, and library budgets shrink with decreases in state funding and endowments, publishers are being forced to consider new ways to connect readers to books. As of today, Google is the only obvious partner in that effort. So the company's role as mediator, filter, and editor of culture and information grows even stronger.

The problems with that role extend well beyond the muddy field of copyright law. To understand those problems and what we can do about them, we need to look further into the nature and effects of the Googlization of knowledge. We must examine the institutions that we rely on to gather, refine, and deliver knowledge to society. And we must explore the extent to which they have been Googlized as well.

SIX THE GOOGLIZATION OF MEMORY

INFORMATION OVERLOAD, FILTERS, AND THE FRACTURING
OF KNOWLEDGE

"I forgot to remember to forget," Elvis Presley sang in 1955. I know that it was 1955 because I just Googled the title and clicked on the link to the Wikipedia entry for the song. Not long ago I would have had to actually remember that Elvis recorded the song as part of his monumental Sun Records sessions in 1955. Then I would have had to flip through a set of histories of blues and country music that sit on a shelf behind me. It might have taken five minutes to do what I did in five seconds. I don't need my own memory any more. And I don't seem to need these books as much as I used to.

This change strikes most of us as a good thing. The costs seem low. The benefits seem high. Our searches for information can be much more efficient and comprehensive now that this teeming collection of documents sits just a few keystrokes away. As a totally wired person, I have access to more information than I could ever know what to do with. So it feels somewhat liberating that I don't have to remember to remember very much. Are we suffering, in this time of constant connectivity and cheap distribution of images, texts, and sounds, from some sort of global cultural malady? Are we drowning in data, unable to distinguish good from bad, true from false? Are we paralyzed by our obsessions to consume, to be aware, and to be connected? What tools help us manage this abundance? What tools hinder our abilities to live well and richly?

The standard description of the difference between knowledge and information does not fully describe our current condition. Knowledge, as Neil Postman explained, involves what, at least pragmatically, is true and good, beautiful and useful. Information always requires interpretation—some form of processing—to be judged so and thus to begin to serve as the basis for knowledge. Too much unprocessed information interferes with the generation and utility of knowledge: it can generate anxiety, wasted effort, and paralysis. It can obscure the valuable and beautiful.[1] It can also diminish respect for the carefully crafted containers of knowledge. As David Shenk explains in his essential book *Data Smog*, "Information, once rare and cherished like caviar, is now plentiful and taken for granted like potatoes."[2] The gentle rejoinder to Shenk's concern, of course, is that caviar was once reserved for the rich and potatoes for the poor. Perhaps the availability of potatoes for the rich and poor alike constitutes an overall improvement. And, after all, it's what you make with the potatoes that really matters. But all information is processed in some way—selected, even roughly, from some collection of signals not deemed relevant or organized enough to even qualify as information. I am not convinced that the standard distinction between information and knowledge helps us understand anything very well. What matters is how we choose what to consider in our daily judgments and choices.

From childhood onward, we have usually allowed others to process the information we receive—to filter it. As technology writer Clay Shirky argues, what we think is information overload is actually a function of "filter failure." When we feel overwhelmed by the quantity of news and information we encounter, it's a sign that we have just not figured out how to manage our flows of information. With discipline, or perhaps with disciplining technology, we can manage to achieve serenity even with Blackberrys in our pockets.[3] Concentration, mental discipline, and time management count as filters. So does Google. If Francis Bacon was correct, and knowledge is an element of power, but not necessarily the source of it, then granting Google the knowledge it needs to do the filtering for us also grants it power. We might be comfortable with that. Clearly, most people are (including me). But we should not be blind to the consequences.

REMEMBERING WITHOUT FORGETTING

The ease of retrieving information with Google might make us too lazy to remember things on our own. I can't remember my mother's phone number. On the other hand, thanks to Google, I can pretend that I never forget, either. I have the potential to connect myself to an abundance of very odd and useless things. But ultimately I choose what elements to remember and comfortably ignore the rest.[4]

My grandfather was born in South India in 1907 and lived to the age of eighty-six. As a Brahmin, he fulfilled his expected role in society as one who memorizes and recites sacred Sanskrit texts. As a young boy, he mastered hundreds of hours of prayers and stories *(slokas)*. Well into his last years he could roll out *sloka*s like Mick Jagger singing "(I Can't Get No) Satisfaction." But his knowledge of these texts was more than mere rote learning: he understood them as well, studying them on paper in Sanskrit and in English translation. He had strong opinions about which translations were best. When I was about ten years old he recited the entire Ramayana in English for me over the course of twelve nights.

Yet my grandfather had cognitive limitations as well. As best I could figure, these limitations were the result of knowing a great deal about a few things and too little about broader fields. He could not fathom how rockets lifted into space or how women could expect to do the work traditionally done by men. I could never convince him that the stars did not determine our fates. He looked on in wonder and awe as the world changed around him, especially after he immigrated to the United States in the late 1970s. But he never expanded his mental frames beyond his impressive scholarly training. My grandfather had a memory so powerful that he would surely be described as a genius by today's standards. Yet he was incapable of thinking clearly about many issues, blinded by his perspective and position. Me? I can Google with the best of them and inform myself about a vast range of topics. So which one of us was the more capable thinker?

In his short story "Funes, His Memory," Jorge Luis Borges writes of the misery of young Ireneo Funes of Argentina, who is cursed with the inability to forget. "He had effortlessly learned English, French, Portuguese, Latin," the narrator tells us. "I suspected, nevertheless, that he was not very good at thinking. To think is to ignore (or forget) differences, to generalize, to abstract."[5] Forgetting is just as important to the act of thinking as remembering. With his inability to forget, Funes simply can't make sense of anything. He can't think abstractly. He can't judge facts by relative weight or seriousness. He is lost in details and can't discriminate between the important and the trivial, the old and the new. Painfully, Funes cannot rest. Google is not just our memory machine; it is also our forgetting machine, because it filters abundance for us.

The costs of such powerful collective memory are higher than we usually assume. Some things, even if we do not wish them forgotten, should at least be put into context. Consider the ordeal of the Vancouver psychotherapist Andrew Feldmar, who tried to cross into the United States to pick up a friend at the Seattle-Tacoma airport in April 2007. At the U.S. border, an agent decided to Google his name. The search yielded a link to an academic article Feldmar had published in 2001, in which he described his experiences with LSD while studying with R. D. Laing in the 1960s. Despite having no criminal record and throwing up no suspicious connections in government databases, the U.S. authorities barred him from entering the United States because he had admitted using a controlled substance illegally.

Before the Web, before Google, that border agent would have had only the standard tools of law enforcement with which to decide whether to prevent Feldmar from crossing the border. But we live in an era of seemingly perfect memory, where any fact can be recalled at will. In fact, this state is far from perfect. Total recall renders context, time, and distance irrelevant. Something that happened forty years ago—whether an example of youthful indiscretion or scholarly discretion—still matters and can come back to haunt someone as if it had happened yesterday.

For most of human history, forgetting has been the default and remembering the challenge. Chants, songs, books, libraries, and even universities were established primarily to overcome our propensity to forget. These aids to memory had physical and economic limitations that in fact served us well. All these technologies of memory also act as filters or editors. They help us remember much by discarding even more. Today, digital information storage and retrieval have made remembering the default state of knowledge and forgetting the accident or exception. So quickly have we have moved from forgetting most things (or at least rendering them hard to access) to remembering them (and making them easy to search) that we have neglected to measure the effects of this change. Just because we have the storage vessels, we feel the need to fill them. Then we engage with networks of data communication that offer disparate elements of our lives to strangers and—perhaps more important—people we would like to know better.

Now that access to so much stuff is so easy, it's easy to abuse small bits of information and blow them up into character-degrading factors. Who among us has not feared being misunderstood or mislabeled because of some indelicate phrase written years ago on some e-mail list or even in an academic paper, only to find that Google has made it accessible to anybody who searches for our name? Even ten years ago we did not consider that words written for a specific audience could easily reach beyond that group and harm us at the hands of an ignorant or malicious reader. Consider the plight of one of my students, who so far has left only a limited digital trail in her short life. A Google search of her name reveals only one element of public significance: a campaign contribution she made in 2008. She worries, not without cause, that this rather flat Google profile may prejudice prospective employers. The costs of such easy proliferation of information may be undramatic but nonetheless trenchant. Collectively, foolishly, we are building a collective memory about as subtle and thoughtful as Funes's own.

As with Funes, the proliferation of data in our lives and the rudimentary filters we use to manage it render us incapable of judging, discriminating, or engaging in deductive reasoning. Inductive reasoning, which one could argue is entering a golden age with the rise of massive databases and the processing power needed to detect patterns and anomalies, is beyond the reach of lay users of the Internet. To deal with these changes, Internet scholar Viktor Mayer-Schönberger suggests we engage in a significant reengineering or reimagining of the default habits of our species: to record, retain, and release as much information as possible. Because we have for centuries struggled against the inertia of forgetting, we can't easily comprehend the momentum and risks of remembering.[6]

MAYBE MEMORY IS NOT THE PROBLEM

In the summer of 2007, the technology writer Nicholas Carr contributed a provocative cover article to the *Atlantic* called "Is Google Making Us Stupid?" In it, Carr made the case that persistent dependence on the Web for intellectual resources and activity is fundamentally rewiring the minds of many people—his own included. "And what the Net seems to be doing is chipping away my capacity for concentration and contemplation," Carr wrote. "My mind now expects to take in information the way the Net distributes it: in a swiftly moving stream of particles. Once I was a scuba diver in the sea of words. Now I zip along the surface like a guy on a Jet Ski."[7]

Carr predicted that we would soon have in-depth psychological and neurological data to support or disprove the hypothesis that Web use undermines the ability to engage in sustained thought. He cited a handful of preliminary studies that show people altering their habits of reading online. But Carr's concerns went beyond that. He was worried that the more we consume online—snippets and links and videos and songs and animations and more snippets of text, each one sending us flitting to another—the less we will be capable of sitting and reading, say, an extended discourse on how Google is affecting our lives.

If the empirical data on which Carr relied were thin and preliminary, his theoretical foundation was all too solid. Despite conflating the general experience of using online media and the form and function of Google, Carr raised in that article many of the same concerns I have voiced in this book: Google expands the reign of technocracy by making us comfortable with it. Google feeds on and then feeds our techno-fundamentalist belief in the benign effects of technological progress. And Google was designed to supplement thought while recording the traces of our thought and exploiting that data in the service of more efficient consumption. But Carr made one point I can't agree with. He proposed that participating in this teeming new environment, designed to overstimulate, somehow fundamentally and irreversibly alters the pathways of our minds.

For this argument Carr invoked the specter of HAL, the computer in *2001: A Space Odyssey*, who wails that his mind is going as Dave, his human adversary, unplugs the memory circuits. Carr also invokes Marshall McLuhan, the grandfather of a particular brand of media theory that posits that dominant communicative technologies mold consciousness and thus create different types of people, such as "typographical man," whose patterns of thought were shaped by the existence of printed texts. McLuhan argued that humans living before or outside writing and printing had (and have) different styles of thought and collective consciousness. Those of us who grew up reading lines on a printed page have much more structured and linear modes of thought as a result of these technologies. Those of us born into electronic media environments undergo a "retribalization," or a return to a premodern mode of thought.[8]

All of these historical assertions are, of course, untestable. Once you overdetermine a set of categories—in this case, modes of thought—you can simply fit whatever small sets you can collect of documented behavior into those categories and proclaim the existence of a "new man" or a "new era." Such historical and anthropological taxonomy has about as much validity as astrology. The plasticity of the human mind, a well-documented phenomenon, means that human brains not only alter over time and with experience but can keep on changing. So if you worry, with Nicholas Carr, that the Web is short-circuiting your capacities to think, you can just retrain your mind to think better. Training, though, is different from Lamarckian adaptation.

Overusing or abusing any tool or technique can leave you numb or foggy. So it's not surprising that people report increased distraction in their lives after adopting technologies that have raised our cultural metabolism. But in making too strong a claim for deep, biological change effected by technology, Carr commits the error of technological determinism.

A year after Carr's article, the futurist Jamais Cascio wrote a rejoinder of sorts. Cascio claimed that electronic media are among the great technological advances that we humans now use to simulate evolution. Instead of relying on the slow winnowing power of natural selection and reproductive advantage, we now invent things that help us deal with life. Google and the Web are on that list. Cascio posits that the noisiness of our digital, connected lives actually trains us to think better by teaching us to discriminate among stimuli. We may feel distracted and overwhelmed, but that's just a function of the inadequacy of our filtering methods and technologies. If Google were better at filtering, as it likely will become, we would live happier, smarter, more sustainable lives. But even today, electronic media operate as "intelligence augmentation," making us smarter, not dumber.[9]

Like Carr, Cascio is half right. He is correct in asserting that technologies (along with social norms and laws) have liberated us somewhat from the eternal cycle of Darwinian pressures. We now invent our way out of life-threatening situations. And even the geeks can breed. The sociologist Lester Frank Ward made a similar argument in 1883, in response to Herbert Spencer's endorsement of social Darwinism.[10] And Cascio is correct to argue, pace Stephen Johnson, that many media forms today, especially video games, are so intellectually demanding that they are demonstrably making us more capable of sustained engagement and tactical, if not philosophical, thought.[11]

Cascio, though, commits an error similar to Carr's. Both assume that technology necessarily and unidirectionally molds us. Cascio assumes that technologies lead us to something certain: the future is already determined, and he knows what it will look like. He is, after all, a futurist by trade. He assumes that technologies drive our abilities and desires, instead of the other way around or, more accurately, in concert with us. According to Cascio's brand of technological determinism, we are always getting better, always rising, never polluting our world or poisoning or fattening or numbing ourselves into submission.

Cascio hints at one of the more profound and potentially disturbing changes to our lives that Google has wrought. When he argues that our filters should and will be stronger, that we may soon resign our powers to edit and ignore to an algorithm, he is flashing on some real and alarming changes that Google has been implementing in its systems of late. Google might not be making us stupid. But we are making Google smarter, because of all the information about our individual interests and proclivities that we allow it to harvest.

The consequences of allowing Google to filter the abundance of information for us by giving it information about us include a narrowing of our focus on the things that matter to each of us and the potential fracturing of our collective knowledge. The effects of Google's increasingly powerful mediation between us and the knowledge that we seek is particularly clear in the domain that I care most about: higher education.

THE GOOGLIZATION OF HIGHER EDUCATION

Learning is by definition an encounter with what you don't know, what you haven't thought of, what you couldn't conceive, and what you never understood or entertained as possible. It's an encounter with the other—even with otherness as such. That is the situation of the searcher in the old-fashioned sense of the term: one who seeks knowledge by encountering the new and different. The kind of filter that Google interposes between an Internet searcher and what a search yields shields the searcher from radical encounters with the other by "personalizing" the results to reflect who the searcher is, his or her past interests, and how the information fits with what the searcher has already been shown to know.

Since 2007, Google has embarked on a consistent process of installing customization technologies in Web Search for its power users (those who register with Google to use services such as Gmail, YouTube, Blogger, Google Books, and iGoogle). Once you register, a cookie is placed in your browser, and Google logs you in by default every time you visit. In 2007, Google switched the default on one important aspect of its search service: automatic customization of search results. "We believe the search engine of the future will be personalized and that it will offer users better results," Marissa Mayer said in an interview in 2007.

Note that Mayer did not express this decision as if Google were the actor choosing among alternatives. Her use of "will" suggests inevitability, as if Google has no choice in the matter. Mayer explained that users' search histories are more valuable than ever to Google's efforts to personalize search results. And she conceded that setting defaults toward personalized search, making users actively opt out of personalization, would condition users to expect customization. "It's a hard sell sometimes," Mayer said. "We're asking them to sign up for a service where we begin to collect data in the form of search history, yet they don't see the benefits of that, at least in its fullest form, for some time. It's one of those things that we think about and struggle with. And that's one reason why we're trying to enter a model where search history and personalized search are, in fact, more expected."[12]

Customization mean means that Google will deliver more results that fit your known locality, interests, obsessions, fetishes, and points of view. That "narrowcasting" of filtered information could be very efficient. If you know what you want, you might get it faster, with the right results higher on the page. It also allows Google to better customize advertisements to you over time and build a richer profile of its best users, those who use multiple Google services. However, if search results are more customized, you are less likely to stumble on the unexpected, the unknown, the unfamiliar, and the uncomfortable. Your Web search experience will reinforce whatever affiliations, interests, opinions, and biases you already possess.

The way we use the Web already offers us ample powers of customization that threaten republican values, such as openness to differing points of view and processes of deliberation. Google, through customization of Web search results, is redoubling those effects.[13] Tailoring search results to reflect who we already are and what we already know fractures us into different discourse communities that know what we know for certain (it's all over the Web, after all), but know different things for certain about the same things. And the customization of search results reflects the consumption imperative so prevalent in Google's design in recent years. This trend toward customization will be great for shopping, but not so great for learning, especially at the college and university level.

In *What Would Google Do?* the media critic Jeff Jarvis posits a vision for a revolution in higher education that follows the contours of Google's values and models. "Who needs a university when we have Google?" Jarvis asks provocatively. He does not, in fact, propose the dissolution of the academy. Instead, he argues, "education is one of the institutions most deserving of disruption—and with the greatest opportunities to come of it."[14]

Jarvis does not fully explain why higher education deserves disruption instead of reform, enhancement, extension, investment, or any number of other words that imply improvement. He identifies teaching, testing, research, and socialization as the chief roles of the university. He then examines these roles and concludes that a dispersed, Internet-based system such as Google would perform all of them better than the status quo does. He asserts that we do not need the "straitjacket of uniformity" of the university campus to accomplish socialization and networking for young people, because those should be lifetime pursuits. He claims that research should be collaborative and open, rather than cloistered in local laboratories. Testing and certification can easily be replicated online. And teaching should be done by subscription, over the Web, by independent contractors who market their services to a broad consumer base, rather than to a group of captive subscribers. "Why are we still teaching students to memorize facts when facts are available through search?"[15]

As an insider and career academic (second generation, at that), I was baffled by these prognoses and prescriptions. In his portrait of the status quo, Jarvis is describing a university I have never seen. The social scenes at all but the most conservative campuses in America are nothing if not petri dishes of shared and personal experimentation. University research has always been collaborative across institutions and national borders, yet it still requires live staff, physical space and equipment, and the purchasing power and infrastructure of a university to fund and manage it all. The practice of memorizing facts did not last long even in primary education (at least in the United States) after John Dewey's reforms in the beginning of the twentieth century.

So I am not sure what Jarvis hopes to disrupt. For one thing, few institutions on earth have been as consistently and spectacularly successful as the American university. Although any student, professor, administrator, or taxpayer could list dozens of things they would like to see changed about these institutions, the fact remains that they have overwhelming endorsement from their market: the best of them turn away four to ten times the number of applicants they admit. And even at less exclusive institutions, such as state technical and teaching universities, quality teaching prevails. It succeeds in the sense of propelling many graduates and their families into the middle class or higher. America's community colleges serve millions who wish to establish a foundation for further study or acquire new or updated career skills. Jarvis, like so many critics of higher education, merely takes the elite institutions as his target and accuses them of the very exclusivity that defines them as elite. He assumes that what happens at Harvard matters to more than just the few thousand people who get to attend it, and he ignores the fact that many of the most important innovations of the past century—from efficient processes of milk pasteurization to drugs that regulate blood clotting during surgery to the free and open-source software that Jarvis celebrates—could only have emerged from universities.

The larger source of my bafflement is the fact that my employer, the University of Virginia, has been succeeding at its mission since Thomas Jefferson founded it in 1819. Google was founded in 1998. Yet Jarvis is so impressed by Google that he prescribes its management and organizational style for the university. I try to avoid making predictions in my scholarly life, but I am willing to bet money that in one hundred years the University of Virginia will remain a premier institution of research and education, and Google will be no more. Virginia might not have beaten Duke in basketball by then, but it will still be producing brilliant graduates and essential research and serving the state of Virginia well.

But Jarvis's greatest error in his commentary on the Googlization of higher education is to ignore the fact that Google itself emerged from universities because of their strengths and values—not despite their weaknesses and maladies. That's why the founders of Google remain so involved in higher education. They make donations to their alma maters, give graduation speeches, sponsor scholarships, recruit voraciously on campuses, and collaborate with universities in every aspect of their business. Google thus is not the answer to the problem of universities: it is the product of the brilliance and success of universities. If anything, universities could be the answer to many of the problems raised by Google.

In fact, the relationship between Google and the universities of the world is more than close—it is uncomfortably familial. In recent years, Google has moved to establish, embellish, or replace many core university services, such as library databases, search interfaces, and e-mail servers. Google's server space and computing power have opened up new avenues for academic research. One experiment, Google Scholar, has allowed nonscholars to discover academic research they might never have encountered, and Google Books has radically transformed both the vision and the daily practices of university libraries. Through its voracious efforts to include more of everything under its brand, Google has fostered a more seamless, democratized, global, cosmopolitan information ecosystem. Yet it has simultaneously contributed to the steady commercialization of higher education and the erosion of standards of information quality.

At a time when cost pressures on universities and their students have spiked and public support for universities has waned, Google has capitalized on this public failure, this erosion or retreat of state commitment. The ubiquity of Google on campus has generated both opportunity and anxiety. Unfortunately, universities have allowed Google to take the lead in and set the terms of the relationship.

There is a strong cultural affinity between Google corporate culture and that of academia. Google's founders, Sergey Brin and Larry Page, met while pursuing PhDs in computer science at Stanford University.[16] The foundational concept behind Google Web Search, the PageRank algorithm, emerged from an academic paper that Brin and Page wrote and published in 1999.[17] Page did his undergraduate work at the University of Michigan and retains strong ties with that institution. Some of the most visionary Google employees, such as the University of California at Berkeley economist Hal Varian, suspended successful academic careers to join the company. So it's not surprising that Google's corporate culture reflects much of the best of academic work life: unstructured work time, horizontal management structures, multidirectional information and feedback flows, an altruistic sense of mission, recreation and physical activity integrated centrally into the "campus," and an alarmingly relaxed dress code. For decades, American universities have been instructed to behave more like businesses. Google is an example of a stunningly successful firm behaving as much like a university as it can afford to.

The core value that Google incorporated from academia is peer review—the notion that every idea, work, or proposition is contingent, incomplete, and subject to criticism and revision by qualified reviewers. This practice is not particular to Google. All open-source or free software projects and much of the proprietary software industry owe their creative successes and quality-control systems to peer review. In fact, the entire Internet is built on technologies that emerged from peer-review processes. But Google, much more than the other major firms engaged in widespread and public distribution of software and information, owes its very existence to an explicit embrace of the concept of peer review.

Google owes its success to the dominance of its Web Search engine and the ability of the company to run simple auctions to place paid advertising spots alongside seemingly organically generated search results. When you type "shoe store" in a Google search box and Google's PageRank algorithm sorts through Web pages that contain the phrase "shoe store," ranking them based on the number of other pages that link to those pages, the result, which takes mere seconds, is a stark list of sources based on relative popularity. In this context, popularity stands in for quality assessment. This is not merely a vulgar, market-based value at work, however. The same principle guides academic citation-review systems. Google's founders were working on citation-analysis projects when they came up with the idea of applying such a system to the chaos that was the World Wide Web.[18]

Popularity turned out to be a highly effective method of filtering and presenting Web search results. As we've seen, Google became the market leader among search engines by outsourcing editorial judgment to the larger collective of Web authors (or, as the Harvard law professor Yochai Benkler puts it, "peer producers").[19] Back in the late twentieth century, every other search engine used some combination of embedded advertising (site owners paid for good placement within searches) and "expert" judgment (search-engine staff determined whether a site was worthy of inclusion in the index). By contrast, as Benkler puts it, "Google harnessed the distributed judgments of many users, with each judgment created as a by-product of making his or her own site useful, to produce a highly valuable relevance and accreditation algorithm."[20]

Of course, the practice of determining the value of a work by its appearances in others' citations (bibliometrics) is a controversial and troublesome topic within academic culture.[21] Widely used in the sciences for decades, the expansion of the principle to measure the presumed "impact" or "value" of scholarship within the humanities has generated widespread criticism, because much of the best work is published in books, rather than in a stable set of indexable journals.[22]

The inclusion of peer review in the corporate culture of Google need not, of course, have come directly from university life. It could have just as easily come from another field that shares a common ancestry with Google: the free and open-source software world. Applications that have emerged from widespread multiauthor, collaborative environments have reshaped every element of the information creation and dissemination process. Almost all e-mail systems, most Web servers, and an increasing number of Web browsers and computer operating systems were built without proprietary claims or controls. Free and open-source software projects and innovators have promoted an ideology of open exchange, constant peer review, and general freedom within a commercial structure that allows for remuneration for services rendered, rather than for computer code delivered. The fact that many of the early innovators of the free and open-source software movement emerged from academia explains the ideological continuities between academic computer science departments, many profitable software firms, powerful amateur communities that build and maintain the Internet and the World Wide Web, and Google itself.[23]

Whatever its source, Google's method of filtering and ranking information, which weighs both the interests of the searcher and the judgments of peer producers of knowledge, has had significant effects on the way people on both sides of the lecture podium understand what goes on in higher education and how to access, present, reflect on, and use knowledge creatively. The Googlization of knowledge has affected students, their professors, university research, and, more broadly, the institutional infrastructure that supports research, teaching, and learning.

THE GOOGLIZATION OF STUDENTS

Paradoxically, the very reliance on the principles of peer review within Google and reliance on the principles of peer review in the Google PageRank algorithm have undermined an appreciation for distinctions between information sources—at least among university students. According to a summary of two user studies conducted among students in the United Kingdom, commercial Internet search services dominate students' information-seeking strategies. The studies found that 45 percent of students choose Google as their prime search technology when doing research for assignments. Only 10 percent consulted the university library catalog first. Students reported that "ease of use" was their chief justification for choosing a Web search engine over more stable and refined search technologies, but they also expressed satisfaction with the results of the searches done with Google and other major search engines.

These results are not surprising. But one particular conclusion should trouble anyone concerned about the influence of Google on the abilities of university students to navigate information: "Students' use of [search engines] now influences their perception and expectations of other electronic resources." In other words, if higher-quality search resources and collections do not replicate the reductive simplicity and orderliness of Google's interface, they are unlikely to attract students in the first place and are sure to frustrate those students who do stumble on them.[24]

A relatively early study from 2002 conducted for the Pew Internet and American Life project found that "nearly three-quarters (73 percent) of college students said they use the Internet more than the library, while only 9 percent said they use the library more than the Internet for information searching."[25] This is a confusing way to frame the question, however, because even at the beginning of the twenty-first century, most academic libraries offered online access to library resources (especially journals) via the Internet. So the question sets up a false distinction. Since 2004, in fact, many libraries have offered direct links from Google Scholar to their library collections when the user connected to a university network. So the notions of "library" and "Internet" have merged significantly for university students in the United States.

The shift toward Google as the first and last stop in research may not be as universal as we assume. A contrasting set of results came from a study of student research behavior at Saint Mary's College in California. This study, published in 2007, showed that "a majority of students began their research by consulting course readings or the library's Web site for on-line access to scholarly journals. To a lesser extent, students used Yahoo!, Google, and Wikipedia as first steps." In addition, the study found that students regarded bibliographies and other aggregated or subject-based research resources as the most fruitful places to start. "A majority of students were not as reliant on search engines as prior research studies have suggested," wrote the study's author, Alison Head. "Only about one in 10 students in our survey reported using Yahoo! or Google first when conducting research. Only two in 10 students in our survey used search engines as a second step."[26] Overall, however, students at Saint Mary's reported themselves to be significantly challenged by research assignments and were frustrated by unclear expectations and an inability to discriminate between sources for quality and relevance. What's clear from these studies is that students need a tremendous amount of guidance through the information ecosystem, and universities are not yet providing them with the necessary tools. Whether students start from course materials, Wikipedia, or Google, they need to know where to go next and why.

In her substantial argument for better information literacy, *The University of Google: Education in the (Post)information Age,* Tara Brabazon of the University of Brighton (U.K.) offers some stories of her students' research habits. "Google, and its naturalized mode of searching, encourages bad behavior," she writes.[27] Brabazon explains that the seductive power of Google—its perceived comprehensiveness and authoritativeness—fools students into thinking that a clumsily crafted text search that yields a healthy number of results qualifies as sufficient research. Even if Google links students to millions of documents heretofore inaccessible, it does nothing to teach them how to use the information they discover or even to distinguish between true or false, dependable or sketchy, polemical or analytical. Because simple Web searches favor simple (and well-established) websites, students are unlikely to discover peer-reviewed scholarship unless they actively select the obscure Google Scholar service; and even then, they must hope that their institution has access agreements with content providers that will allow them to read the full text of the articles they find, because much academic work is confined to paywalled sites.[28]

Brabazon criticizes these practices as an expression of a particular form of literacy—operational literacy—which encourages students to be "code breakers" of complex, multimedia works yet fails to consider other important modes of literacy such as critical literacy, or the ability to judge and distinguish between pieces of information and synthesize them into new, coherent works. Brabazon concludes that universities should not embrace the ideology of "access" and "findability" uncritically but should supplement the ubiquitous power of Google with curricular changes that emphasize the skills of critical literacy. "Critical literacy remains an intervention, signaling more than a decoding of text or a compliant reading of an ideologue's rantings," Brabazon writes. "The aim is to create cycles of reflection." The production of sound arguments, interpretations, and analyses has become more of a challenge in the age of constant connectivity and information torrents.[29]

There is no reason to believe that Google will recede in importance in students' lives any time soon. Nor is there any reason to celebrate Google's pervasive reputation as an unadulterated boon to the process of learning. There is much work to be done to understand what this new information menu offers students and the rest of us.

THE GOOGLIZATION OF SCHOLARSHIP

The effect of Google on college students is replicated in its effect on the scholars who teach them and on their research. The best example of this effect is the way Google Scholar filters and represents the current state of scholarship in a variety of fields.

Google Scholar is an interesting side project for the company. Released in 2004, it serves as a broad but shallow access point to a range of academic work. Google convinced hundreds of suppliers of electronic scholarly resources to open their indexes up to Google's "spiders" so that articles could be scanned, copied, and included in Google's index. Publishers benefit from their articles' receiving enhanced exposure to reading communities beyond academia (and within academia, at institutions that lack full, paid access to certain data collections). The service does something that no other search engine of academic resources does: it offers links to works in areas as diverse as materials science, biophysics, computer science, law, literature, and library science as results of the same keyword search (for instance, "Vaidhyanathan", because there are Vaidhyanathans publishing in all of these areas).

However, according to academic librarians, Google Scholar has been constructed with Google's usual high level of opacity and without serious consideration of the needs and opinions of scholars. The major criticisms include the lack of transparency about how the engine ranks and sorts works, the fact that collections are uneven and results undependable, and the problem that the search interface lacks the detail librarians and scholars demand to find the precise article they need. As with most of Google's services, the greatest strengths of the service—its breadth of coverage and ease of use—generate its greatest flaws: lack of depth and precision. So the service is clearly a boon to students and lay researchers but of limited utility to scholars.

One study of Google Scholar's functions discovered that its index lagged almost a full year behind works published in the leading PubMed collection and concluded that "no serious researcher interested in current medical information or practice excellence should rely on Google Scholar for up-to-date information."[30] Because North American publishers have been most aggressive in including their works in Google Scholar (or perhaps because Google has been most aggressive in attracting North American publishers), many works in languages other than English fail to show up on the first few pages of Google Scholar searches. German literature and social science research, for instance, are heavily under-represented in search results.[31]

As more journals move online, research and citation behavior changes as well. A study published in *Science* in 2008 demonstrated that as more journals came online between 1998 and 2005, scientific literature as a whole cited fewer and newer sources. In other words, forcing scientists to peruse bound volumes of old journals encouraged serendipitous discovery and a deeper acknowledgment of long-term academic debates. Thus, online researchers are more likely to echo a prevailing consensus and to narrow the intellectual foundation on which their research lies.[32]

Google only serves to accentuate this trend. The mystery of why one particular work is ranked above another in Google Scholar searches does not help. Google's "About Google Scholar" site explains that "Google Scholar aims to sort articles the way researchers do, weighing the full text of each article, the author, the publication in which the article appears, and how often the piece has been cited in other scholarly literature. The most relevant results will always appear on the first page."[33] This declaration fails to explain much. The principle at work certainly biases science and technology works above those in the social sciences and humanities, because the lattice of article citations makes up a more solid structure in the sciences than in the humanities, where much of the most influential work appears in books. Also, citation counts do not indicate absolute value, even in the sciences. A high number of citations might indicate that an article stands as prevailing wisdom or consensus within a field and thus serves as foundational; but, just as likely, a high number of citations could indicate that an article is suspect and open to question. These are not equal values, and ranking articles as if they were is troublesome. Finally, because Google Scholar operates by full-text indexing and searching, results are likely to come from divergent collections and fields. A search for "human genome project" yields a large number of metascholarly articles, works that describe or analyze the Human Genome Project from a variety of perspectives. The first-page results are all from major figures in the field, such as James Watson and Francis Collins. But they include no articles about actual research done using the human genome database. For those, one must search for a specific term or gene. A search for "whale oil" could yield results from agriculture journals, ecology journals, and articles about Herman Melville's *Moby Dick*.

Although studies comparing Google Scholar with other commercially available search indexes for scholarly material consistently demonstrate the inadequacies of Google Scholar, it's clear that Google remains front and center in the perceptions of both faculty and students.[34] This makes information-assessment skills more important than ever. In addition, because Google Scholar rankings serve as proxies for citation analyses that assess the contribution of scholars to their fields, they can have a direct effect on academics' employment and promotion prospects. Google Scholar therefore makes the role of librarian central to and more visible within every part of the academic mission. Paradoxically, the more we use Google Scholar, the more we need librarians to help us maneuver through the fog of data and scholarship that it offers.

THE GOOGLIZATION OF RESEARCH

The Googlization of the indexing of scholarly works may seem like a fairly limited issue, but underlying it is a much more troubling concern: the Googlization and hence the further commercialization of the infrastructure supporting academic research. Google's major advantage over almost every other information firm in the world, and certainly over every university, is the massive server space and computing power at its disposal. The scale of Google's infrastructure is a company secret, but its willingness to give each Gmail user two gigabytes of server space to store e-mail is some indication that the capacity of Google's server farms is immense.

Google's remote storage space is large enough and its computers fast enough to host and contribute to some massive collaborative research projects. In October 2007, Google joined with IBM to establish a server farm devoted to research projects that demand both huge data sets and fast processors—expensive ventures for universities to undertake alone. The University of Washington signed up to be the first computer science department to use the Google-IBM resources. It was soon joined by Carnegie Mellon University, the Massachusetts Institute of Technology, Stanford University, the University of California at Berkeley, and the University of Maryland. Researchers at Washington are using servers equipped with suites of open-source software to run complex analyses of Web-posting spam and geographical tagging.[35] In March 2008, the National Science Foundation agreed to vet research proposals for projects that would employ the Google-IBM service.[36]

The benefits to researchers and their universities are clear: no single university can afford to purchase servers and processors on this scale. By computing in the "cloud," using a set of remote servers networked to inexpensive personal computers, researchers from around the globe can collaborate. Big science can be done faster and cheaper if Google, IBM, and universities can combine their brain and computing power.[37]

The benefits to Google and IBM are clear as well: many of the computational problems that academic researchers hope to solve happen to be of interest to these two companies. This project gives them easy access to the knowledge that researchers generate while using these systems.[38] In keeping with Google's traditions and values, Google does not appear to claim exclusive rights to work done with its help. However, university officials who negotiate contracts with Google often must sign nondisclosure agreements to ensure that Google's competitors do not have too clear a picture of what the company is doing with its academic partners.

Computing in the cloud is both radically empowering and potentially worrying. One downside involves the tangle of rights claims that
a widespread collaboration among individual researchers, university
technology-transfer offices, and major computer companies might generate.[39] Such a confusing, complicated set of claims not only risks years
of litigation among the parties but could attract significant antitrust scrutiny as well.

Cloud computing and massive, distributed computation have already
been declared the next great intellectual revolution by *Wired* magazine,
which prides itself on predicting such trends. Its editor, Chris Anderson, wrote in June 2008 that the ability to collect and analyze almost
unimaginable collections of data renders the standard scientific process
of hypothesis, data collection, testing, revision, publication, and further
revision almost obsolete. Anderson wrote:

> Google and like-minded companies are sifting through the most mea-
> sured age in history, treating this massive corpus as a laboratory of the
> human condition. They are the children of the Petabyte Age. . . . At the
> petabyte scale, information is not a matter of simple three- and four-
> dimensional taxonomy and order but of dimensionally agnostic statis-
> tics. It calls for an entirely different approach, one that requires us to
> lose the tether of data as something that can be visualized in its totality.
> It forces us to view data mathematically first and establish a context
> for it later. For instance, Google conquered the advertising world with
> nothing more than applied mathematics. It didn't pretend to know any-
> thing about the culture and conventions of advertising—it just assumed
> that better data, with better analytical tools, would win the day. And
> Google was right.[40]

Needless to say, Anderson's techno-fundamentalist hyperbole belies a
vested interest in the narrative of the revolutionary and transformational
power of computing. But here Anderson has stepped out even beyond
the pop sociology and economics that usually dominate the magazine.
Anderson claims "correlation is enough."[41] In other words, the entire
process of generating scientific (or, for that matter, social-scientific) theories and modestly limiting claims to correlation without causation is
obsolete and quaint: given enough data and enough computing power,
you can draw strong enough correlations to claim with confidence that
what you have discovered is indisputably true.

The risk here is more than one of intellectual hubris: the academy has no dearth of that. Given the passionate promotion of such computational models for science of all types, we run the risk of diverting precious research funding and initiatives away from the hard, expensive, painstaking laboratory science that has worked so brilliantly for three centuries. Already, major university administrations are pushing to shift resources away from lab space and toward server space. The knowledge generated by massive servers and powerful computers will certainly be significant and valuable—potentially revolutionary. But it should not come at the expense of tried-and-true methods of discovery that lack the sexiness of support from Google and an endorsement from *Wired*.

HOW SHOULD UNIVERSITIES MANAGE GOOGLE?

As Google has assumed a progressively greater role in the way that students, faculty, and university administrations pursue knowledge, the company has been calling the shots. Every few months, it seems, it approaches universities with a new initiative that promises stunning returns for the academic equivalent of no money down. Since 2006, for example, Google has been competing with Microsoft and Yahoo to take over university e-mail services, thus locking in students as lifetime Gmail users and allowing the company to mine the content of their e-mail for clues about consumer preferences and techniques for targeting advertisements.[42] The potential of relieving the university of the cost of running e-mail servers and being able to eliminate storage-space restrictions for users is almost too attractive to pass up.

What can and should universities do about these issues? For the answer to that, as for the answer to what we can do about the Googlization of knowledge in general, the Googlization of us, and the Googlization of the world, we need to take a step back and return to considering the prospects for the creation and maintenance of a vital public sphere in a globalized digital age. We should be wary. We should not let one rich, powerful company set the research and spending agenda for the academy at large simply because we—unlike Google—are strapped for cash. The long-term costs and benefits should dominate the conversation. We should not jump at the promise of quick returns or even quick relief. The story of Google's relationship with universities is not unlike the tragedy of Oedipus. Since its birth, Google, overflowing with pride, has been seducing its alma mater—the academy. If Google is the lens through which we see the world, we all might be cursed to wander the earth, blinded by ambition.

CONCLUSION

THE HUMAN KNOWLEDGE PROJECT

In his 1941 short story "The Library of Babel," Jorge Luis Borges describes a universe structured in the form of a library. It is constructed of an infinite number of hexagonal cells. Each cell contains four walls of books arranged at random, with no stable indexing system to guide readers to the valuable or useful ones. Most of the books on the shelves are unreadable. Either they are full of nonsense words and letters, or they are meaningful but in code. But because the library is infinite, by definition it must contain every possible piece of knowledge. Infinite random occurrences of text and symbols should produce poetry, biography, history, and mystery. In addition, every book must necessarily be translated perfectly and in every language somewhere in the stacks and cells. As with his story about Funes, Borges makes the point that amassing vast, infinite collections of information ultimately gets us no closer to wisdom. Even the librarians in the Library of Babel are driven insane by the prospect of perfect, complete knowledge that is frustrated by their inability to navigate the system. They come to believe that somewhere in the library a catalog must exist among the books themselves. After all, if every other possible book must necessarily exist, so must the catalog. The master of this catalog is a mythical figure known as the "Book-Man." The story unfolds with the logical, systematic, and ultimately destructive search for the Book-Man and the catalog of all knowledge. In the Library of Babel, the Book-Man is a myth, a dangerous object of veneration. In our lives, Google is fast assuming the role of Book-Man.[1]

In an interview with the *Wall Street Journal* in August 2010, Google's chief executive officer, Eric Schmidt, made a startling claim about the relationship among people who use Google, the company's search services, and the real world itself. "I actually think most people don't want Google to answer their questions," Schmidt said. "They want Google to tell them what they should be doing next. . . . We know roughly who you are, roughly what you care about, roughly who your friends are."[2] Google, in other words, was moving quickly from a service through which people found information online to one in which it served as an embedded guide to navigating choices, associations, tastes, and the world around us. This means that Google, the most flexible yet powerful information filter we use regularly, could come to exercise inordinate influence over our decisions and values. It would be so closely tailored to reflect the choices we had already made that it could reliably predict how to satiate our established desires. Google would go beyond being Borges's Book-Man: it would be the World-Man. Everything would be Googlized.

IMAGINING A BETTER WAY

To have a healthy global public culture, members of the public must be able to share reliable information about matters of shared concern. Individuals and groups should be able to connect, converse, and collaborate humanistically and humbly. Changes in the economies of the world, the technologies of delivery and exploration, and the role of established institutions have all put new pressures on the public sphere. Google is but one actor in that global ecosystem. It's a central actor, to be sure. It increasingly structures and orders the sources of knowledge and the behavior of people and institutions that use Google. Historically, we have used newspapers, books, and other vessels of knowledge to feed the public sphere. These days, commercial support for journalism and nonfiction book publishing is eroding. As the information ecosystem we have grown accustomed to over the past fifty years dries and crumbles, we owe it to ourselves to invest in and support an environment that will enable experimentation and the emergence of new institutions and voices that can foster local republican values and global democratic culture.

The Internet has been remarkably effective as a medium for distributing materials cheaply and quickly and—to a lesser extent—fostering serious discussion and profound creativity. It's only common sense that we should support policies meant to foster innovation and the cheap, easy acquisition of knowledge. What that infrastructure should look like, however, and how we can achieve it, are questions we need to consider very seriously. Given the Googlization of everything that I've explored in these pages, one of the principal issues we need to consider is the role that Google plays in promoting or preventing the development of a vital global network that increases access to knowledge. The question is not whether Google treats us well but whether this is best we can do. Is the system, as Google has designed and governed it, ideal for all parts of the world and all segments of society? Is it durable and extensible over the long term? Will it let us both preserve and create? Will it let us filter wisely and connect widely?

We may be satisfied with, even excited about, the Googlization of everything. But we should realize that Google is not what it used to be. In recent years, the company has made several major shifts in emphasis and practice. In general, where once Google specialized in delivering information to satiate curiosity, now it does so to facilitate consumption. "Search" as a general concept of intellectual query has mutated into a process of "browsing" for goods and services. Where once users were guided to the unfamiliar, now targeted and customized searches are the default, thus driving us toward the familiar and comfortable. Where once the collection of incoming links generated search results (as imperfect as that system was), now Google accepts more human editing and is starting to recognize brands as indicators of quality in search results.[3] Google gives content from its partners prominent positions in YouTube and Google Books. Under the terms of its settlement with publishers and the Authors' Guild, Google Books could essentially operate vending machines in public libraries throughout the United States. And newspapers are pressuring Google to enter some sort of deal to privilege their content over that of more popular aggregators such as Huffington Post.

Over the next decade, Google will change even more significantly. Personnel will come and go. Projects will start up and end. Investors and board members will express satisfaction with some initiatives and disapproval of others. Google's leaders—Sergey Brin, Larry Page, and Eric Schmidt—could leave the company because of illness or professional differences. Google might fail to make enough money to cover the costs of its commitments and liabilities. Governments might severely restrict Google's ability to turn attention into cash or to dominate the search market. Anything is possible. And whereas institutions such as libraries, states, and universities tend to last for centuries, commercial firms rarely make it through one century. Most die or change unrecognizably within their first two decades. Google is halfway to that point. We should not count on the company being the same old Google, or even being around to serve as well as it has done so far, when it lurches through adolescence.

Clearly, we should not trust Google to be the custodian of our most precious cultural and scientific resources. We should not assume that Google, with its focus on delivering what we want—or think we want— will deliver what we actually need. We made a grand mistake over the past few years. We were relieved to have a big, rich, brave company, one that proclaimed it would not "be evil," to assume responsibility for the digitization and distribution of many of the most precious intellectual and cultural resources our species has produced.

In a sense, we missed an opportunity. About the same time that Google started, we could have coordinated a grand global project, funded by a group of concerned governments and facilitated by the best national libraries, to plan and execute a fifty-year project to connect everybody to everything. At least we could have executed a plan to digitize the major collections of hundred or so major libraries around the world and unify the works under a searchable index. We could have launched something like a "Human Knowledge Project." Now, a dozen years later, it's harder to do that. But it's not impossible. In fact, it's still necessary if we want to pursue the dream of a vital global public sphere.

The very presence and wealth of Google are the greatest impediments are to such a grand global project. Google not only has been crowding out investment in projects that would run along these lines, but has also been crowding out imagination. Google's most attractive feature in its efforts to be the chief agent engaged in generating a global universal library is the speed with which it undertakes projects. As Paul Courant, the head of the libraries at the University of Michigan, writes in support of Google's massive effort to digitize millions of books, "For myself, I'd like to unleash my colleagues and our students on this remarkable resource while I'm still around to see what happens."[4]

Google has three key advantages over some nebulous, long-term public initiative. First, it has the computational power to make great strides toward this effort by itself. Second, it has a revenue-generating system that could help to fund such an endeavor and thus save public entities from having to fund it, especially in the midst of a global recession. Third, by amassing the cultural capital for appearing to foster a grand public service, Google has the incentive to continue this project for the foreseeable future. Google's reputation, so far justified, for building systems that are relatively open and customizable, and for signing nonexclusive contracts to acquire materials, has inoculated it against many concerns about "cornering the market" on knowledge distribution.

Still, it's important to remember that just because Google behaved a certain way between 1998 and 2008 does not mean it will behave that way for the next ten years. As we have seen, Google is changing its nature already. Moreover, Google offers no guarantees of quality, universality, or openness. Without firm regulations, a truly competitive market, or a competing public project, we have no recourse in the event of substandard performance or malfeasance by the company. If this is such an important mission for our species, is it not important enough to promote, debate, and fund publicly? If it's not important enough, then fine. Let's drop the whole idea and allow a fractured, privatized system, with all its inherent inequalities of access, to prevail.

But if we really care enough to dream and work toward a goal of a universally accessible and usable global information ecosystem as the basis for an expanded public sphere, then we should at least muster the political will to pursue it—if not for the sake of the citizens of the future and the system itself, then at least for the sake of politics. After all, ensuring the proper distribution of public goods is what politics is all about.

Fundamentally, we should demand patience, deliberation, and quality over expediency, centralization, and thrift. Leaders of the world might not concur, but I think that the potential of leveling knowledge discrepancies, linking every curious person to quality resources that can help guide us through a complex world, is worth waiting fifty years for and spending millions of dollars to achieve. It's more important to do it right than to do it fast. It's more important to have knowledge sources that will work one hundred years from now than to have a collection of poor images that we can see next week. And it's more important to link poor children in underdeveloped regions with knowledge than to quicken the pace of access for those of us who already live among more information than we could possibly use.

THE HUMAN KNOWLEDGE PROJECT: AN INVITATION

I conclude with an invitation to participate in a project to design an information ecosystem that would outlive Google. This endeavor, which I call the Human Knowledge Project, would identify a series of policy challenges, infrastructure needs, philosophical insights, and technological challenges with a single realizable goal in mind: to organize the world's information and make it universally accessible. I am sure Google won't mind if we copy its mission statement.

Over the next decade, the project would hold a series of meetings to bring together thinkers and designers who can forge a vision and a plan for a just and effective global information ecosystem. I would start small, with a few visionaries mapping out the broad contours of the project. Then I would invite hundreds of interested and talented contributors to work on specific elements of the vision. The Human Knowledge Project should be open, public, global, multilingual, and focused. It should be sensitive to the particular needs of communities of potential knowledge users around the world, yet it should be committed to building a global system that can erase the disparities in knowledge that currently exist between a child growing up in a poor village in South Africa and another growing up in a wealthy city in Canada.

We already have the technologies that can make this happen. What we lack are a legal infrastructure that can let more knowledge flow freely at low or no marginal cost to the user of knowledge, removing impediments such as overly protective and anticompetitive intellectual-property powers; a set of global policies explicitly designed to serve the underserved, closing the digital divide that privileges the wealthy and better educated; a set of protocols or norms that would help us differentiate reliable and useful knowledge from massive distractions and rumor, ending coercive Internet practices that pick winners by favoring some content over others (that is, that violate network neutrality); agreements on technical standards, ensuring the quality and preservation of information worldwide; and a system of global governance, ensuring accountability and transparency throughout the system. These are not easy objectives to achieve. I would anticipate many fights and disagreements about the best way forward. But it's better to have these things argued in a deliberative forum than decided according to the whims of market forces, technological imperatives, and secretive contracts.

Our current information ecosystem is a tangled thicket, consisting of bound, stable, localized, and hierarchical outlets such as old university libraries, commercial publishers, and states; amateur-driven and thus unstable projects such as Wikipedia and blogs; and hypercommercial-ized, data-mined, advertising-directed platforms such as Google. The post-Google agenda of the Human Knowledge Project would be committed to outlining the values and processes necessary to establish and preserve a truly universal, fundamentally democratic global knowledge ecosystem and public sphere.

I foresee public libraries as the nodes of the Human Knowledge Project. Because libraries are increasingly the places where poor people seek knowledge and opportunity via the Internet, we should take advantage of them to connect people with knowledge in the richest and most effective ways possible. In addition, if we rapidly increase funding for libraries around the world, they will spend more on the products that support the public sphere, such as newspapers, magazines, journals, books, videos, recordings, and software. The Human Knowledge Project moves beyond such short-term concerns as how newspapers might become profitable again. And it gets beyond blaming Google, Craigslist, the Huffington Post, and other Web services for the downfall of traditional journalism and publishing. The Human Knowledge Project takes a broad and deep approach in hopes of serving the public's need for knowledge in the best way possible and fostering a flowering of creativity and civic engagement.

I would like to see a plan to fund and support a global network of libraries, staffed by trained professionals, equipped with durable and flexible technology, open to assist people of every station with their inquiries. There is no "global library system" per se. There is not even a standardized national library system in the United States. However, high standards of professionalism and technologies are upheld by professional schools of library science and information in the United States. To realize this global project, the noncommercialized physical space of public libraries and the high ethical and technical standards of professional librarianship are more needed than ever.

The Human Knowledge Project would consider questions of organization and distribution at every level: the network, the hardware, the software, the protocols, the laws, the staff, the administrators, the physical space (libraries), the formats for discrete works, the formats for reference works such as dictionaries and encyclopedias, the formats for emerging collaborative works, and the spaces to facilitate collaboration and creativity. But the Human Knowledge Project would not be an endeavor to crowd out the private sector, any more than the private sector should be allowed to crowd out the Human Knowledge Project. Collaboration with and respect for commercial publishers and distributors would be essential for the maintenance and extension of collections. We should not get locked into the idea that we must protect or preserve any particular firm or industry. We should generate a fertile environment for new ideas to grow, whether commercial, artistic, or scientific.

The idea for the Human Knowledge Project was explicitly inspired by the Human Genome Project. Its story should sound familiar. In the early 1980s, a small group of molecular biologists, led by Robert Sinsheimer of the University of California at Santa Cruz, envisioned a large project that would be the biological equivalent of astronomy's Hubble Telescope—a project so ambitious in scope that it would open up secrets of the natural world that the classic process of close study of a discrete phenomenon could not. Sinsheimer saw the value of what came to be known as "big science." The project's goal was to map the human genome: that is, to identify the location and function of every one of the genes in the human somatic cell. At the time, many scientists assumed that humans have more than 40,000 genes (the number is actually closer to 25,000), so the task seemed quite daunting, perhaps impossible. Using the techniques of the early 1980s, it took several years to determine the genetic sequence of the Epstein-Barr virus, many thousands of times smaller than the human genome. The potential boon of such a database, however, generated sufficient enthusiasm among leading scientists that they were able to generate funding and support for the project.

Still, efforts to sequence the human genome were sporadic, disorganized, uncoordinated across borders, and technologically rudimentary during the first decade of the project. Researchers in Japan, France, and the United Kingdom were pursuing similar projects, but no one had forged a global vision for an open database of information. By the early 1990s researchers such as John Sulston in the United Kingdom had refined some sequencing techniques, making it conceivable that the various researchers could generate a human genome map within a few decades. Enthusiasm grew.[5]

Then an audacious, confident, technologically savvy private actor stepped in and offered to do the job for free—or at least without public funding. Celera, led by the maverick biologist Craig Venter, made promises not unlike Google's: faster, cheaper, better-focused results, with only modest limitations on public access to the data. While earlier working for the public project, by 1990 Venter and his research partner, Mark Adams, had developed a new technique, called expressed sequence tagging, that let them identify genes rapidly. Venter claimed that this new approach "was a bargain in comparison to the genome project" and claimed he could find up to 90 percent of human genes within a few years for a fraction of the cost.[6]

The leader of the Human Genome Project at the time, James Watson, grew enraged when National Institutes of Health officials expressed excitement over Venter's techniques, which Watson saw not only as a cheapening of the mission but also as a route toward the privatization of information. The NIH had already begun securing patents on many of Venter's discoveries. Watson and others considered these actions to be a grave violation of scientific principles because patents could be used to prevent future researchers from sharing knowledge generated by the project. Watson left the project over this dispute. Venter left as well, to found Celera Genomics in 1998 and pursue the privatization of the human genome.

Working with researchers at the Johns Hopkins University, Venter generated another revolutionary technique that sped up the process—whole-genome "shotgun" sequencing. This development generated much debate within the sequencing community, with the new director of the NIH, Francis Collins, arguing for the slow, complete, and more scientifically meaningful approach and others, such as Sulston, pleading to adopt some of Venter's techniques.

The result was that the public project raised its metabolism, adopted new techniques to generate faster results, and increased its funding by rallying public support and invoking concerns about Venter's potential privatization of the data. When Venter declared that Celera could sequence the entire genome within three years, Collins responded by declaring that the Human Genome Project would produce a "rough draft" of the genome within five years. Researchers around the world began coordinating their research and results so that the knowledge of the human genome would belong to the entire species. Ultimately, by late 2000, both the public and the private projects were ready to publish their results, but in different journals and under different terms of access and use. Since that publication, research on the genome and on particular genes continues, all the better for the competition and the expression of political will by some of the most important scientists in the world.[7]

In the aftermath of the race to sequence the human genome, Francis Collins and his colleagues reflected on the lessons they had learned from conducting a grand, global project in the public interest and competing against a high-powered and ambitious private firm. Collins concluded that the keys to success include building teams led by committed and diverse professionals, keeping focused on both the incremental advances and the long-term goal, managing well, establishing and respecting explicit milestones, publishing results quickly, deploying the best technology, and collaborating well with the private sector.[8] In this last factor, Collins and the Human Genome Project failed: they never reached a workable agreement with Celera. But because they exceeded their own expectations, the Human Genome Project succeeded spectacularly nonetheless.

The Human Knowledge Project should encourage private interests such as Google, news organizations, textbook publishers, and scientific organizations to be players in the design and execution of this system. Financial incentives must remain strong, or too few institutions will be willing to take risks to generate new knowledge. However, the goal is not to enrich any particular firm.

The goal of the Human Knowledge Project is to enrich the range of opportunities for knowledge exploitation and to foster creativity and innovation in ways we cannot predict. The only way we are going to accomplish such a long-term project is to mount a political movement for it. If we want to create a vital global public sphere for the digital era by offering the best and the most information to the largest number of people around the world, we will have to make a persuasive case for such a goal. We will have to identify the costs and impediments and confront them directly. We will have to articulate the need and the benefits. We will have to change minds. We will have to change laws. We can't just hope that some big, rich company will do it for us. That's simply irresponsible.

The problem with the Googlization of everything is that we count on Google too much. We trust it too much. We have blind faith in its ability to solve grand problems with invisible technologies. Its stumbles in the Google Books project have already tarnished its aura of invincibility. We have seen how Google's efforts to globalize have met with fierce resistance in places that do not share Google's ideologies. Bad copyright laws have not only prevented other firms and institutions from contributing to the global information ecosystem, but they have also impaired Google's ability to serve us better. And we have seen how Google has played its corporate-responsibility card to deflect attention from troubling actions it takes. Meanwhile, Google is developing more powerful tools to help us shop, without considering that shopping and learning don't always rely on the same standards and practices. Now we must demand more. We must build systems that can serve us better, regardless of which companies and technologies thrive in the next decade. Most important, we should learn to beware of false idols and empty promises. The future of knowledge—and thus the future of the species—depends on getting this right.

ACKNOWLEDGMENTS

The words of Thorstein Veblen sounded in my head as I researched and composed this book. Believe me: that was daunting and weird. I kept saying to myself as I wrote, "What would Veblen think of this?" The summer before I proposed doing a book on Google, I tried to read everything Veblen ever published. In a strange way, this whole project emerged from that experiment. I am convinced that we ignore Veblen at our peril. So this book is an exercise in trying to revive his critical spirit and demonstrate that it can do us much good here at the dawn of the twenty-first century. During the four years that I worked on this book, I resisted the urge to consider my constant connectivity either natural or regular. I focused on how odd it all was and how differently I lived not so long ago. I tried to acknowledge the weirdness of living *la vida Google.*

This book is about living with Google and thinking through Google. To explore these questions, instead of boycotting or living outside Google, I went all in. I spent as much time as possible reading Google's public blogs, talking with people who work there, listening to folks who use it every day, and trying out as many Google services as I was qualified to use. I began using Gmail for e-mail and Google Docs for collaborative writing projects and for presentations in the courses I taught. I joined Orkut (Google's social networking platform, popular in India and Brazil but less so in the United States) and even uploaded my medical records to Google Health, an online repository. For more than four years, I lived every day with and through as many Google products and services as I could. For several weeks, I tried to write this book using Google Docs instead of my default word processing program.

This book would not exist without the cooperation of the people who work at Google and YouTube: in particular, Peter Barron, Dan Clancy, Vint Cerf, Hal Varian, Alex Macgillivray, Glenn Otis Brown, and Jennie Johnson. They welcomed me on several visits, gave me their valuable time, and tolerated my mistakes and overstatements as I presented draft sections of the book on my blog, Googlizationofeverything.com. Most important, they have produced some astounding products that I have used extensively in the research and composition of all my work, not just this book. Google has made my life better and richer.

Bob Stein, Dan Visel, and Ben Vershbow of the Institute for the Future of the Book were early champions of this project and made sure the blog was hosted well and received more attention than perhaps it deserved.

My agent and friend Sam Stoloff talked me through the process of pitching the proposal and selling a complex bundle of rights to various publishers around the world. And when things looked bad, Sam calmly pushed me to make it good and get it done. I can't thank him enough. Bud Bynack, a talented editor helped me forge this into a real book.

The book also benefited from the wisdom and patience of Naomi Schneider of the University of California Press in Berkeley, who saw promise in this project early and endured many false starts. I hope this book lives up to her high expectations.

I worked with two brilliant research assistants in the composition of this work. Alice Marwick is destined to be one of the most important scholars of media in this new century. She has an unparalleled work ethic and an inspiring sense of curiosity. Her critical sensibilities are refined far beyond her years. Sarah Walch is a research librarian of the highest order. She put in many hours helping me refine my thoughts and digging up essential resources for this work. Sarah, who was living and working in Northern California at the time, became my eyes and ears on the fertile ground of Silicon Valley. Most important, Sarah cheered me up and kept me focused at some important points in the research and composition of this book.

Karen Winkler, an editor with the Chronicle Review section of the *Chronicle of Higher Education,* played a major role in the development of this book. She encouraged me to write a long article for her about the risks universities were taking by enabling Google Books. That article generated a lot of attention for me and helped secure the contracts for this book. Michael Wann, technology and science editor at MSNBC.com, invited me to write columns on the Web 2.0 phenomenon for the site. Many of those ideas made it into this work. Michael's encouragement and enthusiasm, and the friendship born during our days together scraping by as underpaid Austin journalists, will always sustain me.

This book could not have been written without the generous support of the University of Virginia, where the curiosity and liberalism of Thomas Jefferson still fills the air. Three deans of the College of Arts and Sciences demonstrated their strong support for my work: Edward Ayers, Karen Ryan, and Meredith Woo. Dean Paul Mahoney and Associate Deans Jim Ryan and Liz Magill of the University of Virginia School of Law also supported me. I owe special thanks to Dotan Oliar, Chris Sprigman, Tom Nachbar, and my students at the law school for all their patience and feedback. My colleagues in the Department of Media Studies—Andrea Press, Bruce Williams, Johanna Drucker, Aniko Bodrokhozy, David Golumbia, Hector Amaya, and Jennifer Petersen—ensured that the department would support me in every conceivable way. Bruce Williams read the manuscript in its entirety and offered much advice that improved it greatly. And Judy McPeak made everything run smoothly. Also at Virginia, Chad Wellmon deserves special thanks for pushing me to think harder about the role of knowledge taxonomy through history. And Deborah Johnson inspired me to think more about the effects of design on privacy and transparency.

This book also owes its existence to the generous support that the Verklin family has given to the Department of Media Studies at the University of Virginia. Several important internal grants helped me conduct research trips and paid for other costs incurred in the completion of the book.

Legal scholars who have helped me work through this material include Randy Picker, Michael Madison, Ann Bartow, Lawrence Lessig, Yochai Benkler, Mark Lemley, Pamela Samuelson, Mahadevi Sundar, Chris Sprigman, Julie Cohen, Molly Van Howeling, Lolly Gasaway, Anupam Chander, Shubha Ghosh, Mike Godwin, and Tim Wu. Neil Netanel and David Nimmer gave me an opportunity to outline my perspectives on Google for their seminar at UCLA Law School. Their students gave me valuable feedback on a draft of part of this book. Oren Bracha did me the great favor of bringing me back to my alma mater, the University of Texas at Austin, to speak about Google Books in its early days. Cass Sunstein assured me I was on the right track with my approach. Frank Pasquale went above and beyond the duties of friendship by engaging with me in conversation on the various blogs to which he contributes about the many facets of Google. Andrew Chin, my dear friend since our early undergraduate years at the University of Texas, read the entire manuscript and helped me avoid some serious mistakes.

The two people who taught me the most about search engines and prompted me to think broadly about how Google affects the world are Helen Nissenbaum of New York University and Michael Zimmer of the University of Wisconsin at Milwaukee. Either of them could have written this book better than I have. I am grateful for their generosity in sharing their ideas, observations, and expertise while I muscled in on their territory. Two wonderful computer scientists, Hal Abelson of MIT and Harry Lewis of Harvard, taught me a tremendous amount about the history and major tenets of their field. Jim Jansen of Penn State University walked me through the growing body of social science on search-engine use. The great danah boyd fed me insights about our shifting conceptions of privacy. Chris Soghoian talked me through technical issues of surveillance and security. Ted Striphas taught me much about the role of books in the twenty-first century. Liz Losh helped me understand the relationship between the state and electronic media. Eszter Hargittai gave me great advice on everything. And Fred Turner shared his brilliant insights into the cultural history of Silicon Valley. Over in Amsterdam, Geert Lovink and Richard Rogers gave me frequent tips and insights into how Google does things in Europe, and they invited me twice to present my work at wonderful conferences in my favorite European city. Konrad Becker in Vienna was also a great help by coordinating global work on search engines for his conferences and published collections. And Lawrence Liang in Bangalore remains a dear friend and inspiration.

As always, Joe Cutbirth, Todd Gitlin, Eric Alterman, Carlo Rotella, Joel Dinerstein, Jay Rosen, Sue Krenek, Sam Penrose, Eric Klinenberg, Lorraine Cademartori, Catherine Collins, Kevin Grauke, Jonathan Silverman, Paul Erickson, and Carolyn de la Peña had my back and cheered me on. Jonathan Lethem talked me through the new challenges of doing something as selfish as writing a book while learning how to be a good father. Political scientist Daniel C. O'Neill has not only supported me with twenty-five years of friendship, but also read my work on China and has given me helpful criticism. David Schenk challenged me to strengthen and refine much of what I had composed too quickly. Susan Orlean and Clive Thompson offered me their thoughts on the work of a writer in the age of Googlization. Jeff Jarvis was a total mensch throughout. He is the best sparring partner a technology writer could ask for.

A few years back I had a very different book proposal waiting on my hard drive. I wanted to write a simple book about a simple subject. I had just recently become a father and earned tenure, so I wanted to write a book from home, in record time, and then move on to the most joyful work of my life. Then I had a pleasant lunch with Nicholas Lemann, dean of the Columbia School of Journalism, at which he asked me what I was writing. I described that quick, simple book project to him. Polite to a fault, Nick did not reveal a lack of interest in the subject. But he did not ask any more questions about it. After a heavy lull in the conversation, I commented, "I have one more thought I have been mulling over," I said. "It's called 'The Googlization of Everything.'" Nick's eyes lit up. "Write that one," he said with a firmness that surprised me. And so I did. I hope my daughter forgives me for the frequent trips to the West Coast and many late nights of writing that followed that fateful lunch.

At that time, my interest in pursuing such a maddening book came from a fascination with the audacity of one young company (then only six years old) daring to declare itself the custodian of hundreds of years of human book learning. But just as influential to me was a single sentence in one book, Yochai Benkler's monumental *Wealth of Networks*. In a chapter that outlines the prospects for what he calls "the networked public sphere," Benkler warns that the Internet might fail in its potential to generate an ideal platform for deliberation because, among other things, "Google could become so powerful on the desktop, in the e-mail utility, and on the Web that it will effectively become a supernode that will indeed raise the prospect of a re-emergence of a mass-media model."[1] I wrote this book to see if that's what has happened. My answer: not yet, but we are getting there. This is my third book, and the third one inspired by the work and words of Yochai Benkler. It's an honor just to hang out in his shadow.

Hundreds of librarians around the world guided and inspired my thoughts on Google and how we use it. Chief among them were Robert Darnton, director of the Harvard University libraries, and Paul Courant, dean of libraries at the University of Michigan. They both generously shared their time and insights. And I cannot say enough about the help given me by the librarians at the University of Virginia. Taylor Fitchett, Ben Doherty, and Leslie Johnston (now at the Library of Congress) deserve special praise.

This book, like all my work, is a love song to all the libraries and librarians I have known. I can't reflect on what I owe to libraries without remembering the hours I spent as a child on the vinyl chairs in the Clearfield Public Library in Amherst, New York. Seated next to me for almost all those hours was my partner in dreams and discovery, my sister Mehala Vaidhyanathan. That library also inspired my younger sister and my favorite librarian, Vedana Vaidhyanathan.

My parents, Virginia and Vishnampet S. Vaidhyanathan, did many wonderful things to enable me to lead this rewarding life, think these thoughts, and do this work. They never told me I could not purchase, borrow, or read any book I wanted. There was no forbidden knowledge. There was nothing to fear. And no book was too expensive. I hope I can be half as generous and brave a parent. Ann Henriksen deserves special thanks for all her love and support to me and our family during my many research and speaking trips.

And to Melissa, Jaya, and our dog, Ellie: Sorry this took so long. I will come down to cook dinner now.

Charlottesville, Virginia
August 2010

NOTES

PREFACE

1. See Amartya Kumar Sen, *Development as Freedom* (Oxford: Oxford University Press, 2001).

2. See Jonathan Zittrain, *The Future of the Internet and How to Stop It* (New Haven, CT: Yale University Press, 2008).

3. See, for example, Jane Mayer, *Dark Side: The Inside Story of How the War on Terror Turned into a War on American Ideals* (New York: Doubleday, 2008). Thomas E. Ricks, *Fiasco: The American Military Adventure in Iraq* (New York: Penguin, 2006); Jeffrey Toobin, *Too Close to Call: The Thirty-Six-Day Battle to Decide the 2000 Election* (New York: Random House, 2001); Alan M. Dershowitz, *Supreme Injustice: How the High Court Hijacked Election 2000* (Oxford: Oxford University Press, 2001); Ron Suskind, *The One Percent Doctrine: Deep Inside America's Pursuit of Its Enemies since 9/11* (New York: Simon & Schuster, 2006); Ron Suskind, *The Price of Loyalty: George W. Bush, the White House, and the Education of Paul O'Neill* (New York: Simon & Schuster, 2004).

4. For a brief description of the costly dynamic tension between anarchy and oligarchy in the digital world, see Siva Vaidhyanathan, *The Anarchist in the*

Library: How the Clash between Freedom and Control Is Hacking the Real World and Crashing the System (New York: Basic Books, 2004).

5. For examples of simplistic, naive visions of how technology works in the world, see Kevin Kelly, *Out of Control: The Rise Of Neo-biological Civilization* (Reading, MA: Addison-Wesley, 1994); Kevin Kelly, *New Rules for the New Economy: 10 Radical Strategies for a Connected World* (New York: Viking, 1998); Nicholas Negroponte, *Being Digital* (New York: Knopf, 1995); Ray Kurzweil, *The Age of Spiritual Machines: When Computers Exceed Human Intelligence* (New York: Viking, 1999).

6. For elaborations of unfounded "generational" thinking, see Jeff Gomez, *Print Is Dead: Books in Our Digital Age* (London: Macmillan, 2008); Neil Howe and William Strauss, *Millennials Rising: The Next Great Generation* (New York: Vintage, 2000).

7. See Harriet Rubin, "Google Offers a Map for Its Philanthropy," *New York Times,* January 18, 2008.

8. See, for example, Randall E. Stross, *Planet Google: One Company's Audacious Plan to Organize Everything We Know,* vol. 1 (New York: Free Press, 2008); David A. Vise and Mark Malseed, *The Google Story* (New York: Delacorte, 2005); John Battelle, *The Search: How Google and Its Rivals Rewrote the Rules of Business and Transformed Our Culture* (New York: Portfolio, 2005); Amy N. Langville and C. D. Meyer, *Google's PageRank and Beyond: The Science of Search Engine Rankings* (Princeton, NJ: Princeton University Press, 2006); Amanda Spink and Michael Zimmer, *Web Search: Multidisciplinary Perspectives, Information Science and Knowledge Management* (Berlin: Springer, 2008). For the most optimistic description of the work Google does in the world (and how other companies might benefit from its example), see Jeff Jarvis, *What Would Google Do?* (New York: Collins Business, 2009). For the most recent and most comprehensive "biography" of the company and a description of the friction the company is causing in the media world, see Ken Auletta, *Googled: The End of the World as We Know It* (New York: Penguin, 2009).

INTRODUCTION

1. Elizabeth Losh, *Virtualpolitik: An Electronic History of Government Media-Making in a Time of War, Scandal, Disaster, Miscommunication, and Mistakes* (Cambridge, MA: MIT Press, 2009).

2. Clay Shirky, "A Speculative Post on the Idea of Algorithmic Authority," Clay Shirky, blog, November 15, 2009, www.shirky.com.

3. Thomas L. Griffiths, Mark Steyvers, and Alana Firl, "Google and the Mind: Predicting Fluency with PageRank," *Psychological Science* 18 (December 2007): 1069–76.

4. Nicholas Carr, "Is Google Making Us Stupid?" *Atlantic*, July 2008, 75–80.

5. I have borrowed this sense of "dangerousness" from Alexander Galloway, who uses the term to describe how Internet protocols, which appear to serve purely anarchistic or libertarian ends, in fact work as technologies of control. See Galloway, *Protocol: How Control Exists after Decentralization* (Cambridge, MA: MIT Press, 2004).

6. For a recent social and technological account of the automobile in the United States, see "Traffic: How We Get from Here to There," Backstory: With the American History Guys, July 18, 2008, www.backstoryradio.org; Peter D. Norton, *Fighting Traffic: The Dawn of the Motor Age in the American City* (Cambridge, MA: MIT Press, 2008). For an enlightening cultural history of the automobile in the United States, see Cotten Seiler, *Republic of Drivers* (Chicago: University of Chicago Press, 2008). For a history of how the airplane radically altered American law, see Stuart Banner, *Who Owns the Sky? The Struggle to Control Airspace from the Wright Brothers On* (Cambridge, MA: Harvard University Press, 2008).

7. Jeff Jarvis, *What Would Google Do?* (New York: Collins Business, 2009); Chris Anderson, *Free: The Future of a Radical Price* (New York: Hyperion, 2009).

8. Anil Dash, "Google's Microsoft Moment," Anil Dash, blog, July 9, 2009, http://dashes.com; David Carr, "How Good (or Not Evil) Is Google?" *New York Times*, June 22, 2009.

9. John Battelle, *The Search: How Google and Its Rivals Rewrote the Rules of Business and Transformed Our Culture* (New York: Portfolio, 2005); Randall E. Stross, *Planet Google: One Company's Audacious Plan to Organize Everything We Know*, vol. 1 (New York: Free Press, 2008); Alexander Halavais, *Search Engine Society* (Cambridge, MA: Polity, 2009).

10. Todd Gitlin, *Media Unlimited: How the Torrent of Images and Sounds Overwhelms Our Lives* (New York: Metropolitan Books, 2001).

11. The phrase is Joseph Schumpeter's. See Schumpeter, *Capitalism, Socialism, and Democracy* (London: Allen and Unwin, 1952), 81.

12. Lucas D. Introna and Helen Nissenbaum, "Shaping the Web: Why the Politics of Search Engines Matters," *Information Society* 16, no. 3 (2000): 169.

13. In another context I have used the term *technocultural imagination* to describe the conditions and habits that contemporary artists have enjoyed since the dissemination of digital technologies and networks. See Siva Vaidhyanathan, "The Technocultural Imagination," in Chrissie Iles et al., *2006 Whitney Biennial: Day for Night* (New York: Whitney Museum of American Art, 2006). In his 1959 manifesto *The Sociological Imagination*, C. Wright Mills instructed social scientists to situate their work between the poles of grand theory and numbing empiricism. "The sociological imagination," Mills wrote, "enables its possessor to understand the larger historical scene in terms of its meaning for the inner life and the external career of a variety of individuals." Thus the "imagineer"

(a term Mills would never have used) can "take into account how individuals, in the welter of their daily experience, often become falsely conscious of their social positions." Mills posits three questions, or lenses, that enable scholars to generate interdisciplinary, influential, and—most of all—interesting work: What are the essential components of a society, and how are they related to each other? What historical changes are affecting a particular part or function of society? Who are the winners and losers in a society, and how did they get to be this way? Mills, *The Sociological Imagination* (New York: Oxford University Press, 1959), 5.

14. Anderson, *Free.*

15. Miguel Helft, "In E-Books, It's an Army vs. Google," *New York Times,* October 7, 2009.

CHAPTER 1. RENDER UNTO CAESAR

1. John Barlow, "Declaring Independence," *Wired* 4, no. 6 (1996): 121, http://wac.colostate.edu/rhetnet/barlow/barlow_declaration.html.

2. Lawrence Lessig, *Code: And Other Laws of Cyberspace* (New York: Basic Books, 1999).

3. I thank James Grimmelmann for this comparative insight from a conversation in 2008 at Georgetown University. See Mary Beard, review of Maria Wyke, *Caesar: A Life in Western Culture, New York Review of Books* 55, no. 20 (2008): 48; Mary Beard, *The Roman Triumph* (Cambridge, MA: Belknap Press, 2007); Maria. Wyke, *Caesar: A Life in Western Culture* (Chicago: University of Chicago Press, 2008); Christopher Kelly, *The Roman Empire: A Very Short Introduction* (Oxford: Oxford University Press, 2006).

4. Even with Google's "safe search" filtering function off (the default state is "moderate" filtering), a search for "facial" is likely to generate a first page with almost every entry devoted to the skin-care technique instead of the sex act. The only two references to the sex act such a search generated from Charlottesville, Virginia, in February 2010 included a Wikipedia entry and the definition of the term on Urbandictionary.com. In the late 1990s, a search for "Asian" on almost any other search engine would have generated torrents of pornography featuring Asian models. Today, such a search on Google generates a first page of links devoted to Asian American history and culture and Asian foods.

5. *Introduction to the Google Ad Auction,* 2009, video online at www .youtube.com; Steven Levy, "Secret of Googlenomics: Data-Fueled Recipe Brews Profitability," *Wired,* May 22, 2009; *Search Advertising: Dr. Hal Varian,* SIMS 141, course in the School of Information, University of California at Berkeley, 2007, video available at www.youtube.com; "Talking Business: Stuck in Google's

Doghouse," *New York Times*, September 13, 2008; "Big Brands? Google Brand Promotion: New Search Engine Rankings Place Heavy Emphasis on Branding," SEOBook, February 25, 2009, www.seobook.com/google-branding; "Corporate Information: Our Philosophy," Google.com, www.google.com/corporate/tenthings.html.

6. Robin Wauters, "Google Flags Whole Internet as Malware," TechCrunch, January 31, 2009, www.techcrunch.com; "Search Is Too Important to Leave to One Company—Even Google," www.guardian.co.uk, June 1, 2009; Liz Robbins, "Google Error Sends Warning Worldwide," *New York Times*, January 31, 2009; Ian Bogost, "Cascading Failure: The Unseen Power of Google's Malware Detection," Ian Bogost, blog, June 12, 2009, www.bogost.com/blog; Jonathan Zittrain, *The Future of the Internet and How to Stop It* (New Haven, CT: Yale University Press, 2008).

7. Barry Schwartz, "First Google Image Result for Michelle Obama Pure Racist," *Search Engine Round Table*, November 13, 2009, www.seroundtable.com/archives/021162.html; David Colker, "Google Won't Exclude Distorted Michelle Obama Image from Its Site," *Los Angeles Times*, November 25, 2009; Judit Bar-Ilan, "Web Links and Search Engine Ranking: The Case of Google and the Query 'Jew'," *Journal of the American Society for Information Science and Technology* 57, no. 12 (2006): 1581.

8. Richard Thaler and Cass Sunstein, *Nudge: Improving Decisions about Health, Wealth, and Happiness* (New Haven: Yale University Press, 2008).

9. Levy, "Secret of Googlenomics."

10. Randall E. Stross, *Planet Google: One Company's Audacious Plan to Organize Everything We Know* (New York: Free Press, 2008), 109–28.

11. Cecilia Kang, "AT&T Accuses Google of Violating Telecom Laws; Google Rejects Claims," Post I.T., blog, September 25, 2009; Amy Schatz, "AT&T Asks for Curbs on Google," WSJ.com, September 26, 2009; John Markoff and Matt Richtel, "F.C.C. Hands Google a Partial Victory," *New York Times*, August 1, 2007.

12. "GOOG: Google Inc Company Profile," CNNMoney.com, August 12, 2010.

13. Ken Auletta, "Annals of Communications: The Search Party," *New Yorker*, January 14, 2008; Rob Hof, "Maybe Google Isn't Losing Big Bucks on YouTube After All," *BusinessWeek*, June 17, 2009; Nicholas Thompson and Fred Vogelstein, "The Plot to Kill Google," *Wired*, January 19, 2009; Eli Edwards, "Stepping Up to the Plate: The Google-Doubleclick Merger and the Role of the Federal Trade Commission in Protecting Online Data Privacy," *SSRN eLibrary*, April 25, 2008, http://papers.ssrn.com; Michael Liedtke, "Guessing Game: How Much Money Is YouTube Losing?" Associated Press, June 17, 2009; "Privacy Group Asks F.T.C. to Investigate Google," *New York Times* Bits Blog, March

17, 2009, http://bits.blogs.nytimes.com; Peter Swire, "Protecting Consumers: Privacy Matters in Antitrust Analysis," Center for American Progress, October 19, 2007, www.americanprogress.org; Miguel Helft, "Yahoo and Google Offer to Revise Ad Partnership," *New York Times,* November 3, 2008; Daniel Lyons, "They Might Be a Little Evil: Why Google Faces Antitrust Scrutiny," *Newsweek,* June 1, 2009.

14.   Miguel Helft, "Google Makes a Case That It Isn't So Big," *New York Times,* June 29, 2009.

15.   Carl Shapiro and Hal Varian, *Information Rules: A Strategic Guide to the Network Economy* (Boston, MA: Harvard Business School Press, 1998).

16.   Amanda Spink et al., "A Study of Results Overlap and Uniqueness among Major Web Search Engines," *Information Processing and Management* 42, no. 5 (September 2006): 1379–91, retrieved from www.sciencedirect.com.

17.   Lawrence Page et al., *The PageRank Citation Ranking: Bringing Order to the Web,* technical report, Stanford University, 1999, http://ilpubs.stanford.edu:8090/422/.

18.   Harry McCracken, "A Brief History of Google Killers," *Technologizer,* May 19, 2009, http://technologizer.com.

19.   Nova Spivack, "Wolfram Alpha Computes Answers to Factual Questions: This Is Going to Be Big," TechCrunch, March 8, 2009, www.techcrunch.com; David Talbot, "Wolfram Alpha and Google Face Off," *Technology Review,* May 5, 2009; Eric Schonfeld, "What Is Google Squared? It Is How Google Will Crush Wolfram Alpha," TechCrunch, May 12, 2009, www.techcrunch.com.

20.   Loren Baker, "Hakia Semantic Search Adds Pubmed Content to Medical and Health Search Engine," *Search Engine Journal,* June 12, 2008.

21.   "Hakia Challenge: IT band," Hakia, July 16, 2009, http://hakia.com.

22.   Miguel Helft, "Bing Delivers Credibility to Microsoft," *New York Times,* July 14, 2009.

23.   Nicholas Thompson and Fred Vogelstein, "The Plot to Kill Google," *Wired,* January 19, 2009.

24.   Chris Anderson, *Free: The Future of a Radical Price* (New York: Hyperion, 2009), 119–34.

25.   Theo Röhle, "Desperately Seeking the Consumer: Personalized Search Engines and the Commercial Exploitation of User Data," *First Monday* 12, no. 9, http://firstmonday.org.

26.   Levy, "Secret of Googlenomics."

27.   Joseph Turow, *Niche Envy: Marketing Discrimination in the Digital Age* (Cambridge, MA: MIT Press, 2006).

28.   *Introduction to the Google Ad Auction;* Levy, "Secret of Googlenomics"; Randall Stross, "Why the Google-Yahoo Ad Deal Is Nothing to Fear," *New York*

Times, September 21, 2008; *Search Advertising: Dr. Hal Varian;* Auletta, "Annals of Communications"; Benjamin Edelman, "How Google and Its Partners Inflate Measured Conversion Rates and Inflate Advertisers' Costs," Ben Edleman—Home, www.benedelman.org/news/051309–1.html.

29. Susan Orlean, personal communication, July 13, 2009.

30. "Browser Statistics," W3schools, www.w3schools.com/browsers/browsers_stats.asp, accessed August 18, 2010.

31. Lester G. Telser, "Why Should Manufacturers Want Fair Trade?" *Journal of Law and Economics* 3 (October 1960): 86–105; Russell Hardin, "The Free Rider Problem," *Stanford Encyclopedia of Philosophy,* http://plato.stanford.edu/entries/free-rider/; Gary Reback, *Free the Market!: Why Only Government Can Keep the Marketplace Competitive* (New York: Portfolio, 2009), 69.

32. Fred G. Gurley, "Unalienable Rights versus Union Shop," *Proceedings of the Academy of Political Science* 26, no. 1 (May 1954): 58–70.

33. Kang, "AT&T Accuses Google of Violating Telecom Laws"; Schatz, "AT&T Asks for Curbs on Google"; Markoff and Richtel, "F.C.C. Hands Google a Partial Victory"; Brad Stone, "The Fight over Who Sets Prices at the Online Mall," *New York Times,* February 8, 2010; Reback, *Free the Market,* 69.

34. *Kelly v. Arriba Soft Corp.* (280 F.3d 934 (CA9 2002) *withdrawn,* refiled at 336 F.3d 811 (CA9 2003).

35. Michael J. Madison, "A Pattern-Oriented Approach to Fair Use," *William and Mary Law Review* 45, no. 4 (2004): 1525–1690; Kathleen K. Olson, "Transforming Fair Use Online: The Ninth Circuit's Productive-Use Analysis of Visual Search Engines," *Communication Law and Policy* 14, no. 2 (2009): 153; Richard Perez-Pena, "Associated Press Seeks More Control of Content on Web," *New York Times,* April 7, 2009; Copyright Law of the United States of America, Sec. 107: *Limitations on Exclusive Rights: Fair Use,* 17 USC, 1976; Siva Vaidhyanathan, *Copyrights and Copywrongs: The Rise of Intellectual Property and How It Threatens Creativity* (New York University Press, 2003).

36. Eric Pfanner, "In Europe, Possible Survival Lessons for U.S. Papers," *New York Times,* March 30, 2009; Eric Pfanner, "In Europe, Challenges for Google," *New York Times,* February 2, 2010.

37. Dirk Smillie, "Murdoch Wants a Google Rebellion," *Forbes,* April 3, 2009, www.forbes.com.

38. Matthew Flamm, "WSJ Publisher Calls Google 'Digital Vampire,'" *Crain's New York Business,* June 24, 2009, www.crainsnewyork.com.

39. Jane Schulze, "Google Dubbed Internet Parasite by WSJ editor," *Australian,* April 6, 2009.

40. "Murdoch Could Block Google Searches Entirely," *Guardian,* November 9, 2009.

41. Dan Farber, "Google's Schmidt: Brands to Clean Up Internet 'Cesspool,'" *CNET News*, October 13, 2008, http://news.cnet.com; Rory Maher, "How Can Google Help Newspapers? How About Some SEO Coaching," *Washington Post*, May 22, 2009; Julie Moos, "Transcript of Google CEO Eric Schmidt's Q&A at NAA," *PoynterOnline*, April 7, 2009, www.poynter.org; Shira Ovide, "Google Responds to AP's Tougher Stance," Digits—Wall Street Journal, April 7, 2009; Zachary M. Seward, "Google Sharing Revenue with Publishers for New Product," *Nieman Journalism Lab*, September 14, 2009, www.niemanlab.org.

42. Charles Mann, "How Click Fraud Could Swallow the Internet," *Wired*, January 2006; *Amit Agarwal—Google AdSense Publisher from India*, 2007, video available at www.youtube.com. The Huffington Post takes only abstracts of commercial news content. But its mastery at optimizing its pages for Google Web Search has made it a frequent user destination for news and much more effective than many of the sources that it aggregates.

43. Todd Gitlin, "Journalism's Many Crises," OpenDemocracy, May 20, 2009, www.opendemocracy.net; Leonard Downie and Michael Schudson, "The Reconstruction of American Journalism," *Columbia Journalism Review*, December 2009, 28–51; John Nichols, "The Death and Life of Great American Newspapers," *Nation*, April 6, 2009, 11; Zachary M. Seward, "How the Associated Press Will Try to Rival Wikipedia in Search Results," *Nieman Journalism Lab*, August 13, 2009; Zachary M. Seward, "Google CEO Eric Schmidt Envisions the News Consumer of the Future," *Nieman Journalism Lab*, November 4, 2009.

44. James Fallows, "How to Save the News," *Atlantic*, June 2010.

45. Miguel Helft, "Google Calls Viacom Suit on YouTube Unfounded," *New York Times*, May 1, 2007; Hof, "Maybe Google Isn't Losing Big Bucks."

46. Richard Alleyne, "YouTube: Overnight Success Has Sparked a Back-lash," *Daily Telegraph*, July 31, 2008; Hof, "Maybe Google Isn't Losing Big Bucks"; Liedtke, "Guessing Game"; *An Anthropological Introduction to YouTube*, 2008, video available on www.youtube.com; Chris Soghoian, "Why Obama Should Ditch YouTube," Surveillance State—CNET News, November 24, 2008, http://news.cnet.com; Chris Soghoian, "White House Exempts YouTube from Privacy Rules," Surveillance State—CNET News, January 22, 2009, http://news.cnet.com; Marcia Stepanek, "Speaking YouTube," Cause Global, July 2, 2009, http://causeglobal.blogspot.com; Siva Vaidhyanathan, "What We Might Lose with GooTube," MSNBC.com, October 27, 2006; Siva Vaidhyanathan, "Me, 'Person of the Year'? No Thanks," MSNBC.com, December 28, 2006.

47. Johnny_mango, "'Lost' Police Incident Report . . . Is This What Heather Wilson 'Lost' 13 Years Ago?" Albloggerque, October 19, 2006, http://albloggerque.blogspot.com; Vaidhyanathan, "What We Might Lose."

48. Vaidhyanathan, "What We Might Lose."

49. Jack Goldsmith and Tim Wu, *Who Controls the Internet? Illusions of a Borderless World* (New York: Oxford University Press, 2006).

50.   Abigail Cutler, "Penetrating the Great Firewall: Interview with James Fallows," *Atlantic,* February 19, 2008; James Fallows, "'The Connection Has Been Reset,'" *Atlantic,* March 2008; Ronald Deibert et al., *Access Denied: The Practice and Policy of Global Internet Filtering* (Cambridge, MA: MIT Press, 2008).

51.   Thomas Frank, *One Market under God: Extreme Capitalism, Market Populism, and the End of Economic Democracy* (New York: Doubleday, 2000).

52.   Francis Fukuyama, *The End of History and the Last Man* (New York: Free Pres, 1992).

53.   Ideology, as the Cambridge University sociologist John Thompson argues, is "meaning in the service of power," or a sense of how symbolic expressions support or challenge structures and habits of social domination. See John Thompson, *Ideology and Modern Culture: Critical Social Theory in the Era of Mass Communication* (Stanford, CA: Stanford University Press, 1990).

54.   David Harvey, *A Brief History of Neoliberalism* (Oxford: Oxford University Press, 2005).

55.   Thomas Frank, *The Wrecking Crew: How Conservatives Rule* (New York: Metropolitan Books, 2008).

56.   Jeffrey Madrick, *The Case for Big Government* (Princeton, NJ: Princeton University Press, 2009).

57.   Paul Krugman and Robin Wells, *Economics* (London: Worth Publishing, 2009).

58.   Carnegie Commission on the Future of Public Broadcasting, *A Public Trust: The Report of the Carnegie Commission on the Future of Public Broadcasting* (New York: Bantam Books, 1979); Laurie Ouellette, *Viewers Like You? How Public TV Failed the People* (New York: Columbia University Press, 2002).

59.   Michael Barbaro and Justin Gillis, "Wal-Mart at Forefront of Hurricane Relief," *Washington Post,* September 5, 2005; Virginia Brennan, *Natural Disasters and Public Health: Hurricanes Katrina, Rita, and Wilma* (Baltimore, MD: Johns Hopkins University Press, 2009); Douglas Brinkley, *The Great Deluge: Hurricane Katrina, New Orleans, and the Mississippi Gulf Coast* (New York: Morrow, 2006); Ivor Van Heerden, *The Storm: What Went Wrong and Why during Hurricane Katrina: The Inside Story from One Louisiana Scientist* (New York: Viking, 2006).

60.   Barbaro and Gillis, "Wal-Mart at Forefront of Hurricane Relief."

61.   Steven Horwitz, *Making Hurricane Response More Effective: Lessons from the Private Sector and the Coast Guard during Katrina,* policy comment, Global Prosperity Initiative (Vienna, VA: Mercatus Center, George Mason University, March 2008).

62.   Robert Pear and Jackie Calmes, "Cost Concerns as Obama Pushes Health Issue," *New York Times,* June 16, 2009.

63.   Steve May, *The Debate over Corporate Social Responsibility* (Oxford: Oxford University Press, 2007); André Habisch, *Corporate Social Responsibility across Europe* (Berlin: Springer, 2005).

64. Milton Friedman, "The Social Responsibility of Business Is to Increase Its Profits," *New York Times Magazine,* September 13, 1970.

65. For an early account of the ways a clumsily regulated Web would fail to foster democratic values if left to the tumult of market forces, see Andrew Chin, "Making the World Wide Web Safe for Democracy: A Medium-Specific First Amendment Analysis," *Hastings Communications and Entertainment Law Journal (Comm/Ent)* 19 (1996): 309.

66. "Regulate Google?" *Brian Lehrer Show,* WNYC TV, July 8, 2009, www .wnyc.org.

67. Jessica Guynn, "Google Facing Challenges to Its Bold Ambitions in Europe," *Los Angeles Times,* February 25, 2010; Adam Liptak, "When American and European Ideas of Privacy Collide," *New York Times,* February 26, 2010; Milton Mueller, "There's More to the Google-Italy Case Than Meets the Eye," Internet Governance Project, February 25, 2010, http://blog.internetgovernance. org; Struan Robertson, "Google Convictions Reveal Two Flaws in EU Law, Not Just Italian Law," Out-Law.com, March 3, 2010, www.out-law.com; Elisabetta Povoledo, "Italian Judge Cites Profit as Justifying a Google Conviction," *New York Times,* April 12, 2010.

68. *Candidates@Google: Barack Obama (Mountainview, California: Google, 2007),* www.youtube.com; Barack Obama, *The Audacity of Hope: Thoughts on Reclaiming the American Dream* (New York: Crown Publishers, 2006).

69. Soghoian, "Why Obama Should Ditch YouTube"; Soghoian, "White House Exempts YouTube"; Chris Soghoian, "White House Acts to Limit YouTube Cookie Tracking," Surveillance State—CNET News, January 23, 2009, http:// news.cnet.com; Chris Soghoian, "Is the White House Changing Its YouTube Tune?" Surveillance State—CNET News, March 2, 2009, http://news.cnet.com.

70. Siva Vaidhyanathan, "Google Net Neutrality Stance Gives 'Net's Future to Corporations," MSNBC.com, August 10, 2010.

71. See Joseph Nye, *The Paradox of American Power: Why the World's Only Superpower Can't Go It Alone* (Oxford: Oxford University Press, 2002); Joseph Nye, *Soft Power: The Means to Success in World Politics* (New York: PublicAffairs, 2004).

CHAPTER 2. GOOGLE'S WAYS AND MEANS

1. Louis C.K. and Conan O'Brien, "Everything's Amazing, Nobody's Happy," *Late Night with Conan O'Brien,* NBC TV, February 19, 2009, available at www.youtube.com.

2. Arthur C. Clarke, *3001: The Final Odyssey,* quoted in Ray Kurzweil, *The Singularity Is Near: When Humans Transcend Biology* (New York: Viking, 2005), 4.

3. Marissa Mayer, *Google I/O '08 Keynote Address,* June 5, 2008, available at www.youtube.com.

4. Ibid.

5. Ibid.

6. John Battelle, *The Search: How Google and Its Rivals Rewrote the Rules of Business and Transformed Our Culture* (New York: Portfolio, 2005).

7. Otis Port and Neil Gross, "A Search Engine Gets a Search Engine," *Business Week,* September 28, 1998.

8. Marshall Robin, "Don't Take It Out on Your PC," *Press* (Christchurch, New Zealand), December 15, 1998.

9. Sam Vincent Meddis, "Find a Career, Laugh a Lot, or Pay a Visit to the E-Quarium," *USA Today,* December 16, 1998.

10. Max Frankel, "The Way We Live Now," *New York Times,* November 21, 1999.

11. Peter H. Lewis, "Searching for Less, Not More," *New York Times,* September 30, 1999.

12. Ibid.

13. Chris Anderson, *Free: The Future of a Radical Price* (New York: Hyperion, 2009).

14. Jeff Jarvis, *What Would Google Do?* (New York: Collins Business, 2009). Google's astounding record as a commercial entity has understandably garnered almost daily attention on business pages in recent years. Its stock price soared in value after its initial offering in 2004, and in the autumn of 2007 it peaked at more than $600 per share. Its annual revenue has more than quadrupled since the initial public offering. Revenues—largely from advertising placements—were $3.87 billion in the second quarter of 2007, up 58 percent from the same quarter in 2006. Since its initial public offering, Google has aggressively acquired other firms, like the video-hosting site YouTube and the Internet advertising company DoubleClick. In 2009 the core service of Google—its Web search engine—handled more than 70 percent of the Web search business in the United States and more than 90 percent in much of Europe, and grew at impressive rates elsewhere around the world.

15. Thorsten Joachims et al., "Accurately Interpreting Clickthrough Data as Implicit Feedback," *Proceedings of the 28th Annual International ACM SIGIR Conference on Research and Development in Information Retrieval* (Salvador, Brazil: ACM, 2005), 154–61.

16. B. J. Jansen and U. Pooch, "A Review of Web Searching Studies and a Framework for Future Research," *Journal of the American Society for Information Science and Technology* 52, no. 3 (2001): 235–46; Amanda Spink and Bernard J. Jansen, *Web Search: Public Searching on the Web* (Dordrecht: Kluwer Academic Publishers, 2004); Caroline M. Eastman and Bernard J. Jansen, "Coverage,

Relevance, and Ranking: The Impact of Query Operators on Web Search Engine Results," *ACM Transactions on Information Systems* 21, no. 4 (2003): 383–411; Eszter Hargittai, "The Social, Political, Economic, and Cultural Dimensions of Search Engines: An Introduction," *Journal of Computer-Mediated Communication* 12, no. 3 (2007): 767–77.

17.   Bing Pan et al., "In Google We Trust: Users' Decisions on Rank, Position, and Relevance," *Journal of Computer-Mediated Communication* 12, no. 3 (2007): 801–23.

18.   Bernard J. Jansen and Amanda Spink, "How Are We Searching the World Wide Web? A Comparison of Nine Search Engine Transaction Logs," *Information Processing and Management* 42, no. 1 (January 2006): 248–63.

19.   Deborah Fallows, *Search Engine Users*, January 23, 2005, Pew Research Center and American Life Project, www.pewinternet.org.

20.   S. Fortunato et al., "Topical Interests and the Mitigation of Search Engine Bias," *Proceedings of the National Academy of Sciences of the United States of America* 103, no. 34 (August 22, 2006): 12684–89.

21.   Susan L Gerhart, "Do Web Search Engines Suppress Controversy?" *First Monday* 9, no. 1 (January 5, 2004), http://firstmonday.org.

22.   William James, *Pragmatism* (Buffalo, NY: Prometheus, 1991); Charles Peirce, *Charles S. Peirce: The Essential Writings* (Amherst, NY: Prometheus Books, 1998); Charles S. Peirce and Peirce Edition Project, *The Essential Peirce: Selected Philosophical Writings* (Bloomington: Indiana University Press, 1992); Richard Rorty, *Contingency, Irony, and Solidarity* (Cambridge: Cambridge University Press, 1989).

23.   Peirce, *Charles S. Peirce.*

24.   William James, *Pragmatism and Other Writings* (New York: Penguin Books, 2000), 88–89.

25.   Rorty, *Contingency, Irony, and Solidarity.*

26.   Lucas D. Introna and Helen Nissenbaum, "Shaping the Web: Why the Politics of Search Engines Matters," *Information Society* 16, no. 3 (2000): 169.

27.   Eric Goldman, "Search Engine Bias and the Demise of Search Engine Utopianism," *SSRN eLibrary*, March 29, 2006, http://papers.ssrn.com.

28.   Ibid.

29.   Judit Bar-Ilan, "What Do We Know about Links and Linking? A Framework for Studying Links in Academic Environments," *Information Processing and Management* 41, no. 4 (July 2005): 973–86.

30.   Joseph Reagle, "In Good Faith: Wikipedia Collaboration and the Pursuit of the Universal Encyclopedia," Joseph Reagele, 2008, http://reagle.org/joseph/blog; Joseph M. Reagle, "Do as I Do: Authorial Leadership in Wikipedia," *Proceedings of the 2007 International Symposium on Wikis* (Montreal: ACM, 2007), 143–56.

31. Andrew Famiglietti, "Wikipedia and Search: Some Quick Numbers," Hackers, Cyborgs, and Wikipedians, blog, March 4, 2009, http://blogs.bgsu.edu/afamigl.

32. Nicholas Carr, "All Hail the Information Triumvirate!" Rough Type: Nicholas Carr's Blog, January 23, 2009, www.roughtype.com.

33. See Siva Vaidhyanathan, "The Digital Wisdom of Richard Sennett," *Chronicle of Higher Education*, May 23, 2008. If you skim the past ten years or so of *Wired* magazine in search of the names of the intellectuals who have influenced digital culture, you would encounter many notables: Sherry Turkle, Mark Granovetter, Lawrence Lessig, Clay Shirky, Pamela Samuelson, and, of course, the patron saint of digital media theory, Marshall McLuhan. One name you would not encounter in a search of the *Wired* archives is Richard Sennett. Usually characterized as a public sociologist of the analog world, Sennett has been slighted as a theorist of things digital. Wikipedia, which tends to wax enthusiastic about the new and digital, offers Sennett only 489 words. In contrast, Granovetter, a Stanford sociologist of social networks with a much smaller following than Sennett's among those who read their news and commentary on paper, has 812 words in his Wikipedia profile. Lessig has 3,127 words in his.

34. Frank A. Pasquale, *Rankings, Reductionism, and Responsibility,* Seton Hall Public Law Research Paper No. 888327, Seton Hall University, 2006.

35. Judit Bar-Ilan, "Web Links and Search Engine Ranking: The Case of Google and the Query 'Jew'," *Journal of the American Society for Information Science and Technology* 57, no. 12 (2006): 1581.

36. "Google: An Explanation of Our Search Results," Google.com, www.google.com/explanation.html, accessed August 12, 2010.

37. "ADL Praises Google for Responding to Concerns about Rankings of Hate Sites," press release, Anti-Defamation League, April 22, 2004, www.adl.org.

38. Judit Bar-Ilan, "Google Bombing from a Time Perspective," *Journal of Computer-Mediated Communication* 12, no. 3 (2007), http://jcmc.indiana.edu.

39. Goldman, "Search Engine Bias."

40. John Paczkowski, "Google and the Evolution of Search, I: Human Evaluators," *Digital Daily,* June 3, 2009, http://digitaldaily.allthingsd.com.

41. Randall E. Stross, *Planet Google: One Company's Audacious Plan to Organize Everything We Know* (New York: Free Press, 2008).

42. Steven Shapin, *The Scientific Life: A Moral History of a Late Modern Vocation* (Chicago: University of Chicago Press, 2008).

43. Thorstein Veblen, *The Engineers and the Price System* (New Brunswick, NJ: Transaction Books, 1983).

44. Walter Kirn, "Life, Liberty and the Pursuit of Aptitude," *New York Times Magazine,* July 5, 2009.

45.   Kevin J. Delaney, "Google Adjusts Hiring Process as Needs Grow," *Wall Street Journal,* October 23, 2006.

46.   Nicholas Lemann, *The Big Test: The Secret History of the American Meritocracy* (New York: Farrar Straus and Giroux, 1999).

47.   Neil Postman, *Technopoly: The Surrender of Culture to Technology* (New York: Knopf, 1992).

48.   Langdon Winner, *Autonomous Technology: Technics-out-of-Control as a Theme in Political Thought* (Cambridge, MA: MIT Press, 1980).

49.   Fred Turner, *From Counterculture to Cyberculture: Stewart Brand, the Whole Earth Network, and the Rise of Digital Utopianism* (Chicago: University of Chicago Press, 2006).

50.   Fred Turner, "Burning Man at Google: A Cultural Infrastructure for New Media Production," *New Media Society* 11, nos. 1–2 (2009): 73–94.

51.   Yochai Benkler, *The Wealth of Networks: How Social Production Transforms Markets and Freedom* (New Haven, CT: Yale University Press, 2006).

52.   Dalton Conley, *Elsewhere, U.S.A.* (New York: Pantheon Books, 2009).

53.   Siva Vaidhyanathan, "Interview with Vint Cerf of Google," The Googlization of Everything, blog, January 2, 2009, www.googlizationofe verything.com.

54.   Mayer, *Google I/O '08 Keynote Address.*

55.   Joe Nocera, "On Day Care, Google Makes a Rare Fumble," *New York Times,* July 5, 2008.

56.   "Corporate Information—Our Philosophy," Google.com, www .google.com/corporate/tenthings.html, accessed August 12, 2010.

57.   "Does Google Violate Its 'Don't Be Evil' Motto?" *Intelligence Squared,* National Public Radio, November 26, 2008, available at www.npr.org.

58.   See, for example, Martin Wachs, *Curbing Gridlock: Peak-Period Fees to Relieve Traffic Congestion* (Washington, DC: National Academies Press, 1994); Bo Carlberg, Ola Samuelsson, and Lars Hjalmar Lindholm, "Atenolol in Hypertension: Is It a Wise Choice?" *Lancet* 364, no. 9446 (2004): 1684–89.

59.   Gordon E. Moore, "Cramming More Components onto Integrated Circuits," *Electronics* 38, no. 8 (1965). For a critical analysis of Moore's law, see Ilkka Tuomi, "The Lives and Death of Moore's Law," *First Monday* 7, no. 11 (November 2002), http://firstmonday.org.

60.   Timothy H. Dixon et al., "Space Geodesy: Subsidence and Flooding in New Orleans," *Nature* 441, no. 7093 (2006). Also see Ivor van Heerden, *The Storm: What Went Wrong and Why during Hurricane Katrina: The Inside Story from One Louisiana Scientist,* ed. Mike Bryan (New York: Viking, 2006).

61.   For an excellent historical account of the follies of missile defense and the ideologies and corruptions that have kept the dream alive through two decades

and billions of dollars, see Frances FitzGerald, *Way Out There in the Blue: Reagan, Star Wars, and the End of the Cold War* (New York: Simon & Schuster, 2000).

62.   Reinhold Niebuhr, *The Irony of American History* (Chicago: University of Chicago Press, 2008), 160.

63.   "Retraction: Ileal-Lymphoid-Nodular Hyperplasia, Non-specific Colitis, and Pervasive Developmental Disorder in Children," *Lancet* 375, no. 9713 (February 6, 2010): 445; Kate Kelland, "Lancet Retracts Paper Linking Vaccine to Autism," *Washington Post*, February 3, 2010.

64.   Kugel Allison, "Jenny McCarthy on Healing Her Son's Autism and Discovering Her Life's Mission," PR.Com, October 9, 2007, www.pr.com/article/1076.

65.   When I conducted a search on Google for "Autism vaccinations" on October 26, 2009, in Charlottesville, Virginia, the top two sites listed posited a connection between vaccination and autism. The third result, from the U.S. Centers for Disease Control, authoritatively denied the link. Most of the rest of the results were journalistic accounts of the so-called debate over vaccinations.

66.   Frank Ahrens, "2002's News, Yesterday's Sell-Off," *Washington Post*, September 9, 2008.

67.   Tom Petruno, "Tribune, Google Trade Blame in United Airlines Stock Fiasco," *Los Angeles Times*, September 9, 2008.

68.   Amy Fry, "Information Is Power—Even When it's Wrong," ACRLog, blog, September 11, 2008, http://acrlog.org.

69.   John Letzing, "Tribune Blames Google for Damaging News Story," Marketwatch.com, September 10, 2008.

70.   Cass Sunstein, *Going to Extremes: How Like Minds Unite and Divide* (Oxford: Oxford University Press, 2009).

71.   For a long time I was a Google evangelist. Back in 1999 and 2000 I must have told more than a hundred people, including my closest friends and family, that Google was the best possible way to find stuff on the Web. When I first encountered Google in early 1999, I was teaching history at Wesleyan University. Mostly, I was scrambling to finish my dissertation—which became my first book. Because most of my research drew on sources available on microfilm, search engines had not yet become an integral part of my professional life. I was aware of the techno-utopian conversations about electronic archives and the global delivery of knowledge, but I didn't think very hard about them. I had a book to write and sell. The Web, for me, was a platform for self-promotion. And existing search engines, like Yahoo, were not helping in that effort.

Since about 1995 I had been using Yahoo and AltaVista for my Web navigation. I had a brief and passionate involvement with a much better and faster Web search service, Northern Light, until, facing a revenue shortage, it became a specialized portal for corporate clients (and remains so today). I first learned about Google from an e-mail list called Red Rock Eater, written and edited by Phil Agre, a professor of information studies at UCLA. Like many Web geeks of the late 1990s, I read Agre's newsletter religiously. If he liked Google, chances were good that I would as well.

Unlike everything else on the Web at that time, Google lacked clutter. It was simple, fast, and effective. Before Google essentially solved the problem of managing and filtering the Web for us, we relied on the pages we liked and trusted to provide links to other pages we might like and trust. But Google was aggregating all of that linking and clicking, making it a general process of ranking and linking. It was brilliant.

And then, within hours of using Google for the first time, I started thinking through the consequences of Google becoming the institution that governs the Web. I had no idea how quickly that notion would grow into an obsession.

While composing this book I often used my blog, Googlization of Everything, to solicit feedback and comments from Web users. Back in July 2008 I posted a simple query: "Do you remember the first time you used Google? When was it? How did you hear about Google? What was your first impression?" The response was overwhelming: 216 people posted their stories to my blog, and 36 more posted comments to BoingBoing, the most popular blog in the world, after it linked to my query.

From the website developer and critic Waldo Jaquith:

It's difficult to properly emphasize how truly terrible search engines were in 1998. AltaVista and HotBot were as good as it got, and that's saying very little. Results were basically sorted randomly. Choosing a search engine was really based on faith more than anything else. . . . And then along came Google.

From the author Clay Shirky:

Late 90s—I'd been the CTO of a web shop in Manhattan, and we'd always spend a lot of time with new clients on the "nav bar issue"—what was the best set of links to put in the home page navigation? . . . we spent a *lot* of time studying Yahoo's front-page taxonomy—the whole Web, broken down into 14 top-level categories. And then I saw Google, which had no taxonomy at all. just search. I . . . switched immediately, as many of us did in those days, but I didn't realize what a big deal it was until 2000. I was at a geek dinner of two dozen people, hosted by Tim O'Reilly, on a completely different subject. . . . At that dinner, Tim said "I know this doesn't have anything to do with the matter at hand, but out of curiosity, how many people here use Google?" Every hand went up.

From library consultant Karen Coyle:

I was chatting with the brother of one of the Google founders. He told me that his brother was working on a new search engine that would be better than anything ever seen before. I tried to argue that it would still be limited by the reality of the full-text search. I probably looked at Google when it was first made available, and I was pretty un-impressed. Just more keyword searching. Today I use it constantly, but I'm very aware of the fact that it works quite well for nouns and proper nouns (people, companies, named things), and less well for concepts. . . . . I think of it as a giant phone book for the Internet, not as a classification of knowledge.

Many of the people who responded to my query were information or Web professionals. They were certainly the earliest to embrace Google and recognize its value. They quickly spread the word to their immediate friends and family. From there, it grew to span the world within five years. We were so thrilled to find so much, so easily, that we hardly stopped to ask questions. We became true believers.

CHAPTER 3. THE GOOGLIZATION OF US

1. Lev Grossman, "Time's Person of the Year: You," *Time,* December 13, 2006.

2. See Robert L. Mitchell, "What Google Knows about You," *Computer World,* May 11, 2009.

3. Michael Zimmer, "Privacy on Planet Google: Using the Theory of Contextual Integrity to Clarify the Privacy Threats of Google's Quest for the Perfect Search Engine," *Journal of Business and Technology Law* 3 (2008): 109.

4. "Privacy Policy: Google Privacy Center," Google.com, www.google.com/privacypolicy.html, accessed March 11, 2009.

5. Paul Ohm, "Broken Promises of Privacy: Responding to the Surprising Failure of Anonymization," *SSRN eLibrary,* August 13, 2009, http://papers.ssrn.com.

6. "Privacy Policy," Google.com. March 11, 2009.

7. Arshad Mohammed, "Google Refuses Demand for Search Information," *Washington Post,* January 20, 2006.

8. *Charlie Rose Show,* 2009, available at http://video.google.com.

9. Richard Thaler and Cass Sunstein, *Nudge: Improving Decisions about Health, Wealth, and Happiness* (New Haven, CT: Yale University Press, 2008), 109.

10. Ibid., 3.

11. *Google Search Privacy: Plain and Simple,* 2007, www.youtube.com.

12. Louise Story and Brad Stone, "Facebook Retreats on On-Line Tracking," *New York Times,* November 30, 2007.

13. Warren St. John, "When Information Becomes T.M.I.," *New York Times,* September 10, 2006.

14.   Jenna Wortham, "Facebook Glitch Brings New Privacy Worries," *New York Times*, May 5, 2010; Laura M. Holson, "Tell-All Generation Learns to Keep Things Offline," *New York Times*, May 8, 2010.

15.   Emily Nussbaum, "Say Everything: Kids, the Internet, and the End of Privacy: The Greatest Generation Gap since Rock and Roll," *New York*, February 12, 2007.

16   dana boyd and Eszter Hargittai, "Facebook Privacy Settings: Who Cares?" *First Monday* 15, no. 8 (2010), www.uic.edu/htbin/cgiwrap/bin/ojs/index.php/fm/article/view/3086/2589.

16.   Helen Nissenbaum, *Privacy in Context: Technology, Policy, and the Integrity of Social Life* (Stanford, CA: Stanford Law Books, 2010).

17.   Michael Zimmer, "The Quest for the Perfect Search Engine: Values, Technical Design, and the Flow of Personal Information in Spheres of Mobility," PhD diss., New York University, 2007.

18.   I am basing the notion of privacy interfaces on the work of the foremost philosopher of privacy and ethics in online environments, Helen Nissenbaum. See her most influential work on the subject, "Privacy as Contextual Integrity," *Washington Law Review* 79, no. 1 (2004): 101–39. Also see Nissenbaum, *Privacy in Context: Technology, Policy, and the Integrity of Social Life* (Stanford, CA: Stanford Law Books, 2010).

19.   Helen Nissenbaum, "Protecting Privacy in an Information Age: The Problem of Privacy in Public," *Law and Philosophy* 17, no. 5 (1998): 559–96.

20.   Daniel Solove, *The Future of Reputation: Gossip, Rumor, and Privacy on the Internet* (New Haven, CT: Yale University Press, 2007). Solove's earlier book, *The Digital Person: Technology and Privacy in the Information Age*, set the standard for explaining what is at stake in online data collection and analysis. In it, Solove walks us through the construction of "digital dossiers" in the "person to firm" and "person to state" interfaces and outlines the potentials for abuse. *The Digital Person* is significant because it came out long enough after September 11, 2001, to take into account the U.S. government's notorious Total Information Awareness program and other efforts at behavioral profiling. It supplemented the best previous book of social and media theory applied to massive digital data collection and private-sector surveillance, Oscar Gandy's *The Panoptic Sort*. But 2004 was a long time ago in matters of government surveillance. Solove could not have predicted the revelation in 2005 that the NSA was monitoring American phone calls through an illegal secret program that relied on the cooperation of the major telecommunication companies.

21.   James Rule, *Privacy in Peril* (Oxford: Oxford University Press, 2007).

22.   James Rule, *Private Lives and Public Surveillance: Social Control in the Computer Age* (New York: Schocken Books, 1974).

23. Ibid.

24. In May 2008, Google announced it would deploy special tricycles to extend Street View to roads and alleys in which cars would have trouble navigating. The tricycle experiment began in Italy but was soon used throughout Europe. See Google, "Trike with a View," Press Centre, May 18, 2009, www.google.co.uk/intl/en/press/pressrel/20090518_street_view_trike .html.

25. Elinor Mills, "Are Google's Moves Creeping You Out?" *CNET News,* June 12, 2007.

26. Siva Vaidhyanathan, "Ever Use Google Street View for Something Important?" Googlizationofeverything, blog, March 29, 2009, www.googliza tionofeverything.com.

27. Ibid.

28. Cory Doctorow, *Little Brother* (New York: Tor Teen, 2008).

29. Cory Doctorow, quoted in Vaidhyanathan, "Ever Use Google Street View?"

30. Jemima Kiss, "Google Wins Street View Privacy Case," *Guardian,* February 19, 2009.

31. "Google Eyes Canada Rollout of Discreet Street View," Reuters, September 24, 2007, http://uk.reuters.com; "Google's Street View Blurred by Canadian Privacy Concerns," CanWest News Service, www.canada.com.

32. Tamsyn Burgmann, "Google to Blur Faces in Canadian Street View," *Star* (Toronto), April 5, 2009. One Conservative member of Parliament, Pierre Poilievre of Ontario, switched positions on Street View. At first he questioned the propriety and utility of the service. Less than a week later he wrote an op-ed piece advocating the service and complaining that Canadian law seemed to impede it. See Michael Geist, "Poilievre Changes His Tune on Privacy and Google Street View," Michael Geist, April 2, 2009, www.michaelgeist.ca/content/ view/3797/125/. See also Vito Pilieci, "MP wants Google Boss to Explain Street Cameras," *Ottawa Citizen,* March 30, 2009; Pierre Poilievre, "Pierre: Updating the Law to Deal with Google," *National Post,* April 2, 2009.

33. Kevin J. O'Brien, "Google Threatened with Sanctions over Photo Mapping Service in Germany," *New York Times,* May 20, 2009.

34. "Hamburg Threatens Google Street View Ban," *Local: Germany's News in English,* May 18, 2009, www.thelocal.de.

35. Kevin J. O'Brien, "New Questions over Google's Street View in Germany," *New York Times,* April 29, 2010.

36. Mike Harvey, "Greece Bans Google Street View," *TimesOnline,* May 13, 2009, http://technology.timesonline.co.uk.

37. "Japanese Group Asks Google to Stop Map Service," Reuters, December 19, 2008.

38. James, "More Sensational News from Japan about the Dangers of Google Street View," *Japan Probe,* January 11, 2009.

39. Chris Salzberg and Higuchi Osamu, "Japan: Letter to Google about Street View," Global Voices Online, August 8, 2008, http://globalvoicesonline.org.

40. Stephen Kamizura, "Google Forced to Retake All Street View Images in Japan," *DailyTech,* May 18, 2009, www.dailytech.com; "Google to Reshoot Street Views of Japanese Cities," *Japan Today,* May 14, 2009, www.japantoday.com.

41. Jo Adetunji, "Google Hit by Privacy Protests over Its Tour of British Cities," *Guardian,* March 21, 2009.

42. Alex Chitu, "Google's Market Share in Your Country," Google Operating System: Unofficial News and Tips about Google, blog, March 13, 2009, http://googlesystem.blogspot.com.

43. Jane Merrick, "Google Street View Forced to Remove Images," *Independent,* March 22, 2009.

44. Ibid.; Urmee Khan, "Google Removes Picture of Naked Child from Street View," *Daily Telegraph,* March 22, 2009; "Public Urged to Report Google Street View Fears," *Independent,* March 21, 2009.

45. Andy Dolan and Eddie Wrenn, "Watch Out Broughton! Street View Fans Plan to Descend on 'Privacy' Village for Photo Fest," *Daily Mail,* April 4, 2009.

46. Khan, "Google Removes Picture."

47. Paul Harris, "Watchdog Calls for Tighter Google Privacy Controls," *Guardian,* April 20, 2010.

48. Peter Barron, personal communication, April 21, 2009.

49. Jeffrey Rosen, *The Naked Crowd: Reclaiming Security and Freedom in an Anxious Age* (New York: Random House, 2004); B. Yesil, "Watching Ourselves," *Cultural Studies* 20, no. 4 (2006): 400–416.

50. "Britain Is 'Surveillance Society,' " BBC News, November 2, 2006, http://news.bbc.co.uk.

51. "Report Says CCTV Is Overrated," *Guardian,* June 28, 2002; Alan Travis, "Police and CCTV: Pictures Too Poor, Cameras in Wrong Place," *Guardian,* October 20, 2007.

52. "Britain Is 'Surveillance Society.' "

53. Sarah Lyall, "Britons Weary of Surveillance in Minor Cases," *New York Times,* October 25, 2009.

54. Eric Schmidt, presentation at Princeton Colloquium on Public and International Affairs, 2009, video available at www.youtube.com.

55. Amartya Sen, *Development as Freedom* (Oxford: Oxford University Press, 2001); Amartya Sen, *Identity and Violence: The Illusion Of Destiny* (New York: W. W. Norton, 2007).

56. Herbert Schiller, *Communication and Cultural Domination* (White Plains, N.Y.: M.E. Sharpe, 1976). John Tomlinson, *Cultural Imperialism: A Critical Introduction* (Baltimore, MD: Johns Hopkins University Press, 1991).

57. Steven Feld, "A Sweet Lullaby for World Music," *Public Culture* 12, no. 1 (January 1, 2000): 145–71.

58. David Rothkopf, "Praise of Cultural Imperialism?" *Foreign Policy*, no. 107 (1997): 38–53.

59. Tyler Cowen, *Creative Destruction* (Princeton, NJ: Princeton University Press, 2002).

60. Siva Vaidhyanathan, "Remote Control: The Rise of Electronic Cultural Policy," *Annals of the American Academy of Political and Social Science* 597 (January 2005): 122–33; Siva Vaidhyanathan, *The Anarchist in the Library: How the Clash between Freedom and Control Is Hacking the Real World and Crashing the System* (New York: Basic Books, 2004).

61. Edward Herman and Robert McChesney, *The Global Media: The New Missionaries of Corporate Capitalism* (London: Continuum, 2001).

62. John Thompson, *Ideology and Modern Culture: Critical Social Theory in the Era of Mass Communication* (Stanford, CA: Stanford University Press, 1990).

63. Peter Barron, personal communication, April 21, 2009.

64. Michel Foucault, *Discipline and Punish: The Birth of the Prison* (New York: Pantheon Books, 1977).

65. See, for example, Oscar H. Gandy, *The Panoptic Sort: A Political Economy of Personal Information* (Boulder, CO: Westview Press, 1993); David Lyon, *Theorizing Surveillance: The Panopticon and Beyond* (Cullompton, U.K.: Willan Publishing, 2006); Satu Repo and Canadian Centre for Policy Alternatives, *Teacher Surveillance: The New Panopticon* (Ottawa: Canadian Centre for Policy Alternatives, 2005); Mark Andrejevic, *iSpy: Surveillance and Power in the Interactive Era* (Lawrence: University Press of Kansas, 2007). For a refreshing approach to studying surveillance without the Panopticon model, see Kevin Haggerty, "Tear Down the Walls: On Demolishing the Panopticon," in Lyon, *Theorizing Surveillance*.

66. B. Brower, review of Sonia Combe, *Une société sous surveillance: Les intellectuels et la Stasi*, in *Totalitarian Movements and Political Religions* 2 (2001): 88–92; Gary Bruce, "The Prelude to Nationwide Surveillance in East Germany: Stasi Operations and Threat Perceptions, 1945–1953," *Journal of Cold War Studies* 5, no. 2 (May 1, 2003): 3–31; Sonia Combe, *Une société sous surveillance: Les intellectuels et la Stasi* (Paris: Albin Michel, 1999).

67. Chris Anderson, *The Long Tail: Why the Future of Business Is Selling Less of More* (New York: Hyperion, 2006).

68. Eric Lichtblau, *Bush's Law: The Remaking of American Justice* (New York: Pantheon Books, 2008).

CHAPTER 4. THE GOOGLIZATION OF THE WORLD

1. Amit Agarwal, "French Town Changing Name to Improve Ranks in Google," Digital Inspiration, February 25, 2009, www.labnol.org; Mark Milian, "French Town Eu Considers Changing Name for Web Search Visibility," *Los Angeles Times*, February 25, 2009.

2. Rachel Donadio, "Larger Threat Is Seen in Google Case," *New York Times*, February 25, 2010; Jessica Guynn, "Google Facing Challenges to Its Bold Ambitions in Europe," *Los Angeles Times*, February 25, 2010.

3. Nazila Fathi, "Iran Disrupts Internet Service ahead of Protests," *New York Times*, February 11, 2010.

4. Farhad Manjoo, "How the Internet Helps Iran Silence Activists," *Slate*, June 25, 2009; Miguel Helft and John Markoff, "Google, Citing Cyber Attack, Threatens to Exit China," *New York Times*, January 13, 2010.

5. John Ribeiro, "Google Placates India, China with Different Map Versions," *PC World*, October 23, 2009.

6. Miguel Helft and David Barboza, "Google Shuts China Site in Dispute over Censorship," *New York Times*, March 22, 2010.

7. Miguel Helft and David Barboza, "Google's Plan to Turn Its Back on China Has Risks," *New York Times*, March 23, 2010; John Markoff, "Cyberattack on Google Said to Hit Password System," *New York Times*, April 19, 2010; John Markoff and Ashlee Vance, "Software Firms Fear Hackers Who Leave No Trace," *New York Times*, January 20, 2010.

8. Harry Lewis, "Does Google Violate Its 'Don't Be Evil' Motto?" *Intelligence Squared*, National Public Radio, November 26, 2008, www.npr.org.

9. Esther Dyson, "Does Google Violate Its 'Don't Be Evil' Motto?"

10. Andrew Shapiro, *The Control Revolution: How the Internet Is Putting Individuals in Charge and Changing the World We Know* (New York: PublicAffairs, 1999), 6–7. Also see Gladys Ganley, *Unglued Empire: The Soviet Experience with Communications Technologies* (Norwood, NJ: Ablex, 1996).

11. Richard Oliver, *What Is Transparency?* (New York: McGraw-Hill, 2004), 27.

12. Marshall McLuhan, *The Gutenberg Galaxy: The Making of Typographic Man* (Toronto: University of Toronto Press, 1962); Marshall McLuhan, *Understanding Media: The Extensions of Man* (New York: Routledge, 2008); Elizabeth Eisenstein, *The Printing Press as an Agent of Change: Communications and Cultural Transformations in Early Modern Europe* (Cambridge: Cambridge University Press, 1979); Elizabeth L. Eisenstein, "An Unacknowledged Revolution Revisited," *American Historical Review* 107, no. 1 (February 2002): 87–105; Bernard Bailyn, *The Ideological Origins of the American Revolution*, enlarged ed. (Cambridge, MA: Belknap Press of Harvard University Press, 1992).

13.   Gordon Wood, *The Radicalism of the American Revolution* (New York: Knopf, 1992); Adrian Johns, "How to Acknowledge a Revolution," *American Historical Review* 107, no. 1 (February 2002): 106–25; Adrian Johns, *The Nature of the Book: Print and Knowledge in the Making* (Chicago: University of Chicago Press, 1998).

14.   Tony Judt, *Postwar: A History of Europe since 1945* (New York: Penguin, 2005), 585–605.

15.   Ibid., 628–29. Also see Brian Hanrahan, "How Tiananmen Shook Europe," BBC News, June 5, 2009, http://news.bbc.co.uk.

16.   Siva Vaidhyanathan, "Introduction: Rewiring the 'Nation': The Place of Technology in American Studies," *American Quarterly* 58, no. 3 (September 2006): 555–67; Siva Vaidhyanathan, *The Anarchist in the Library: How the Clash between Freedom and Control Is Hacking the Real World and Crashing the System* (New York: Basic Books, 2004).

17.   Robert Darnton, "Censorship, a Comparative View: France, 1789—East Germany, 1989," *Representations* 49 (Winter 1995): 40. See also Robert Darnton, *The Literary Underground of the Old Regime* (Cambridge, MA: Harvard University Press, 1982); Robert Darnton, *The Forbidden Best-Sellers of Pre-revolutionary France* (New York: W.W. Norton, 1995); Vaidhyanathan, *The Anarchist in the Library*.

18.   Jim Yardley, "Chinese Nationalism Fuels Tibet Crackdown," *New York Times*, March 31, 2008; Edward Wong, "China Admits Building Flaws in Quake," *New York Times*, September 5, 2008; Austin Ramzy, "Failed Government Policies Sparked Tibet Riots," *Time*, May 26, 2009.

19.   "Dissent in China: A Stab at Reform," *Economist*, June 4, 2009; John Pomfret, "After Tiananmen, How Did the Communists Stay in Power?" *Washington Post*, June 7, 2009; Susan Shirk, *China: Fragile Superpower* (Oxford: Oxford University Press, 2007); David Shambaugh, *China's Communist Party: Atrophy and Adaptation* (Berkeley: University of California Press, 2009).

20.   "Global Internet Freedom Consortium," 2008, www.internetfreedom.org/Background, accessed August 13, 2010.

21.   Ben Einhorn and Bruce Elgin, "The Great Firewall of China," *Business-Week*, January 12, 2006; Howard W. French, "Great Firewall of China Faces Online Rebels," *New York Times*, February 4, 2008.

22.   Aldous Huxley, *Brave New World* (London: Chatto & Windus, 1932); George Orwell, *Nineteen Eighty-Four* (Boston: Houghton Mifflin Harcourt, 2008); Neil Postman, *Amusing Ourselves to Death: Public Discourse in the Age of Show Business* (New York: Penguin, 2006).

23.   Kristen Farrell, "Big Mamas Are Watching: China's Censorship of the Internet and the Strain on Freedom of Expression," *Michigan State Journal of International Law* 15 (2007): 577; Rebecca MacKinnon, "Asia's Fight for Web Rights,"

Far Eastern Economic Review 171, no. 3 (2008): 49; Shaojung Sharon Wang and Junhao Hong, "Discourse behind the Forbidden Realm: Internet Surveillance and Its Implications on China's Blogosphere," *Telematics and Informatics* 27, no. 1 (February 2010): 67–78; K. O'Hara, "'Let a Hundred Flowers Bloom, a Hundred Schools of Thought Contend': Web Engineering in the Chinese Context," in *China's Information and Communications Technology Revolution: Social Changes and State Responses*, ECS E-Prints Repository, 2009, http://eprints.ecs.soton.ac.uk/17189/.

24.   J. Zittrain and B. Edelman, "Internet Filtering in China," *IEEE Internet Computing* 7, no. 2 (2003): 70–77; Joel Schectman, "Countering China's Internet Censors," *BusinessWeek*, June 3, 2009; Abigail Cutler, "Penetrating the Great Firewall: Interview with James Fallows," *Atlantic*, February 19, 2008; James Fallows, "'The Connection Has Been Reset,'" *Atlantic*, March 2008; Rebecca MacKinnon, "Flatter World and Thicker Walls? Blogs, Censorship and Civic Discourse in China," *Public Choice* 134, no. 1 (January 1, 2008): 31–46; "The Party, the People and the Power of Cyber-talk," *Economist*, April 29, 2006, 27–30.

25.   "Global Internet Freedom Consortium."

26.   Fallows, "'The Connection Has Been Reset.'"

27.   "The Party, the People and the Power of Cyber-talk."

28.   William A. Cohn, "Yahoo's China Defense: How Western Companies Are Helping China to Filter Democracy," *New Presence* 10, no. 2 (2007): 30–33.

29.   Neil Haddow and G. Elijah Dann, "Just Doing Business or Doing Just Business: Google, Microsoft, Yahoo! and the Business of Censoring China's Internet," *Journal of Business Ethics* 79, no. 3 (2008): 219–34.

30.   William Thatcher Dowell, "The Internet, Censorship, and China," *Georgetown Journal of International Affairs* 7 (Summer/Fall 2006): 111; Amnesty International, *Undermining Freedom of Expression in China: The Role of Yahoo!, Microsoft, and Google* (London: Amnesty International UK, July 2006).

31.   Elliot Schrage, testimony before the Subcommittee on Asia and the Pacific, and the Subcommittee on Africa, Global Human Rights, and International Operations Committee on International Relations, United States House of Representatives, February 15, 2006, Official Google Blog, http://googleblog.blogspot.com/2006/02/testimony-internet-in-china.html

32.   Joel Schectman, "Countering China's Internet Censors," *BusinessWeek*, June 3, 2009.

33.   Amnesty International, *Undermining Freedom of Expression in China*; Justine Nolan, *The China Dilemma: Internet Censorship and Corporate Responsibility*, University of New South Wales Faculty of Law Research Series (2008): 57; J.S. O'Rourke IV, B. Harris, and A. Ogilvy, "Google in China: Government Censorship and Corporate Reputation," *Journal of Business Strategy* 28, no. 3 (2007): 12–22.

34. Matt Looney and Evan Hansen, "Google Pulls Anti-scientology links," CNET News, March 21, 2002, http://news.cnet.com.

35. Schrage, Testimony of Google Inc.; Steven Levy, "Google and the China Syndrome," *Newsweek*, February 13, 2006, 14; "Here Be Dragons," *Economist*, January 28, 2006, 59–60.

36. Nolan, *The China Dilemma*, 57.

37. Ibid.

38. Iris Hong, "Google Boosts China Revenues but Falls Back in Share of Searches," Telecomasia.net, June 8, 2009, www.telecomasia.net.

39. "Google Q1 China Market Share Falls to 20.9 Pct," Caijing.com.cn, June 8, 2009, http://english.caijing.com.cn.

40. Reuters, "Google Exit Appears to Benefit Top China Rival, Baidu," *New York Times*, April 29, 2010.

41. Mao Lijun, "Baidu in Dock over Alleged Blacklisting," *China Daily*, June 6, 2009; "Google China to Push Music Tracks," BBC News, March 30, 2009, http://news.bbc.co.uk; Bruce Einhorn, "Google Hits a Chinese Wall," *Business-Week*, September 10, 2007, 43; Normandy Madden, "Google Is Clearly King of Search—Except in China," *Advertising Age*, January 22, 2007, 18.

42. MacKinnon, "Flatter World and Thicker Walls?"

43. Vaidhyanathan, *The Anarchist in the Library*; Andrew Feenberg, "From Essentialism to Constructivism: Philosophy of Technology at the Crossroads," www-rohan.sdsu.edu/faculty/feenberg/talk4.html, accessed August 12, 2010; Andrew Feenberg and Alastair Hannay, *Technology and the Politics of Knowledge* (Bloomington: Indiana University Press, 1995).

44. Rebecca MacKinnon, "The Green Dam Phenomenon: Governments Everywhere Are Treading on Web Freedoms," *Wall Street Journal*, June 18, 2009.

45. Siva Vaidhyanathan, "Copyright as Cudgel," *Chronicle of Higher Education*, August 2, 2002; M. Lesk, "Copyright Enforcement or Censorship: New Uses for the DMCA?" *IEEE Security and Privacy* 1, no. 2 (2003): 67–69.

46. Jürgen Habermas, *Between Facts and Norms: Contributions to a Discourse Theory of Law and Democracy* (Cambridge, MA: MIT Press, 1996); Jürgen Habermas, *The Theory of Communicative Action* (Boston: Beacon Press, 1984); Craig Calhoun, *Habermas and the Public Sphere* (Cambridge, MA: MIT Press, 1992); Bent Flyvbjerg, "Habermas and Foucault: Thinkers for Civil Society?" *British Journal of Sociology* 49, no. 2 (June 1998): 210–33; Jürgen Habermas, "Further Reflections on the Public Sphere," in Calhoun, *Habermas and the Public Sphere*, 421–57; John Thompson, *Habermas: Critical Debates* (Cambridge, MA: MIT Press, 1982).

47. John Keane, *Global Civil Society?* (Cambridge: Cambridge University Press, 2003), 9.

48. A broader definition of civil society would include for-profit firms such as Sony Universal, ExxonMobil, and Google itself. We could even construct a

list of global "uncivil" society actors that would include Al Qaeda, organized crime syndicates, and those who participate in human trafficking. Keane includes commercial actors as elements of global civil society, but I think including them dilutes the analysis of noncommercial actors who forge remarkable connections without compensation. Each set of actors should be considered separately first so that we can then examine the effects of one on the other. See John Keane, *Global Civil Society?* (Cambridge: Cambridge University Press, 2003), 20. See also Anthony Appiah, *Cosmopolitanism: Ethics in a World of Strangers*. (New York: W. W. Norton, 2006); Gillian Brock and Harry Brighouse, *The Political Philosophy of Cosmopolitanism* (Cambridge: Cambridge University Press, 2005); Martha Nussbaum, *The Clash Within: Democracy, Religious Violence, and India's Future* (Cambridge, MA: Belknap Press of Harvard University Press, 2007).

49. Jürgen Habermas, "The Public Sphere: An Encyclopedia Article," in *Media and Cultural Studies: Keyworks,* ed. Meenakshi Durham and Douglas Kellner (Malden, MA: Blackwell Publishers, 2001), 102–7.

50. Jürgen Habermas, *The Structural Transformation of the Public Sphere: An Inquiry into a Category of Bourgeois Society* (Cambridge, MA: MIT Press, 1989).

51. Ibid. I use the word *revolution* cautiously. It is far too early to assess the effects of the Internet in a balanced and sober manner. Hyperbole and fear still dominate the discussions of the effects of the Internet on culture, societies, politics, and economics. In addition, the Internet hype may have distracted scholars from another revolution. I believe that the proliferation of the magnetic cassette tape and player in the 1970s has had a more profound effect on daily life in all corners of the earth than the Internet has so far. See Peter Lamarche Manuel, *Cassette Culture: Popular Music and Technology in North India* (Chicago: University of Chicago Press, 1993).

52. Habermas, *Between Facts and Norms*. This work extends and revises the work Habermas initiated in the 1960s, before he took his "linguistic turn" into considerations of communicative competence in the 1970s. See Habermas, *The Theory of Communicative Action;* also see Douglas Kellner, "Habermas, the Public Sphere, and Democracy: A Critical Intervention," www.gseis .ucla.edu/faculty/kellner/papers/habermas.htm, accessed March 27, 2010. For critical perspectives on Habermas and public-sphere theory, see Calhoun, *Habermas and the Public Sphere;* Bruce Robbins and the Social Text Collective, *The Phantom Public Sphere* (Minneapolis: University of Minnesota Press, 1993).

53. Yochai Benkler, *The Wealth of Networks: How Social Production Transforms Markets and Freedom* (New Haven, CT: Yale University Press, 2006), 212–61.

54. Marshall McLuhan, *The Global Village: Transformations in World Life and Media in the 21st Century* (New York: Oxford University Press, 1989). Some media theorists like Mark Poster and Jodi Dean are critical of efforts to associate a print-centered nostalgic phenomenon with the cacophony of cultural

and political activities in global cyberspace. Others, like Yochai Benkler and Howard Rheingold, see the practice of "peer production" and the emergence of impressive and efficient organizational practices as a sign that Habermas's dream could come true in the form of digital signals and democratic culture. See Mark Poster, "The Net as a Public Sphere?" *Wired,* November 1995; Howard Rheingold, *The Virtual Community: Homesteading on the Electronic Frontier* (Cambridge, MA: MIT Press, 2000); Howard Rheingold, *Smart Mobs: The Next Social Revolution* (Cambridge, MA: Perseus Publishing, 2002); Craig J. Calhoun, "Information Technology and the International Public Sphere," in *Digital Directions,* ed. D. Schuler (Cambridge, MA: MIT Press), 229–51; Jodi Dean, "Cybersalons and Civil Society: Rethinking the Public Sphere in Transnational Technoculture," *Public Culture* 13, no. 2 (2001): 243–65; Manuel Castells, ed., *The Rise of the Network Society,* 2nd ed. (Oxford: Blackwell Publishers, 2000). The law professor Michael Froomkin has argued that the aspect of the Internet that best exemplifies the Habermasian spirit is the open generation of the protocols themselves. See A. Michael Froomkin, "Habermas@Discourse.Net: Toward a Critical Theory of Cyberspace," *Harvard Law Review* 116, no. 3 (January 2003): 749–873.

55. Benedict Anderson, *Imagined Communities: Reflections on the Origin and Spread of Nationalism,* rev. ed. (London: Verso, 1991); Lincoln Dahlberg, "Rethinking the Fragmentation of the Cyberpublic: From Consensus to Contestation," *New Media Society* 9, no. 5 (October 1, 2007): 827–47.

56. Nate Anderson, "How Wide Is the World's Digital Divide, Anyway?" *Ars Technica,* July 1, 2009.

57. Eszter Hargittai, "The Digital Reproduction of Inequality," in *Social Stratification,* ed. David Grusky (Boulder, CO: Westview Press, 2008); Eszter Hargittai and Amanda Hinnant, "Digital Inequality: Differences in Young Adults' Use of the Internet," *Communication Research* 35, no. 5 (October 1, 2008): 602–21; Neil Selwyn, "Reconsidering Political and Popular Understandings of the Digital Divide," *New Media Society* 6, no. 3 (June 1, 2004): 341–62.

58. Richard Rapaport, "Bangalore," *Wired,* February 1996.

59. Lawrence Liang, "The Other Information City," World-Information .org, March 2, 2005, http://world-information.org/wio/readme/992003309/1115043912.

60. Ibid.

61. Ibid.

62. "About the Brazilianization of India: An Interview with Ravi Sundaram," in Geert Lovink, *Uncanny Networks: Dialogues with the Virtual Intelligentsia* (Cambridge, MA: MIT Press, 2004), 125; Liang, "The Other Information City."

63. Ippolita Collective, *The Dark Side of Google*, Ippolita.net, 2007 http://ippolita.net/google.

64. Miguel Helft, "Amid Iran Turmoil, Google Adds Persian to Translation Service," *New York Times* Bits Blog, June 19, 2009, www.nytimes.com.

65. Madelyn Flammia and Carol Saunders, "Language as Power on the Internet," *Journal of the American Society for Information Science and Technology* 58, no. 12 (2007): 1899–1903.

66. See "Google's Market Share in Your Country," Google Operating System: Unofficial News and Tips about Google, http://quick-proxy.appspot.com/googlesystem.blogspot.com/2009/03/googles-market-share-in-your-country.html, accessed August 21, 2010.

67. Judit Bar-Ilan and Tatyana Gutman, "How Do Search Engines Respond to Some Non-English queries?" *Journal of Information Science* 31, no. 1 (February 1, 2005): 13–28.

68. Liwen Vaughan and Yanjun Zhang, "Equal Representation by Search Engines? A Comparison of Websites across Countries and Domains," *Journal of Computer-Mediated Communication* 12, no. 3 (2007), http://jcmc.indiana.edu.

69. Wingyan Chung, "Web Searching in a Multilingual World," *Communications of the ACM* 51, no. 5 (2008): 32–40; Fotis Lazarinis et al., "Current Research Issues and Trends in Non-English Web Searching," *Information Retrieval* 12, no. 3 (2009): 230–50.

70. "Google's Market Share in Your Country."

71. Choe Sang-Hun, "Crowd's Wisdom Helps South Korean Search Engine Beat Google and Yahoo," *New York Times*, July 4, 2007.

72. "S. Korea May Clash with Google over Internet Regulation Differences," *Hankyoreh*, April 17, 2009; Kim Tong-hyung, "Google Refuses to Bow to Gov't Pressure," *Korea Times*, April 9, 2009.

73. Marcus Alexander, "The Internet and Democratization: The Development of Russian Internet Policy," *Demokratizatsiya* 12, no. 4 (Fall 2004): 607–27; Ronald Deibert et al., *Access Denied: The Practice and Policy of Global Internet Filtering* (Cambridge, MA: MIT Press, 2008).

74. Jennifer L. Schenker, "Yandex Is Russian for Search—and More," *BusinessWeek*, November 29, 2007; Jason Bush, "Where Google Isn't Goliath," *BusinessWeek: Online Magazine*, June 26, 2008; Alexander, "The Internet and Democratization."

75. "Google's Market Share in Your Country."

76. Ojas Sharma, "Where is India's Google?" *SiliconIndia*, May 22, 2009, www.siliconindia.com.

77. See Adoni Alonso and Iñaki Arzoz, *Basque Cyberculture: From Digital Euskadi to CyberEuskalherria* (Reno: Center for Basque Studies, University of Nevada–Reno, 2003).

78.   Rosemary J. Coombe, *The Cultural Life of Intellectual Properties: Authorship, Appropriation, and the Law* (Durham, NC: Duke University Press, 1998); Rosemary J. Coombe and Andrew Herman Coombe, "Rhetorical Virtues: Property, Speech, and the Commons on the World Wide Web," *Anthropological Quarterly* 77, no. 3 (2004); Robyn Kamira, *Indigenous Peoples: Inclusion in the World Summit for the Information Society* (Geneva: World Summit on the Information Society, 2002); Ian McDonald, "Unesco-Wipo World Forum on the Protection of Folklore: Some Reflections and Reactions" (Redfern, NSW: Australian Copyright Council, 1997).

79.   Michael F. Brown, *Who Owns Local Culture?* (Cambridge, MA: Harvard University Press, 2003).

80.   McDonald, "Unesco-Wipo World Forum."

81.   Vaidhyanathan, *The Anarchist in the Library;* see also Shanthi Kalathil and Taylor C. Boas, *Open Networks, Closed Regimes: The Impact of the Internet on Authoritarian Regimes* (Washington, DC: Carnegie Endowment for International Peace, 2003).

82.   Coombe and Coombe, "Rhetorical Virtues."

83.   Seyla Benhabib, "The Liberal Imagination and the Four Dogmas of Multiculturalism," *Yale Journal of Criticism* 12, no. 2 (1999): 401.

84.   Peter L. Bergen, *Holy War, Inc.: Inside the Secret World of Osama Bin Laden* (New York: Free Press, 2001).

CHAPTER 5.   THE GOOGLIZATION OF KNOWLEDGE

1.   Stephen Gaukroger, *Francis Bacon and the Transformation of Early-Modern Philosophy* (Cambridge: Cambridge University Press, 2001).

2.   Kevin Kelly, "Scan This Book!" *New York Times Magazine*, May 14, 2006, 42.

3.   Ibid.

4.   See John Updike, "The End of Authorship," *New York Times Book Review,* June 25, 2006.

5.   See Neil Netanel, "Google Book Search Settlement," Balkinization, blog, October 28, 2008, http://balkin.blogspot.com. Also see James Grimmelmann, "Author's Guild Settlement Insta-Blogging," The Laboratorium, blog, October 28, 2008, http://laboratorium.net; Lawrence Lessig, "On the Google Book Search agreement," Lessig Blog, October 29, 2008, http://lessig.org/blog; Paul Courant, "The Google Settlement: From the Universal Library to the Universal Bookstore," Au Courant, blog, October 28, 2008, http://paulcourant.net; Open Content Alliance, "Let's Not Settle for this Settlement," Open Content Alliance (OCA), blog, November 5, 2008, www.opencontentalliance.org.

6.   Pamela Samuelson, "Reflections on the Google Book Search Settlement," Kilgour Lecture, University of North Carolina, April 14, 2009, available at www .slideshare.net/naypinya/reflections-on-the-google-book-search-settlement-by-pamela-samuelson; Pamela Samuelson, "Legally Speaking: The Dead Souls of the Google Booksearch Settlement," O'Reilly Radar, April 17, 2009, http://radar. oreilly.com; Pamela Samuelson, "Google Book Settlement 1.0 Is History," Huffington Post, September 24, 2009, www.huffingtonpost.com.

7.   Lessig, "On the Google Book Search Agreement."

8.   *Lawrence Lessig on the Google Book Search Settlement—"Static Goods, Dynamic Bads,"* August 9, 2009, video available at www.youtube.com. Also see Lessig, "For the Love of Culture," *New Republic,* January 26, 2010.

9.   Robert Darnton, "Google and the Future of Books," *New York Review of Books,* February 12, 2009.

10.   Andrew Jacobs, "Google Apologizes to Chinese Authors," *New York Times,* January 12, 2010.

11.   Andrew Albanese, "Deal or No Deal: What If the Google Settlement Fails?" *Publishers Weekly,* May 25, 2009; Tim Barton, "Saving Texts from Oblivion: Oxford U. Press on the Google Book Settlement," *Chronicle of Higher Education,* June 29, 2009; Ben Hallman, "Do Justice Department Objections Spell Doom for Google's Online Book Deal?" *AmLaw Litigation Daily,* September 20, 2009; Miguel Helft, "In E-Books, It's an Army vs. Google," *New York Times,* October 7, 2009; Steve Lohr and Miguel Helft, "New Mood in Antitrust May Target Google," *New York Times,* May 18, 2009; Daniel Lyons, "They Might Be a Little Evil: Why Google Faces Antitrust Scrutiny," *Newsweek,* June 1, 2009; Randal C. Picker, "The Google Book Search Settlement: A New Orphan-Works Monopoly?" *SSRN eLibrary,* April 16, 2009, http://papers.ssrn.com; Randal C. Picker, "Assessing Competition Issues in the Amended Google Book Search Settlement," *SSRN eLibrary,* November 16, 2009, http://papers.ssrn.com; Samuelson, "Google Book Settlement 1.0 Is History."

12.   Sergey Brin, "A Library to Last Forever," *New York Times,* October 9, 2009.

13.   Ibid.

14.   "UC Libraries Partner with Google to Digitize Books Press Release," press release, University of California Office of the President, August 9, 2006, www.universityofcalifornia.edu/news/2006/aug09.html. See also Scott Carlson, "U. of California Will Provide Up to 3,000 Books a Day for Google to Scan," *Chronicle of Higher Education,* September 8, 2006; Scott Carlson and Jeffrey R. Young, "Google Will Digitize and Search Millions of Books from 5 Top Research Libraries," *Chronicle of Higher Education,* January 7, 2005.

15.   Michael Gorman and John P. Wilkin, "One College Librarian Worries about 'Atomizing' Books," *Chronicle of Higher Education,* June 3, 2005.

16. Cooperative Agreement, University of Michigan, available at www .lib.umich.edu/files/services/mdp/um-google-cooperative-agreement.pdf. See also Elisabeth Hanratty, "Google Library: Beyond Fair Use?" *Duke Law and Technology Review* 10 (2005), www.law.duke.edu/journals/dltr.

17. "Google Checks Out Library Books," press release, Google Inc., December 14, 2004, www.google.com/press/pressrel/print_library.html.

18. For an argument that Google's library project cannot help but promote book sales, see Cory Doctorow, "Why Publishing Should Send Fruit-Baskets to Google," post on BoingBoing, February 14, 2006, www.boingboing.net. For questions and doubts about the quality and effectiveness of Google's book search service in general, see Siva Vaidhyanathan, "The Great Unanswered Question: Can Google Do It Right?" www.nyu.edu/classes/siva/archives/002811.html (February 20, 2006).

19. See, for example, *Lexmark International, Inc. v. Static Control Components, Inc.*, 387 F.3d 522 (6th Cir. 2004); *Chamberlain Group, Inc. v. Skylink Techs, Inc.*, 292 F. Supp. 2d 1040 (N.D. Ill. 2003).

20. Copyright Act, 17 U.S.C. § 106 (2006).

21. Robert P. Merges, "Contracting into Liability Rules: Intellectual Property Rights and Collective Rights Organizations," *California Law Review* 84 (1996): 1293; Ariel Katz, "The Potential Demise of Another Natural Monopoly: Rethinking the Collective Administration of Performing Rights," *Journal of Competition Law and Economics* 1, no. 3 (September 1, 2005): 541–93; Ariel Katz, "The Potential Demise of Another Natural Monopoly: New Technologies and the Administration of Performing Rights," *Journal of Competition Law and Economics* 2, no. 2 (June 1, 2006): 245–84; Picker, "Assessing Competition Issues"; Samuelson, "Legally Speaking."

22. Picker, "The Google Book Search Settlement."

23. See generally Ganesan Shankaranarayanan and Adir Evan, "The Metadata Enigma," *Communications of the ACM* 49, no. 88 (2006).

24. Geoffrey Nunberg, "Google's Book Search: A Disaster for Scholars," *Chronicle of Higher Education*, August 31, 2009.

25. As it turned out, the distribution of billions of copyrighted music files via the Internet did not destroy the commercial music industry. More important, the behavior of more than seventy million people who offered and received copyrighted files without payment did not undermine the foundations of copyright. The system continues to work. Songwriters still write. Producers still produce. Distributors still distribute. Lawyers still sue. Downloaders still download. We learned three essential truths from the downloading debate: a shared file is not a lost sale; there is a significant difference between a crisis and a moral panic; and culture is not a zero-sum game. See Siva Vaidhyanathan, *The Anarchist in the Library: How the Clash between Freedom and Control Is*

Hacking the Real World and Crashing the System (New York: Basic Books, 2004), 43–50.

26. *MGM Studios, Inc. v. Grokster Ltd.*, 380 F.3d 1154, 1158 (9th Cir. 2004).

27. Brief for Media Studies Professors as Amici Curiae Supporting Respondents at 4, 10, *MGM Studios, Inc. v. Grokster Ltd.*, 380 F.3d 1154 (9th Cir. 2004) (No. 04-480).

28. Lawrence Lessig makes a similar point in one of his earliest blog posts on the Google library project, in which he notes that if the project were ruled to be massive infringement, it might endanger all of Google's enterprises. This is essentially my premise as well, although I derive a very different and more conservative conclusion from it. See Lawrence Lessig, "Google Sued," Lessig Blog, September 22, 2005, www.lessig.org/blog.

29. *Field v. Google Inc.*, 412 F. Supp. 2d 1106, 1124 (2006); *Kelly v. Arriba Soft Corp.*, 336 F.3d 811, 817–22 (2003); see also "Google Free to Cache: Court," Red Herring, March 7, 2006, www.redherring.com.

30. John Battelle, *The Search: How Google and Its Rivals Rewrote the Rules of Business and Transformed Our Culture* (New York: Portfolio, 2005); Khoi D. Dang, "Kelly v. Arriba Soft Corp.: Copyright Limitations on Technological Innovation on the Internet," *Santa Clara Computer and High Technology Law Journal* 18, no. 2 (2002): 389–403.

31. Considerations of how norms influence copyright regulation and practices are essential to a full understanding of the relationship among cultural communities, industries, markets, and regulatory systems. See Ann Bartow, "Electrifying Copyright Norms and Making Cyberspace More Like a Book," *Villanova Law Review* 48 (2003): 101–206.

32. Madison considers this a good bet. I do not. See Michael J. Madison, "Google Print II," Madisonian Blog, October 20, 2005, http://madisonian.net/archives/2005/10/20/google-print-ii/.

33. David Bollier, *Silent Theft: The Private Plunder of Our Common Wealth* (New York: Routledge, 2002); Niva Elkin-Koren et al., *The Commodification of Information* (The Hague: Kluwer Law International, 2002); Benjamin Kaplan, *An Unhurried View of Copyright, Republished (and with Contributions from Friends)*, ed. Iris C. Geik et al. (New York: Matthew Bender, 2005); Lawrence Lessig, *Code and Other Laws of Cyberspace* (New York: Basic Books, 1999); Lawrence Lessig, *Free Culture: The Nature and Future of Creativity* (New York: Penguin, 2004); Lawrence Lessig, *The Future of Ideas: The Fate of the Commons in a Connected World* (New York: Random House, 2001); Jessica Litman, *Digital Copyright: Protecting Intellectual Property on the Internet* (Amherst, NY: Prometheus, 2001); Kembrew McLeod, *Freedom of Expression: Overzealous Copyright Bozos and Other Enemies of Creativity* (New York: Doubleday, 2005); Kembrew McLeod, *Owning Culture: Authorship, Ownership, and Intellectual Property Law* (New York: Peter Lang Publishing, 2001);

Siva Vaidhyanathan, *Copyrights and Copywrongs: The Rise of Intellectual Property and How It Threatens Creativity* (New York: New York University Press, 2001); Vaidhyanathan, *The Anarchist in the Library*; Siva Vaidhyanathan, "Copyright as Cudgel," *Chronicle of Higher Education*, August 2, 2002.

34.   See Paul Ganley, "Google Book Search: Fair Use, Fair Dealing, and the Case for Intermediary Copying," unpublished manuscript, available at http://papers.ssrn.com/so13/papers.cfm?abstract_id=875384.

35.   Siva Vaidhyanathan, "A Risky Gamble with Google," *Chronicle of Higher Education*, December 2, 2005; Vaidhyanathan, "The Great Unanswered Question"; Siva Vaidhyanathan, "The Googlization of Everything and the Future of Copyright," *University of California at Davis Law Review* 40, no. 3 (2007): 1207–31; Paul Courant, "Quick Response to Siva Vaidhyanathan," Au Courant, blog, November 6, 2007, http://paulcourant.net.

36.   See generally Jonathan Band, "The Google Library Project: Both Sides of the Story," *Plagiary* 2 (2006); William Patry, "Google, Revisited," The Patry Copyright Blog, September 23, 2005, http://williampatry.blogspot.com; Fred von Lohmann, "Authors Guild Sues Google Electronic Frontier Foundation," Electronic Frontier Foundation, September 20, 2005, www.eff.org/deeplinks/archives/003992.php; Doctorow, "Why Publishing Should Send Fruit-Baskets to Google"; Lawrence Lessig, *Digital Video: Is Google Book Search Fair Use?* January 8, 2006, video available at www.youtube.com.

37.   *Limitations on Exclusive Rights: Fair Use*, 17 U.S.C. § 107 (2005).

38.   See, for example, *Campbell v. Acuff-Rose Music, Inc.*, 510 U.S. 569, 585 (1994); *Ty, Inc. v. Publications International, Ltd.*, 292 F.3d 512, 515, 523 (7th Cir. 2002).

39.   See *Campbell v. Acuff-Rose Music, Inc.*, 510 U.S. at 578–79.

40.   Ibid.

41.   Michael J. Madison, "A Pattern-Oriented Approach to Fair Use," *William and Mary Law Review* 45 (2004): 1525–1671.

42.   See, for example, *Ty, Inc. v. Publications International, Ltd.*, 292 F.3d 512, 515, 523 (7th Cir. 2002); Madison, "A Pattern-Oriented Approach,"1530; Georgia Harper, "Google This," October 19, 2005, www.utsystem.edu/ogc/INTELLEC-TUALPROPERTY/googlethis.htm.

43.   Lawrence Lessig, "Google Sued," Lessig Blog, September 2005, http://lessig.org/blog.

44.   David Weinberger, *Small Pieces Loosely Joined: How the Web Shows Us Who We Really Are* (Reading, MA: Perseus Books Group, 2002).

45.   Open Content Alliance, "Let's Not Settle for this Settlement," Open Content Alliance (OCA), blog, November 5, 2008, www.opencontentalliance.org.

46.   I must disclose that I served as a paid consultant for such a consortium organized by Oxford University Press in 2004. The project ended abruptly when

its leaders learned of Google's plans to undermine its potential market. Oxford University Press paid me a onetime fee of $1,000 before the project folded. I did not expect any subsequent compensation regardless of the prospects of the project. I did, however, support the aims of the project before I signed on as a consultant.

CHAPTER 6. THE GOOGLIZATION OF MEMORY

1. Neil Postman, *Amusing Ourselves to Death: Public Discourse in the Age of Show Business* (New York: Penguin, 2006).

2. David Shenk, *Data Smog: Surviving the Information Glut* (San Francisco: Harper Edge, 1997).

3. Clay Shirky, *Web 2.0 Expo NY: It's Not Information Overload; It's Filter Failure,* video, September 19, 2008, available at www.youtube.com. Also see Clay Shirky, *Cognitive Surplus: Creativity and Generosity in a Connected Age* (New York: Penguin, 2010).

4. Jeffrey Olick, *The Politics of Regret: On Collective Memory and Historical Responsibility* (New York: Routledge, 2007).

5. Jorge Borges, "Funes, His Memory," in *Collected Fictions* (New York: Viking, 1998).

6. Viktor Mayer-Schönberger, *Delete: The Virtue of Forgetting in the Digital Age* (Princeton, NJ: Princeton University Press, 2009).

7. Nicholas Carr, "Is Google Making Us Stupid?" *Atlantic,* July 2008, 56–63.

8. Marshall McLuhan, *The Gutenberg Galaxy: The Making of Typographic Man* (Toronto: University of Toronto Press, 1965); Marshall McLuhan, *The Global Village: Transformations in World Life and Media in the 21st Century* (New York: Oxford University Press, 1989); Marshall McLuhan, *Understanding Media: The Extensions of Man* (New York: Routledge, 2008).

9. Jamais Cascio, "Get Smart," *Atlantic,* July 2009, 94–100.

10. Lester Ward, *Dynamic Sociology* (New York: D. Appleton and Company, 1883).

11. Steven Johnson, *Everything Bad Is Good for You* (New York: Penguin, 2006).

12. Gord Hotchkiss, "Marissa Mayer Interview on Personalization," Out of My Gord, blog, February 23, 2007, www.outofmygord.com.

13. Cass Sunstein, *Republic.com 2.0* (Princeton, NJ: Princeton University Press, 2007).

14. Jeff Jarvis, *What Would Google Do?* (New York: Collins Business, 2009), 210.

15. Ibid., 211–15.

16.   Randall E. Stross, *Planet Google: One Company's Audacious Plan to Organize Everything We Know* (New York: Free Press, 2008), 8–10.

17.   Lawrence Page et al., *The PageRank Citation Ranking: Bringing Order to the Web,* Technical Report, Digital Libraries Project, Stanford University, 1999, http://ilpubs.stanford.edu:8090/422/.

18.   John Battelle, *The Search: How Google and Its Rivals Rewrote the Rules of Business and Transformed Our Culture* (New York: Portfolio, 2005).

19.   Yochai Benkler, *The Wealth of Networks: How Social Production Transforms Markets and Freedom* (New Haven, CT: Yale University Press, 2006).

20.   Yochai Benkler, "Coase's Penguin, or, Linux and the Nature of the Firm," *Yale Law Journal* 112, no. 3 (2002): 369–446.

21.   Daniel O. O'Connor and Henry Voos, "Laws, Theory Construction and Bibliometrics," *Library Trends* 30, no. 1 (1981): 9–20; see also Christine Kosmopoulos and Denis Pumain, "Citation, Citation, Citation: Bibliometrics, the Web and the Social Sciences and Humanities," *Cybergeo: European Journal of Geography* 411 (December 17, 2007), www.cybergeo.eu. Also see Dean Hendrix, "An Analysis of Bibliometric Indicators, National Institutes of Health Funding, and Faculty Size at Association of American Medical Colleges Medical Schools, 1997–2007," *Journal of the Medical Library Association* 96, no. 4 (October 1996): 324–34.

22.   Umut Al, Mustafa Sahiner, and Yasar Tonta, "Arts and Humanities Literature: Bibliometric Characteristics of Contributions by Turkish Authors," *Journal of the American Society for Information Science and Technology* 57, no. 8 (April 13, 2006): 1011–22. Also see A. Archambault and E. Gagné, *Research Collaboration in the Social Sciences and Humanities: Bibliometric Indicators* (Ottawa: Social Sciences and Humanities Research Council of Canada, 2004).

23.   Steve Weber, *The Success of Open Source* (Cambridge, MA: Harvard University Press, 2004).

24.   Jillian R. Griffiths and Peter Brophy, "Student Searching Behavior and the Web: Use of Academic Resources and Google," *Library Trends* 53, no. 4 (Spring 2005): 539–54.

25.   Steve Jones and Mary Madden, *The Internet Goes to College: How Students Are Living in the Future with Today's Technology* (Washington, DC: Pew Research Center, Internet and American Life Project, September 15, 2002), www.pewinternet.org.

26.   Alison J. Head, "Beyond Google: How Do Students Conduct Academic Research?" *First Monday* 12, no. 8 (August 2007), http://firstmonday.org.

27.   Tara Brabazon, *The University of Google: Education in the (Post) Information Age* (Aldershot, U.K.: Ashgate, 2007), 16.

28.   Ibid., 45.

29.   Ibid., 28–30.

30. Rita Vine, "Google Scholar," *Journal of the Medical Library Association* 94, no. 1 (January 2006): 97–99.

31. Philipp Mayr and Anne-Kathrin Walter, "An Exploratory Study of Google Scholar," *On-line Information Review* 31, no. 6 (2007): 814–30.

32. James A. Evans, "Electronic Publication and the Narrowing of Science and Scholarship," *Science* 321, no. 5887 (July 18, 2008): 395–99.

33. "About Google Scholar," Google Scholar website, http://scholar.google .com/intl/en/scholar/about.html, accessed August 13, 2010.

34. Burton Callicott and Debbie Vaughn, "Google Scholar vs. Library Scholar: Testing the Performance of Schoogle," *Internet Reference Services Quarterly* 10, nos. 3–4 (April 27, 2006): 71–88; Peter Jasco, "As We May Search: Comparison of Major Features of the Web of Science, Scopus, and Google Scholar Citation-Based and Citation-Enhanced Databases," *Current Science* 89, no. 9 (November 10, 2005): 1537–47.

35. "Google and IBM Announce University Initiative to Address Internet-Scale Computing Challenges," press release, Google Inc., October 8, 2007, www .google.com/intl/en/press/pressrel/20071008_ibm_univ.html.

36. "NSF Partners with Google and IBM to Enhance Academic Research Opportunities," American Association for the Advancement of Science, press release, March 13, 2008, www.eurekalert.org/pub_releases/2008–03/nsf-npw031308.php.

37. Jeffrey Young, "3 Ways Web-Based Computing Will Change Colleges," *Chronicle of Higher Education,* October 24, 2008.

38. Steve Lohr, "Google and I.B.M. Join in 'Cloud Computing' Research," *New York Times,* October 8, 2007.

39. Young, "3 Ways Web-Based Computing Will Change Colleges."

40. Chris Anderson, "The End of Theory: The Data Deluge Makes the Scientific Method Obsolete," *Wired,* June 23, 2008.

41. Ibid.

42. Jeffrey Young, "Google Expands Its Bid to Run Student E-Mail Systems," *Chronicle of Higher Education,* October 20, 2006.

CONCLUSION

1. Jorge Luis Borges, "The Library of Babel," in *Collected Fictions* (New York: Viking, 1998); William Bloch, *The Unimaginable Mathematics of Borges' Library of Babel* (Oxford: Oxford University Press, 2008).

2. Holman W. Jenkins, "Opinion: Google and the Search for the Future," *Wall Street Journal,* August 14, 2010.

3. Dan Farber, "Google's Schmidt: Brands to Clean Up Internet 'Cesspool,'" *CNET News,* October 13, 2008, http://news.cnet.com; "Google Brand Update

Means Authority Websites Are Hogging the Rankings," StuckOn—Search Engine Optimisation, July 15, 2009, www.stuckon.co.uk; "Big Brands? Google Brand Promotion: New Search Engine Rankings Place Heavy Emphasis on Branding," SEOBook, blog, February 25, 2009, www.seobook.com; "What Google Can Do to Make the Web Less of a 'Cesspool,'" paidContent.org—Washingtonpost.com, May 5, 2009, www.washingtonpost.com.

4. Paul Courant, "Quick Response to Siva Vaidhyanathan," Au Courant, blog, November 6, 2007, http://paulcourant.net.

5. Leslie Roberts, "Controversial from the Start," *Science* 291, no. 5507 (February 16, 2001): 1182a–88.

6. Leslie Roberts, "Gambling on a Shortcut to Genome Sequencing," *Science* 252, no. 5013 (June 21, 1991): 1618–19.

7. Roberts, "Controversial from the Start"; Daniel J. Kevles and Leroy E. Hood, *The Code of Codes: Scientific and Social Issues in the Human Genome Project* (Cambridge, MA: Harvard University Press, 1992); Francis S. Collins, Michael Morgan, and Aristides Patrinos, "The Human Genome Project: Lessons from Large-Scale Biology," *Science* 300, no. 5617 (April 11, 2003): 286–90; Francis S. Collins, "Medical and Societal Consequences of the Human Genome Project," *New England Journal of Medicine* 341, no. 1 (July 1, 1999): 28–37; John Sulston, *The Common Thread: A Story of Science, Politics, Ethics, and the Human Genome* (Washington, DC: Joseph Henry Press, 2002); Siva Vaidhyanathan, *The Anarchist in the Library: How the Clash between Freedom and Control Is Hacking the Real World and Crashing the System* (New York: Basic Books, 2004).

8. Collins, Morgan, and Patrinos, "The Human Genome Project."

ACKNOWLEDGMENTS

1. Yochai Benkler, *The Wealth of Networks: How Social Production Transforms Markets and Freedom* (New Haven, CT: Yale University Press, 2006), 261.

INDEX

academia, Google's relations with: and affinity between academia and Google, 186–87; agenda set by Google in, 197–98; and commercialization, 186, 194; and Google Books, 150–53, 155, 158, 162–65, 169, 171–72, 186, 203; and Google Scholar, 186, 190–94; and Google's technological infrastructure, 186, 194–97; legal aspects of, 195–96; and obsolescence of educational institutions, 184–86; and obsolescence of scientific methodology, 196–97; and peer review, 187–89, 191; and scholars' use of Google, 192–94; and students' use of Google, 189–92, 197; and university presses, 171–72

Adams, Mark, 208

advertising space, Google as provider of: and AdSense, 34; and AdWords, 26, 30; and auction program, 14, 26, 27, 28, 30, 52, 74, 187; and blogs, 34; as company's primary activity, 16, 26, 130; and contextual advertising, 27, 28; earnings from, 27; government regulation of, 18, 25; and malware, 14; and news media search results, 33–35; and proposal to collaborate with Yahoo, 18, 25; small firms' interests served by, 27–28; and sponsored results, 26, 60; and use of personal information, 9, 26, 83

Agre, Phil, 234n71

airline's financial status reported erroneously, via Google, 78–79

Ajaxwrite (Web-based word processor), 29

Alpha. *See* Wolfram Alpha

AltaVista, 19, 57, 233n71

Amazon, 11, 31, 82, 112, 157, 163

America Online (AOL), 47

Anderson, Benedict, 137

Anderson, Chris, 113, 196

anonymization, of IP addresses, 86

Anti-Defamation League, 65, 66

anti-Semitism, 47, 64–66, 130

antitrust laws, 11, 45, 153, 162, 196

Apple corporation, 11, 29

Aptocracy, 68–69

Argentina, 142

Association of American Publishers, 152, 161

Atlantic magazine, 179

AT&T, 49
attention of users, as Google's chief product, 26, 27, 70
Australia, 134, 146, 147
Authors' Guild, 152, 161, 202
automotive technology, 4–6
aviation technology, 4–5

Bacon, Francis, 149
Baidu (search engine), 127, 132–33
Band, Jonathan, 169
Barron, Peter, 106–7, 110
Basque nationalism, 146
Beacon program, on Facebook, 90–92
Belgium, 106, 141
Benhabib, Seyla, 147, 148
Benkler, Yochai, 71, 137, 188, 245n54
Bentham, Jeremy, 111, 112
Berlin Wall, fall of, 122
bibliometrics. *See* citation-review systems
Bing (search engine), 21, 24, 25
Blair, Tony, 40, 104, 108
Blogger, 16, 47, 86, 118, 129, 148, 183
blogs: and free rider problem, 34; and Google's AdSense service, 34; hyperlinks used in, 62; and present author's Googlization of Everything blog, 234n71
Bloomberg news service, 78, 79
BoingBoing, 234
books: digitization of, 11, 157, 172; online access to, 11, 150–51, 157. *See also* Google Books
Borges, Jorge Luis, 177, 199
Boring, Aaron and Christine, 100–101
boyd, danah, 92
Brabazon, Tara, 191
brain, human, 3, 179, 180–81
Brazil, 14, 16, 121, 122, 142
Brin, Sergey, 67, 71, 144, 156, 186–87, 202
Broughton, England, 104–5
Brown, Gordon, 108
Burma, 131
Burning Man, 70–71
Bush, George W., 41–42, 69
Business Week, 56

Canada, 42, 95, 101, 102, 144, 146, 147, 237n32
Carnegie Mellon University, 195
Carr, Nicholas, 179–81
Cascio, Jamais, 181–82
Ceauşescu, Nicolae, 121
Celera corporation, 208–9
cell phones. *See* mobile phones

censorship, Google's participation in, 15, 36, 47, 65, 74, 134; in China, 10, 117–21, 127–34; and YouTube content, 37–39, 116, 118
Cerf, Vint, 73
Cheney, Dick, 97
Child Online Protection Act, 87
Chile, 142
Chin, Denny, 154
China, 14, 25, 39, 74, 107; Baidu search engine in, 127, 132–33; Cultural Revolution in, 124; economic relations in, 119, 124–25; Gmail accounts of dissidents hacked in, 116, 118; Google Books challenged in, 153; Google Maps reflecting border claims of, 117; Google's market share in, 132–33, 142; Google's relations with government of, 9–10, 74, 117–21, 128–34; Great Leap Forward in, 124; Internet content censored in, 10, 39, 74, 117–21, 125–34; political relations in, 121, 124–28
choice architecture, 88
ChoicePoint, 96–97, 112
Chrome operating system, 17, 24, 25
Cisco, 127
citation-review systems, 56, 188, 193–94
civil society, global, 135, 138, 140, 141, 145, 148
C.K., Louis, 51
Clarke, Arthur C., 53
Clinton, Bill, 40, 41, 57
Clinton, Hillary, 118, 119
cloud computing, Google services using, 17, 24, 29, 195–96
Cohen, Sacha Baron, 66
Collins, Francis, 208–9
Colombia, 142
Comcast, 49
Comedy Central, 35
commercialization: of academic research, 194; of libraries, 153, 154, 164, 186; of public sphere, 136
Communism, fall of, 121–23
competitors, Google's, 15, 16, 17, 18–20, 27, 28–30; and book digitization, 162, 172; and cross-subsidization, 29; and search engines, 16, 20–25, 55–57, 132–33, 142–45. *See also* foreign markets, Google's share in
Conley, Dalton, 71
content providers, Google's relations with, 26, 30, 46–48; and free rider problem, 30–36

contextual advertising, 27, 28
cookies, 9, 21, 86, 89, 183
copyright: and cache copies, 166–67; in China, 132; and Digital Millennium Copyright Act, 38; in Europe, 32; four-factor test of, 169, 170; and free rider problem, 31–32, 166; and Google Books project, 10, 155, 159–61, 163, 166–71, 172; of music, 132, 166, 170, 249n25; and "notice and takedown" process, 47, 130; and transformative vs. derivative use, 170; and YouTube, 18, 35–36, 37, 38. *See also* fair use
corporate responsibility, 42–44, 210
counterculture, sixties, 70
Courant, Paul, 203
Coyle, Karen, 234–35n71
critical literacy, 191
cross-subsidization, 29
Cuil (search engine), 21–22
cultural imperialism, 109–10
customization, Google services offering, 138, 141, 183, 203; and search results, 27, 132, 147, 148, 183–84, 202. *See also* localized search results
Czechoslovakia, 121, 123

Dante Alighieri, 76, 77
Darnton, Robert, 124, 153
Darwinism, social, 148, 181
data mining, 96–97, 197
Dean, Jodi, 244n54
default settings: and customized search results, on Google, 183; for privacy, on Facebook, 90–92; for privacy, on Google, 86–90, 106, 114
de la Peña, David, 99–100
democratic revolutions of 1989, 121–24
Denmark, 142
Dewey, John, 185
Digital Millennium Copyright Act, 38
diversity of services, Google's, 16–17
Doctorow, Cory, 100, 152, 159, 169
"Don't be evil" (Goggle's motto), 2, 8, 10, 46, 59, 74–77, 120
DoubleClick, 18, 229n14
Drummond, David, 116
Dyson, Esther, 76, 120, 133

earnings, Google's. *See* financial status, Google's
East Germany, 108, 112, 113, 121, 123
economic relations: in China, 119, 124–25; and corporate responsibility, 42–44; and

free rider problem, 31; and Google's profitability during downturn, 17–18; and market failure, 40–41; and market fundamentalism, 39–40, 43; and neoliberalism, 40; and public failure, 40–42; state intervention in, 39–40, 43, 44
Egypt, 47, 143
Eldritch Press, 157
e-mail service, Google's. *See* Gmail
employees, Google's: and attitudes toward company, 72–74, 75; layoffs experienced by, 18; number of, 18; as technocrats, 67–71
encryption, 116, 125, 126
England. *See* United Kingdom
English-language Web sites, 141, 142
eschatology, techno-fundamentalist, 55
Europe: Google Books challenged in, 153; Google News content aggregation challenged in, 32; Google Street View in, 102, 104–8, 237n24; government regulation in, 47; market fundamentalism in, 39, 40; privacy policy in, 87
European Union, 25, 115
Excite (Internet portal), 56

Facebook, 16, 43, 82, 90–92, 99, 112, 116, 118
fair use: and European law, 32; and Google Books project, 153, 160–61, 162, 165–66, 168–70, 172; and YouTube, 38
faith in Google, users', xii, xiii, xiv, 2–5, 50, 53, 55, 59–60, 75, 77, 80; dangers of, 5–6, 77–81. *See also* trust bias
Farsi language, 141
fax machines, 121, 123
FCC. *See* Federal Communication Commission (FCC)
Federal Communication Commission (FCC), 18, 49
Federal Emergency Management Agency (FEMA), 41–42
Feldmar, Andrew, 177
FEMA. *See* Federal Emergency Management Agency (FEMA)
filters, 7, 175–76, 178–79, 182
financial status, Google's, 17–18, 229n14; and earnings from advertising, 27, 229n14
Finland, 142
Firefox, 17, 29, 30
Fleetwood Mac, 113
Flickr, 82
foreign markets, Google's share in, 25, 132–33, 141–45, 229n14
forgetting, of information, 174, 176–79

Foucault, Michel, 111, 112
founders, Google's, 67, 156, 186–87, 202
France, 14, 25, 47, 115, 130, 142, 146, 153
Frankel, Max, 56
free market, 45, 46
free rider problem, 30–36, 166
free speech, 109, 110; in China, 120, 130,
    131
free trade, 109
Froomkin, Michael, 245n54

Gandy, Oscar, 236n20
gang-related online video, 110
Ganley, Paul, 168, 169, 172
Gaukroger, Stephen, 149
Germany, 14, 25, 47, 65–66, 102, 108, 112,
    113, 121, 122, 123, 130, 134, 142, 153
global civil society, 135, 138, 140, 141, 145,
    148, 243–44n48
globalization, 108–10, 111, 146
Gmail, 3, 16, 19, 67, 86, 90, 129, 143, 183;
    Chinese dissidents' use of, 116, 118;
    Iranian dissidents' use of, 116; students'
    use of, 197
"God," search results for, 63–64
Google bombing (search-engine optimiza-
    tion), 66
Google Book service: and antitrust laws,
    153, 162; authors' response to, 152, 153,
    154, 156, 161, 162, 163, 173, 202; Chinese
    response to, 153; copyright issues raised
    by, 10, 155, 159–61, 163, 166–71, 172;
    European response to, 153; and fair use,
    153, 160–61, 162, 165–66, 168–70, 172;
    four-factor analysis of, 169; initial project
    of, 156–60; legal actions resulting from,
    48, 154, 156, 160–62, 165–66, 168; librar-
    ies' participation in, 17, 23, 152–53, 155,
    158–60, 162–66, 169, 171, 186, 202, 203;
    and misapplication of Web standards
    to books, 152, 167, 171; noncommercial
    service preferable to, 169, 171–72; and
    out-of-print books, 153, 154, 156, 161–62,
    171; and partner program, 157, 159; and
    privatization of knowledge, 152, 153,
    155, 164–65; and public domain, 157, 158,
    159; and public failure, 44, 155; public
    project preferred to, 203–4; publishers'
    response to, 11, 17, 48, 152–54, 156–63,
    165–68, 170–73, 202; and registered users,
    183; and rights registry, 161, 162; and
    royalty payments, 161, 172, 173; and univer-
    sities' participation in, 150–53, 155, 158,
    162–65, 169, 171–72, 186

Google Checkout, 16
Google Docs, 24, 29
Google Earth, 17
Google headquarters, 49, 72, 187
Google Maps, 106, 107, 117
Googlemobiles, 98, 104–5
Google News, 32–35, 44, 78, 79, 148
Google Scholar, 186, 190–94
Google Street View, 17, 48, 98–108, 111,
    237nn24,32
Google Voice, 16
Google Web Search. See search engine,
    Google; search results, Google
Gorbachev, Mikhail, 122–23
GoTo (search engine), 27
Graham, Christopher, 106
Granovetter, Mark, 231n33
Great Britain. See United Kingdom
Greece, 102
Grokster, 166
Grossman, Lev, 82
Gurunet (search engine), 57

Habermas, Jürgen, 135–37, 146, 147,
    245n54
hackers, 116, 118, 135, 140, 159
Hakia (search engine), 23
Hargittai, Eszter, 92
Harper, Jim, 76
Harvard University libraries, 153, 158
Havel, Václav, 121
Hawthorne, Nathaniel, 95
health-care reform, 42
health records, online access to, 17
higher education. See academia
Hindu fundamentalism, 135, 140
Hinton, Les, 33
Honecker, Erik, 121
Hong Kong, 119, 142
Hotbot (search engines), 57
Huffington Post, 34, 202, 226n42
Human Genome Project, 194, 207–8
Human Knowledge Project, 11, 204–10
human rights, xii, 9, 10, 118–20, 127–28, 129,
    130, 131–33, 143
Hungary, 121, 141, 142
Huxley, Aldous, 125
hyperlinks: significance of, 62; used in
    ranking search results, 61, 62, 69; Web
    crawlers' use of, 47

IBM corporation, 195
iGoogle, 86, 183
imperialism, 2, 109, 111

India, 9, 16, 47; global civil society in, 139–41; Google Maps reflecting border claims of, 117; Google search results in, 138–39; Google's market share in, 144–45
Indonesia, 131
information: distinguished from knowledge, 175; filters of, 175–76, 178–79; Google's aim of organizing and providing access to, 2, 10, 84, 110
infrastructural imperialism, 2, 109, 111, 130, 131, 134
Intelligence Squared (radio program), 76
Internet: design of, 14; governability of, 13–14; liberal states' involvement in, 39, 134; skills required for use of, 138; socio-economically differentiated access to, 137–38; sociopolitical change promoted by, xii–xiii, 120, 123–24, 128; state censorship of, in China, 39, 74, 117–21, 125–34; state censorship of, in Europe, 134
Internet Explorer, 29–30
IP (Internet Protocol) addresses, 84, 86
Iran, 16, 116, 141
Italy, 14, 47–48, 116, 142

James, William, 60, 61, 62
Japan, 25, 142; Google Street view resisted in, 102–4, 108, 111
Jaquith, Waldo, 234n71
Jarvis, Jeff, 76, 184–86
"Jew", search results for, 64–66
Johns Hopkins University, 208
Johnson, Stephen, 181
Jordan, 143
journalism. *See* news media
Judt, Tony, 122, 123
Justice Department, U.S., 87, 153

Katrina, Hurricane, 41–42, 77
Keane, John, 135, 244n48
Kelly, Kevin, 150–51, 152
Kirn, Walter, 68–69
knowledge: access to, 149–50; commercialization of, 153, 154; distinguished from information, 175; fragmentary state of, 138, 139; and Human Knowledge Project proposal, 204–10; and power, 149; privatization of, 152, 153, 155, 164–65, 208–9
Korea. *See* South Korea

languages. *See* linguistic diversity; natural language
Latvia, 141, 142

laws and legislation, 18, 20, 32, 87, 116, 131. *See also* copyright; privacy; regulation, government
lawsuits, 32, 36, 101, 156, 163, 166, 167, 168
Lehrer, Brian, 44–45
Lennon, John, 64
Lessig, Lawrence, 152, 153, 169, 170, 231n33, 250n28
Lewis, Harry, 76, 120
Lewis, Peter, 57
Liang, Lawrence, 139, 140
liberalism, 109
liberal state, 39, 113
libraries: and Human Knowledge Project proposal, 206; Internet's effect on students' use of, 190–91; as participants in Google's Book Search project, 17, 23, 152–53, 155, 158–60, 162–66, 169, 171, 186, 202, 203
"Library of Babel" (Borges), 199–200
linguistic diversity, 141–45
Lithuania, 141, 142
Li Zhi, 127
local-culture movements, 145–48
localized search results, 28, 64, 129, 138–39, 143
local norms, Google's adherence to, 98, 102, 104, 108, 110

Machiavelli, Niccolò, 149
MacKinnon, Rebecca, 134
Madison, Michael, 167, 170
Magi, Oscar, 48
Major, John, 108
Malaysia, 107
Malkin, Michelle, 38–39
Mandarin language, 118–19, 132, 141
market failure, 40–41
market fundamentalism, 39–40, 43, 109, 113
market segmentation, 113
market share, international. *See* foreign markets
Marx, Karl, 68
Massachusetts Institute of Technology (MIT), 195
Mayer, Marissa, 53–54, 73, 87, 88, 89, 183
Mayer-Schönberger, Viktor, 179
McCarthy, Jenny, 77–78
McLuhan, Marshall, 137, 180, 231n33
medical information, online sources of, 23. *See also* health records, online access to
memory, human, as information filter, 174–79
metadata, 79, 80, 164, 165

Microsoft corporation: advertising business of, 27; and Bing, 21, 24, 25; in competition with Google, 17, 19, 24–25, 27, 29, 197; and cross-subsidization, 29; early search engine of, 57; and government regulation, 44; and Internet Explorer, 29–30; as multinational, 9; and Open Content Alliance, 172; and Windows, 17, 24; and Word, 29
military technology, 70
Mills, C. Wright, 221–22n13
mission statement, Google's, 10, 58, 205
mobile-phone systems, Google's interest in, 17, 18, 49, 119
monopoly, Google as, 19, 20, 152. *See also* antitrust laws
Moore's law, 76
motto, Google's. *See* "Don't be evil" (Goggle's motto)
Mozilla Foundation, 17, 29
MTV, 35
Murdoch, Rupert, 32–35
music, copyright of, 132, 166, 170, 249n25
Muslims: attacked by Hindus in India, 140; caricatured on YouTube, 38–39
MySpace, 82, 83

National Institutes of Health (NIH), 208
National Public Radio, 76, 120
natural language, search results based on, 23
Naver (search engine), 143, 145
neoliberalism, 40, 120, 148
Netherlands, 106, 141
Netscape, 29
network effect, 19–20
network neutrality, 18, 45, 49
New Mexico, 37–38
New Orleans, 41–42, 77
news media: Google covered in, 56–58, 150, 153, 156, 179, 196, 200; Google's competition with, 11, 32–35; misled by Google search results, 78–80
New York magazine, 92
New York Public Library, 158
New York Review of Books, 153
New York Times, 44, 56–58, 156
New York Times Book Review, 151
New York Times Magazine, 150
Nickelodeon, 35
Niebuhr, Reinhold, 77
Northern Light (search engine), 233n71
notice and takedown process, 47, 48
Nussbaum, Emily, 92

Obama, Barack, 16, 37, 42, 49
O'Brien, Conan, 51
Open Content Alliance, 162, 172
open-source software, 17, 29, 49, 185, 187, 188–89, 195
optimization, search-engine, 66, 115
Orbison, Roy, 170
Orkut, 16
Orlean, Susan, 29
Orwell, George, 125
Osamu Higuchi, 103
Oxford University, 158

Page, Larry, 67, 71, 156, 186–87, 202
PageRank system, 21, 23, 58, 60, 61–64, 66, 74, 171, 187
Paine, Thomas, 122
Pakistan, 117
Panopticon, 9, 111–12
Patry, William, 169
peer producers, 71, 188, 189, 245n54
peer review, 187–89, 191
Peirce, Charles Sanders, 60, 61
personal information: ChoicePoint's use of, 96–97; Facebook's use of, 90–92; Google's use of, 9, 26, 58, 59, 83–90, 163
personalization, of search results. *See* customization
Picker, Randall, 76
Poland, 121, 141
political relations: and corporate responsibility, 43–44; and democratic revolutions of 1989, 121–24; and global public sphere, 135–38; and Google Maps, 117; and Google's relations with Chinese government, 117–21, 128–34; and Google's relations with Obama administration, 49, 119; and mass surveillance, 97–98; role of culture in, 147–48; technology's impact on, xii, 121–24; and YouTube, 16, 37–39, 49
pornography, 14, 57, 67, 87, 134, 222n4
Portugal, 142
Poster, Mark, 244n54
Postman, Neil, 69–70, 175
pragmatic theory of truth, 60–62
Presley, Elvis, 174
pride, sin of, 76–77
printing press, sociopolitical impact of, 122, 180
print on demand, 171

privacy: and Facebook's default settings, 90–92; and Google Books, 163; and Google's anonymization of IP addresses, 86; and Google's collection of personal information, 26, 83–90, 163; and Google's default settings, 86–90, 106, 114; Google's opposition to laws protecting, 18; Google's policy on, 84–86; and Google's registered users, 86; and Google Street View, 98–108, 111; meaning of, 87, 93; and person to firm interface, 94, 236n20; and person to peer interface, 94; and person to power interface, 94; and person to public interface, 94–96; and person to state interface, 94–95, 236n20. *See also* surveillance

privatization of knowledge, 152, 153, 155, 164–65, 208–9

profiles, personal. *See* personal information

profits, Google's. *See* financial status, Google's

Project Gutenberg, 157

public failure, 6, 40–42, 44, 155, 186

public good, 4, 32, 40, 44, 74

public interest, 18, 44, 49, 97

public sphere, 4, 11, 122, 135–38, 145–48, 150, 197, 201, 203, 204, 206, 209, 216

publishers' response to Google Books, 11, 17, 48, 152–54, 156–63, 165–68, 170–73, 202

PubMed database, 193

Putin, Vladimir, 143

quality control, by Google, 14–15, 35, 36, 65–67, 156

Quero, 25

Rambler (search engine), 144

Random House, 157

Reagan, Ronald, 40

Red Rock Eater (e-mail newsletter), 234n71

registered users, of Google, 67, 86, 90, 183

regulation, government, 10, 11, 18, 20, 25, 44–49

relevance, of search results, 7, 21, 32, 57, 59, 61, 63, 65, 66, 138, 171, 188, 193. *See also* customization; localized search results

remembering, of information, 174–79

responsibility for content, Google's, 46–48, 65–67, 116. *See also* corporate responsibility

Rheingold, Howard, 245n54

Romania, 121, 141

Rorty, Richard, 60–61

Rose, Charlie, 87

Rosen, Jay, 121

Rule, James, 96, 97

Russia, 14, 25, 142, 143–44

Safari, 29

safe search, 15, 222n4

Saint Mary's College, in California, 190

Samuelson, Pamela, 231n33

satellite images, 17

Saudi Arabia, 131

Schmidt, Eric, 44–46, 49, 108, 200, 202

Schrage, Elliot, 129

Science (periodical), 193

scientific research, search engines used for, 22, 192–94

Scientology, 134

search engine, Google: algorithm used in, 7, 23, 52, 60, 61, 62, 65, 66, 69, 171, 182, 187; and company's expanded mission, 16; competitors of, 16, 20–25, 55–57, 132–33, 142–45; operating principles of, 20–21, 23, 65, 66, 69; technological basis of, 54, 195; trade secrets relating to, 87

search results, Google: bias in, 7, 62–64; compared to citation-review systems, 56, 188, 193–94; customized, 27, 132, 147, 148, 183–84, 202; and free rider problem, 30–36; human intervention in, 65–67, 202; hyperlinks as factor in, 61, 62, 69; localized, 28, 64, 129, 138–39, 143; and news media, 32–35; optimization of, 66, 115; and PageRank, 21, 23, 58, 60, 61–64, 66, 74, 171, 187; and pornography, 14, 57, 67, 222n4; and precise comprehensiveness, 59; quality control of, 14–15, 35, 36, 65–67; ranking of, 21, 23, 56, 57, 58, 61–64, 66, 69, 74, 171, 187; registered users' influence on, 67; and relevance, 7, 21, 32, 57, 59, 61, 63, 65, 66, 138, 171, 188, 193; and safe search, 15, 222n4; and semantic analysis, 23; and sponsored results, 26, 60; and users' gratification, 52–55; users' trust in, 3, 58–60; Wikipedia represented in, 63, 64, 66, 222n4. *See also* censorship

semantic searches, 22–23

Sennett, Richard, 231n33

seven deadly sins, 76, 77

sexually explicit content, 38. *See also* pornography

Shell Oil corporation, 131

Shenk, David, 175
Shirky, Clay, 175, 231n33, 234n71
Shi Tao, 127
Silicon Valley, 56, 70–71
Sinsheimer, Robert, 207
Skype, 16
social networking, 16, 17–118, 90–92, 95, 116
social responsibility, 42–44
Solove, Daniel, 95, 96, 236n20
Souter, David, 170
South Africa, 121, 122, 128
South Korea, 25, 142–43, 145
Soviet Union, 121–23
Spain, 142, 146
speed, priority placed on, 51–54
Spencer, Herbert, 181
sponsored results, 26, 60
Stanford University, 56, 158, 187, 195
"Star Wars Kid," 95–96
stock market, 79, 229n14
Street View. See Google Street View
students' use of Google, 189–92, 197
Sulston, John, 207, 208
Sundaram, Ravi, 140
Sunstein, Cass, 88
surveillance: consumer choices facilitated by, 112–13; and data mining, 96–97; and Google Street View, 98–108; government, 97, 107, 112, 113, 236n20; individualism compatible with, 112–13; mass, 92–94, 96, 97, 107–8; Panopticon model of, 9, 111–12; and Total Information Awareness program, 236n20
Switzerland, 142

Taiwan, 142
technocracy, 8, 67–71, 180
technocultural imagination, 8, 221n13
techno-fundamentalism, 40, 50, 55, 75, 76–77, 109, 113, 120, 128, 151, 180, 196
technology, sociopolitical change promoted by, xii–xiii, 4–5, 8, 120, 121–24, 128, 133, 179–82, 244n51
telecommunications companies, 15, 18, 49
television, 31, 58, 112, 123
terrorism, 5, 37, 107
Thailand, 17
Thaler, Richard, 88
Thatcher, Margaret, 40, 108
Thinkfree (Web-based word processor), 29
third-party content, Google's responsibility for, 3, 47
Thomson, Robert, 33
Tibet, 11, 124, 125

Time magazine, 82
Total Information Awareness program, 236n20
trade secrets, Google's, 87, 195
translation, automatic, 141, 145
transparency, governmental, 97, 120
tricycles, used for Google Street View, 237n24
trust bias, 58–60
truth, pragmatic theory of, 60–62
Turkle, Sherry, 231n33
Turner, Fred, 70, 71
Turow, Joseph, 113
Twitter, 99, 116, 117
2 Live Crew, 170
2001: A Space Odyssey, 180

UNESCO, 146
United Kingdom: Google Books copyright case in, 168; Google Street View resisted in, 104–8; Internet censorship in, 134; mass surveillance in, 107–8; YouTube content removed in, 110
universalization, 108, 109, 110, 111, 117
universities, Google's relations with. See academia, Google's relations with
University of California, 3, 158, 187, 207
University of Maryland, 195
University of Michigan, 158, 187, 203
University of Virginia, 158, 185–86
University of Washington, 195
University of Wisconsin, 158
university presses, 171–72
Updike, John, 151
USA Today, 56

Varian, Hal, 187
Veblen, Thorstein, 68
Venezuela, 142
Venter, Craig, 208–9
Verizon, 49
Viacom, 18, 35–36, 47
video, Web-based, 16, 37, 49. See also YouTube
video games, 181
virtual private networks (VPNs), 126
voice-over-Internet providers (VoIP), 16
von Lohmann, Fred, 169

Wagner, Dana, 19, 20
Wall Street Journal, 33, 34, 200
Walmart, 42
Wang Xiaoning, 127
Ward, Lester Frank, 181

Watson, James, 194, 208
Weber, Max, 147
Weinberger, David, 171
Wikipedia, 8, 23, 63, 64, 190, 191, 222n4
Wilson, Heather, 37–38
Windows, Microsoft, 17, 24
Wired magazine, 196, 231n33
Wolfram, Stephen, 22
Wolfram Alpha (search engine), 22, 24
Word, Microsoft, 29
World Intellectual Property Organization
    (WIPO), 146
World Trade Organization, 146
World Wide Web, Google's dominance of,
    xi, 1–3, 7, 13–15, 17, 25, 229n14
Writely (Web-based word processor), 29

Yahoo: in competition with Google, 19, 197;
    as Internet portal, 56; and Open Content
    Alliance, 172; in partnership with Micro-
soft, 24; political repression in China
facilitated by, 127–28, 131; and proposal
to collaborate with Google, 18, 25; search
engine of, 20, 24, 233n71; students' use
of, 190, 197
Yandex, 144
YouTube: Chinese censorship of, 118;
    and copyright, 18, 35–36, 37; cultural
    significance of, 37; and daily number of
    views, 37; gang-related content on, 110;
    and global public sphere, 148; Google's
    acquisition of, 3, 16, 37, 229n14; Google's
    management of, 36, 37, 39; Google's
    responsibility for content on, 47–48, 110,
    116, 130; and network effect, 19; and
    political relations, 16, 37–39, 49; rate of
    uploads to, 37; and registered users, 90,
    183; and sexually explicit content, 38

Zoho (Web-based word processor), 29

Text: 10/14 Palatino
Display: Univers Condensed Light 47 and Bauer Bodoni
Compositor: Toppan Best-set Premedia Limited
Indexer: Andrew Joron
Printer and binder: Sheridan Books Inc.